– THE SHIFT –

The Next Evolution in Baseball Thinking

Russell A. Carleton

TRIUMPH
BOOKS

Library of Congress Cataloging-in-Publication Data available upon request.

This book is available in quantity at special discounts for your group or organization. For further information, contact:

> Triumph Books LLC
> 814 North Franklin Street
> Chicago, Illinois 60610
> (312) 337-0747
> www.triumphbooks.com

Printed in U.S.A.
ISBN: 978-1-62937-544-1
Design by Meghan Grammer

To my father, who took me to my first baseball game, and my mother, who learned about baseball so that she could have something to talk about with six-year-old me.

– CONTENTS –

– *FOREWORD* –

I STILL REMEMBER THE FIRST TIME I READ RUSSELL Carleton. The cloistered world of baseball analysis treated the notion of intangibles with equal measures of doubt and disdain, and here was this guy—at no less than Baseball Prospectus, the online bastion of statistical dogmatism—wielding a scythe, happy to play the devil in the details.

"Sabermetricians do not understand the human element of the game," he wrote in early 2010, and I was hooked, not just because I'd waited years for someone to offer a rejoinder to the analysts who treated players like robots and games like static events instead of the living, breathing beasts they are. This was something greater. He was marrying numbers and psychology, the baseball world's version of a blind date gone wrong. He was ipecac for those who had red-pilled themselves in to believing there was but one lens through which to view the baseball world, whose bible was the Book of Bill James.

Russell's work, and by extension this book, is unlike anything I've ever seen, and it comes at the perfect time, as Newton's Third Law reverberates across Major League Baseball. This year marks *Moneyball*'s 15th anniversary, and nearly every team finds itself in a similar place with regards to proprietary numbers. It isn't groupthink so much as a natural plateau of analytics. Only so much variation will exist when brilliant people educated similarly try to tackle similar data sets. The equal and opposite reaction is those brilliant people trying to understand what they missed during analytics' ascent. And it's piggybacking on so much of what Russell understands as well as anyone.

Take coaching. Front offices have long considered coaches as much of a nuisance as a tangible addition to understanding the game. The most worthless coaches engage in pop psychology full of vacuous suggestions and offer chestnuts that have spent decades roasting on an open fire. Executives today are starting to test the open-mindedness of coaches, trying to figure out who cares about extracting marginal advantages from certain situations, understand who can communicate and teach and lead. No longer is it simply about having information; the best coaches describe it, explain it, sell it. They are about to inherit a generation of players reared in an objective baseball world. Their job isn't to remind the players of a bygone era; it's to prepare for the one coming.

We live in a world in which teams are actively studying the brain. A handful of clubs today test the mental acuity of prospective draft picks, minor league players, and even major leaguers using games on handheld devices. Those who score best get drafted higher and pushed to the major leagues more quickly, their brain treated like a 100-mph fastball, a unique skill that portends success. Some teams are starting to research brain waves in hopes of better understanding whether there's an objective measurement to determine who's likelier to play better in high-pressure moments. If the numbers can't tell us who's definitively clutch, maybe the brain can.

These truths have been found for years by Russell. His brain works differently than any of his peers'. He asks smarter questions than mainstream sportswriters and more empathetic ones than those dabbling in sabermetrics. He's kind enough to warn readers of an impending dive into wonkiness and talented enough to guide them through without a misstep. He believes the game deserves better than the narrative contrivances that for so long represented how baseball's story was told.

The internecine war between scouts and stats? It's not just dead. It barely existed. For every grizzled scout bellyaching about the nerds taking over, another recognized that nerds were going to win the whole time. The scouts who survived understand the value of analysts. The analysts who care for layers of depth to complement their reports turn to scouts. Their relationship is symbiotic, and the most capable master both languages and serve as conduits when the inevitable disagreement arrives.

When a vacuum exists, laughable scenarios germinate. A few years back, a player regaled me with a story about his team's effort to integrate analytics to its daily scouting reports. The team wanted to shift its defense more, so the front office prepared documents that showed the spray charts of a batter's last 200 at-bats. The coaching staff balked. There were too many dots. So a new report arrived, with 100 at-bats of data. Nope. Too busy still. Only with a sample of 50—far too small to glean anything substantive—did the coaches accept the new complement.

The player was incredulous. How could this organization be so willfully ignorant? And while that's a perfectly fair question—not to mention one that's been resolved since then with a management overhaul—it's not the sort Russell bothers to ask, because that's more a rhetorical gripe. He wants to know what caused the organization not to do it. What are the ill effects a sabermetrically deficient franchise might suffer because of a simple lack of curiosity? Does organizational inertia keep bad actors from changing their ways?

In a sport obsessed with the micro, he is the macro. Information is everything, and while baseball has defined information as numbers, statistics, and the branches of those family trees, information also encompasses behavior, history, processes, systems, biases, communication, and, perhaps most important, decision-making.

That's really what this book is about, and it's what makes it unlike anything I've ever read. It's a psychological exegesis dressed in a baseball uniform. It's a study of human nature—of its triumphs and fallibilities, its strengths and weaknesses, its power and powerlessness—and how baseball falls prey to the very same patterns exhibited in other areas of life. It's an appeal to learn from these lessons—learn as a game and learn as people. It's a text for its moment.

I've spent almost 15 years now trying to understand baseball better, and even though I immerse myself in it every day, its wide universe often proves too unwieldy to contextualize. Its greatest gift is the thinkers who transcend that, who look beyond the obvious, who challenge themselves and the wide array that loves the game, too, to do better by it. To drag it not kicking and screaming into a new era but spirit it through whatever barriers may still exist.

Fear not, purists: This book reaffirms the human element exists. Now sit back, relax, and let a brain doctor use a few numbers, a little bit of savoir-faire, and a whole lot of experience to explain how.

— **JEFF PASSAN**

Prairie Village, Kansas

December 15, 2017

– *INTRODUCTION* –

Rule 1

Baseball is a game between two teams of nine players each, under direction of a manager, played on an enclosed field in accordance with these rules, under jurisdiction of one or more umpires.

—Official Rules of Major League Baseball, Rule 1.01

I'VE BROKEN THE *REAL* RULE 1 OF BASEBALL A GRAND TOTAL of one time in my life. *Never willingly leave a baseball game early (unless you absolutely have to).* Sure enough, I picked exactly the wrong day to do it. It was August 5, 2001, and I was in my native Cleveland, home from college for the last part of summer break before heading back to school. Earlier that day, my buddy from high school—we'll call him "Steve," because that's his name—called me and recited the most wonderful poem in the English language. "I have two tickets to the game tonight. Wanna go?"

The Indians were playing the Seattle Mariners, a team that would eventually win 116 games during the regular season, and three out of five from the Indians in the American League Division Series that October. I actually hesitated before saying yes. Normally, I wouldn't have, but the next day was special. Early in the morning, I was scheduled to fly to Atlanta to be with my girlfriend, Tanya, for her birthday, and I didn't want to be tired. We all learn to make sacrifices for what we love, and for a baseball game, I was willing to be tired.

The outlook wasn't brilliant for the Cleveland nine that day. Dave Burba (famous for being "the guy we got for Sean Casey") and Mike Bascik (who would eventually become the answer to the trivia question: Who gave up Barry Bonds's record-breaking 756th career home run?) had combined to give up 12 runs by the end of the third inning. By the fifth, the Indians found themselves on the wrong end of a 14–2 score. Steve and I had a few philosophical moments during that fifth inning. We openly discussed Rule 1, but wondered if it really applied to a game that was this much of a laugher. Perhaps the parenthetical (unless you absolutely have to) applied to lost causes. Plus, I had a morning flight and a girlfriend to think about. Steve asked me if I really liked this woman, because that's what two men do when they're watching a baseball game. They talk about relationships.

In the top of the sixth inning, the public address announcer at Jacobs Field informed us that Jolbert Cabrera would be taking care of second-base duties for the rest of the game. Indians manager Charlie Manuel had given up. Maybe it was time for us to follow suit. I did some mental math and figured that if we left right then, I could make it home and get seven good hours of sleep. I'd be at the airport in the morning, refreshed for my flight, and be in Tanya's arms by lunchtime singing "Happy Birthday" to her, even if it meant leaving before singing "Take Me Out to the Ballgame." I proposed that we leave. Steve agreed and we headed out across the Tower City walkway to the train station.

It was the biggest mistake of my life.

Russell Branyan hit a home run to lead off the bottom of the seventh inning, which was nice because it meant that if the Indians could somehow hit three grand slams, they'd win. I heard about the home run, and an eventual two-run single by—who else?—Jolbert Cabrera from the guy sitting in front of us on the train. He had a Walkman (hello, 2001!) and would occasionally do a little silent but noticeable fist pump when the Indians scored a run. Steve and I were busy recounting stories from high school, because that's what two men who have left a baseball game early do. They talk about the good old days.

The Indians weren't quite done that night. Jim Thome and Marty Cordova homered in the eighth inning to make the score a more respectable 14–8, and as I walked in the front door of my parents' house, Omar Vizquel doubled in Einar Diaz to make it 14–9. My dad, who was watching the game on TV, asked why I'd left the game early. He quoted Rule 1. And *as he said that*, a pitch from Mariners reliever Norm Charlton got past catcher Tom Lampkin, and Indians center fielder Kenny Lofton, who had been on third, charged home. The ball ricocheted off the wall behind home plate back to Lampkin, who collected the ball in time to throw back to Charlton who had raced 60 feet and six inches to cover home. Lofton was the second out and now the bases were empty. Soon, the lowly Cabrera went down on strikes. "That's why," I pointed. My dad nodded.

In theory, I should have gotten ready for bed right then. Maybe I should have called Tanya and told her I was looking forward to seeing her the next day, but baseball is a terrible mistress. The 2001 Indians were still an offensive juggernaut, as they had been for most of my adolescence in the 1990s, and even though I had skipped out on this game earlier in the night, I could still watch the ninth inning on TV. The Indians were down five, but "maybe" is the most seductive word in baseball.

There are certain events in life that defy probability. In 1988, as the hobbled Kirk Gibson rounded the bases after his famous home run to win Game 1 of the World Series, legendary broadcaster Vin Scully proclaimed, "In a year that has been so improbable, the impossible has happened." Gibson's home run was always within the realm of the possible, but the odds were so remote that when it actually happened—and happened on that particular stage—it seemed magical. That night, I witnessed my own Kirk Gibson moment. In the ninth, the Indians again faced Charlton, and Eddie Taubensee let fly a single to the wonderment of all. After Jim Thome flew out to right and Russell Branyan struck out, Marty Cordova tore the cover off the ball. And when the dust had lifted and the fans saw what occurred, there was Marty safe at second, and Eddie a-hugging third.

I should have been there in the stadium for what came next. Wil Cordero walked the bases loaded and Einar Diaz singled to score Taubensee and Cordova. What had once been a 14–2 deficit was now a 14–11 save situation and the Mariners brought closer Kazuhiro Sasaki into a game that had once seemed like a foregone conclusion. Sasaki gave up a single to Lofton to load the bases once more. There were now two outs and the Indians were still down three runs as Omar Vizquel came to the plate. As the clock on my parents' VCR rolled around to 11:00 PM, I was locked in. Oh baseball, why must you do this to me?

I had an odd feeling about what would happen next. It wasn't exactly *déjà vu*. It was a premonition. Or maybe it was just a thought so crazy that it could only happen in a dream or a baseball game. The scientist in me knows that it was really just wishful thinking, but in my mind, I saw the switch-hitting Vizquel pulling one down the first-base line to clear the bases. Somewhere around 11:10 PM, I jumped higher into the air than I ever had before or since. On a 3-2 pitch, Vizquel made my dreams come true. The game was tied 14–14. To this day, I sometimes queue up that highlight and audibly squeal in delight.

There was a problem. I had broken Rule 1 with the intention of being rested for the next morning. The game was tied and at this point, I had to see this one through. Up stepped the lowly Jolbert Cabrera to put an exclamation point on one of *those* nights in baseball history. Except it didn't happen that way. He grounded to third. The game was going to extra innings. I faced a choice.

Though in truth, there was no choice. I was going to be there, if only through the magic of television. It took until about 12:30 in the morning until—who else?—Jolbert Cabrera drove in the winning run in the bottom of the 11th. The penance was extracted. I was tired the next day, but happy. I made it to Atlanta, and thankfully, Tanya understood when I fell asleep that afternoon.

✱   ✱   ✱

"BASEBALL IS A GAME...."

Games are defined by their rules, and rules create spaces outside the normal bounds of reality. Baseball is an odd activity when you look at it out of context. Why is that man running 90 feet in a straight line and then turning left to run another 90 feet? In the real world, that man is—at best—strange. In the space known as "baseball," he just hit a double! Rules turn mad dashes into meaninful events.

There are two ways to win at any game. One is to read the rulebook and become good at the skills that are listed there. In baseball, that means being the person who can throw the fastest fastball or hit the ball the farthest. When baseball players practice, that's usually what they focus on—hitting, fielding, and pitching— the physical aspects of the game. The same stuff I was terrible at when I was a kid.

There's a second way to win a game, one that always brings about a few raised eyebrows. In between the rules, there are always spaces. The infield shift has never been illegal. The rules of baseball dictate where the pitcher and catcher have to stand (or squat), but say nothing about the other seven fielders. They may all huddle together in left field if they choose to, but for years, teams would unquestioningly put two infielders to the left of second base and two to the right, because that's the way it had always been done. Yet, somewhere along the line, a small mutation appeared, and the shift came into being.

In any game, there are always cheaters. They use their creative powers to figure out ways to do the things that the rules explicitly say that they can't. It takes a different kind of creativity to see—and then see past—that imaginary line up the middle that no one, not even the rulebook, ever talked about. There are two sets of rules in any game: the ones that are written down and the social norms that fill the vacuum when the rules fall silent. As teams began to shift more often, the shift itself became the focus of a moral debate. Was that cheating? It felt a little dirty. It was technically legal, but social norms do not take kindly to the word "technically." It's easier to change the written rules than the unwritten ones. In the written rules, the change can be negotiated and everyone knows what's being negotiated. What happens when someone tries to break the rules that aren't written down or even spoken of? That's where baseball becomes a thinking game.

Baseball at once walks the fine line of being a game that "never changes" despite being a game ever in flux. It's not rapid change; that illusion of permanence has to come from somewhere. Most of the written rules haven't changed in a century and a half, but in 10 years Major League Baseball has seen the average team go from scoring 4.80 runs per game in 2007 to 4.32 in 2012 to 4.65 in 2017. If someone out there is reading this book in the year 2027, the game will have changed again, despite the fact that the bases will still be 90 feet apart.

Baseball is a game. Games create their own ecosystems. Over time, all ecosystems change, even if we don't want them to.

There's a lot of downtime in baseball, which means that there's a lot of time for incubating the tiny mutations that can shape the game. It takes three hours to play one game and six months of nearly daily installments to play a whole season. There's a lot of time to think, not just between each pitch, but night after night and plane ride after plane ride. A baseball season is more like a six-month mantra. There are a thousand little things that happen over and over again, and you can pick any one of them to fixate on as you meditate. You can think about the implications of throwing a fastball vs. a curveball in a thousand different situations, and it's not entirely academic to obsess about it. The pitchers on your team have to make that decision a thousand times in the space of a week, the same way that they had to the week before and the week before that. A game and even a season could turn on any of those pitches.

Baseball is a thinking game. Maybe it's even an obsessing game. It is most certainly a shifting game.

WHEN I WAS SIX, I WANTED TO BE THE THIRD BASEMAN FOR the Cleveland Indians and with apologies to the incumbent at the position, Brook Jacoby, I was clearly the better option. Unfortunately, my baseball career ended in seventh-grade rec league summer softball due to a tragic lack of talent. It probably should have ended before that. Even though my dream never really came true, baseball has a way of staying in the blood. The problem is that even at six, when you're asked what you want to be when you grow up, "obsessive baseball junkie" isn't an acceptable answer. I had to come up with an alternate plan.

After college, I moved to Chicago to attend graduate school in child and adolescent clinical psychology. I was going to be a therapist. I lived on the North Side, and in the summer of 2003 (the Bartman Year), I started watching Cubs games because my still-then-girlfriend Tanya had traveled to her native Russia for a few weeks. To fill the time, I took up working out at the campus gym and the Cubs were always on the TV right in front of the elliptical machine that I liked. It helped when, just before the trade deadline, the Cubs acquired Kenny Lofton, who had played for the Indians teams I had adored growing up in the 1990s. I suppose I'll never be able to lay claim to being a true Cubs fan, but I was 23, living in a new city, and my girlfriend was out of the country. It was probably cheating on both my girlfriend and the Indians, but the Cubs became my unrequited crush.

That was an interesting year to be a fan of baseball. In 2003, author Michael Lewis released the book *Moneyball*, which chronicled the adventures of the Oakland A's and their then–general manager (later president) Billy Beane. Beane and his front office workers had used advanced statistical methods to look for small edges that could help the A's compete with the rest of the league on a shoestring budget. I ended up reading the book accidentally. I was working on a research project that would eventually become my dissertation, and I spent a lot of time interviewing adolescents in public libraries about stressful events in their lives. For half of the two-hour meeting, the teen completed a packet of fill-in-the-bubble forms. It meant that I often had an hour or so on my hands and a room full of books at my disposal. One day, I happened to see *Moneyball* on the "New Books" shelf. It was about baseball, so I picked it up.

Moneyball—the book and the portmanteau that forms its title— has become a cultural shorthand for many things, both inside and outside of baseball. It's become a euphemism for the systematic analysis of data that leads to a counterintuitive finding, even though this process had long been known as "research." Somewhere within its pages, I had a moment of clarity. I was in the middle of a research-based graduate program, taking advanced statistics and research methodology classes. I spent large amounts of time collecting data on and thinking deeply about how to explain human behavior. Surely, baseball couldn't be *that* different. Baseball players were just humans behaving, and if baseball had one thing going for it, it had plenty of data. The rest was just some data-processing tricks, and I knew how to do that.

Moneyball led me to find a small but growing group of people— baseball outsiders like me—who were doing their own statistically based research and then publishing it at websites like Baseball Prospectus. A lot of the research was truly brilliant work. In fact, as I started doing my own work, real Major League teams started to hire some of those early writers. That was when I decided to create a secret double life for myself. I was a graduate student who needed a hobby that didn't cost any money. I had access to everything I needed. For a good amount of time in graduate school, when I was supposed to have my dissertation data set open, I was instead working on a very different data set. I had found my muse. Maybe if the whole therapist thing didn't work out, Billy Beane would hire me.

I GREW UP IN THE 1980S AND '90S, DURING THE GOLDEN age of "cheating" in video games. I first had an Atari 2600, then an 8-bit Nintendo, and eventually I moved on to (from today's perspective) hilariously bad PC games. I'm not much of a gamer anymore, but I can appreciate how far video games have come. In some sense, I'm lucky that I grew up in the days when they were sophisticated enough to where I could play something that looked like baseball (or football or a spaceship that for some reason needed to shoot a bunch of other spaceships) on the screen, but primitive enough that I could figure out all of the game's weaknesses and exploit them. I didn't even have to go to the arcade and spend all my quarters. Everything was right there on my television. I don't think people truly appreciate the impact that bad video games had on baseball or the world in general.

Maybe the most important cultural legacy of the video game is the idea of one-player mode. Most real-world games are multi-player. They pit two (or more) people against each other within some rule structure and the players compete until there's a winner. While you're playing the game—assuming that your friends actually want to win—there is no space to stop the game, back up, and try something a little different to see if you can get an edge that way. Before one-player mode, most games were *social* experiences. There was etiquette to consider. You didn't take every last advantage and run up the score, even if you could, especially if you still wanted to be friends with the person after the game was over.

When video games came along, though, there was no other person (in one-player mode, anyway) whose feelings you had to worry about. Suddenly, the opposing pitcher or the Russian army or the pathway to Willamette Valley was controlled by a computer. When I was growing up, it was a rather stupid computer. If I messed up, I could try again, either through the magic of the "save" button, or through hundreds of repetitions. The computer didn't care if I bent the rules, nor did it really change its strategy to compensate once I figured it out its weaknesses. On top of that, the games were all standardized and that meant that there was an army of other people who were trying to beat the same artificial intelligence that I was. The social aspect of game playing was turned on its ear. Now two people could play a game against "the computer" and instead of being adversaries, they could collaborate to find ways to win. One-player mode ushered in an era of the game itself as the opponent. Games were now puzzles to be solved. Etiquette could be replaced by ruthless efficiency. There had always been a small group of people who studied different games to try to find an edge, but now that sort of game-breaking was something that could be done for fun by 10-year-olds.

There was always a point in those limited early video games where beating the computer in a straight-up match wasn't even a question anymore, but with a going rate of $30 to $40 for a new

8-bit Nintendo cartridge, sometimes I had to make do with the ones I already had. So, I ran little experiments. Maybe it was taking on a ridiculous handicap or maybe challenging myself to run up an even higher score. Sometimes it involved just trying something new to see if it could be done. If my experiment didn't work, I could hit "reset" and try again.

There are probably a lot of people reading this book who are products of that shift. We lived through an era in which *breaking* a game (rather than *playing* a game) became not only possible, but socially acceptable. It's not that big a leap to start applying those same principles to all games, even games where there was an opponent. Some of us just happened to be baseball fans.

I REMEMBER THE DAY THAT I STARTED SKETCHING OUT MY first baseball research projects. I was in a once-a-week three-hour class on cognitive psychology. Three hours is a long time to be thinking about anything, especially thinking about how people think. In class, we were learning about a concept known as signal detection theory. Humans sometimes need to design a test for figuring out whether something—a disease, a sound—is present or absent. We want a test that says "yes" when the disease really is present and "no" when it isn't. We want to be able to detect whether our phones really did beep so that we can answer our friend who just texted, but we also want to ignore the phone when it *isn't* beeping so as not to have to do that awkward "I thought it was my phone, but it wasn't" dance. Since there are two ways to be correct, there are also two ways to be wrong. I can grab the phone, even though it didn't really beep (a Type I error) or I can miss a real beep when someone's trying to reach me (a Type II error).

It reminded me of the strike zone. A batter is trying to determine whether the pitch coming toward him will eventually be called a strike or a ball. If it's a strike, he probably (not always) wants to swing at it. If it's a ball, he probably (not always) wants to let it go because swinging at something out of the strike zone usually results in a swing and miss or a weak grounder to second. We want a batter who makes fewer mistakes (i.e., strikes), but we can also look at the *kind of mistakes* that he makes. Is he more likely to swing at everything (and miss a lot) or is he overly patient and takes a lot of pitches, some for called strikes? Is he good at finding a balance between those two extremes? There are numbers that can be calculated in this signal detection framework that tell us both how good a hitter is at detecting which pitches were good to swing at, and another number that tells us how well the batter balances the "too much vs. too little" problem. I had created my very first baseball statistic, a crude measure of plate discipline, and it was about understanding the mindset of a batter as he made a rather important decision.

If there's something that the field of sabermetrics—a term that loosely refers to the study of baseball through the scientific method—has been accused of, it's been idolizing numbers and ignoring the human element of baseball. If sabermetricians really are ignoring the human element, then it's a wasted opportunity. Baseball is a wonderfully rich human data set. As a psychologist—a term that loosely refers to people who study human thought and behavior—I look at baseball and I see a mind game. If you want to understand the game, it's important to understand the very human dynamics of those people wearing funny pajamas and running around that odd box we call a baseball field.

The human element is all over baseball. It's embedded in Rule 1.01 if you look closely. I propose that there's room to explore that human side of the game, to do it using good scientific method, and to discover some very fun and exciting things about the game—and maybe about humans in general—along the way.

"...BETWEEN TWO TEAMS OF NINE PLAYERS EACH...."

Baseball is an odd game. The big trophy at the end of the year goes to the team that won the World Series. It's also a game where the fundamental unit of play is the one-on-one pitcher-versus-batter confrontation. Even once the ball is hit into play, it's not much of a team game. In basketball or football, a player might not handle the ball itself, but he usually has a job as a blocker or a decoy, and the ball could go to him at any moment. In baseball, the fielders are mostly just accomplishing their individual jobs and then passing the ball on to the next person who has his job to do. It's telling that when something goes awry on a fielding play, the scorer must assign an "error" to an individual player. It's one person's fault, rather than the team's. Baseball is a team game played by nine individuals.

Those nine players have to take turns. Only one of them may shape the game at a time from the batter's box, and it's whoever's name appears next on a list. The best hitter in the league has zero effect on what happens in the game until it's his turn again. Or does he? Perhaps the last time he was up, he made the pitcher throw 12 pitches, and now the pitcher is a little more tired than he would have been. Maybe that little bit of fatigue means that the pitcher leaves a hanging curve out over the plate for the number seven hitter, who hits the ball into the second deck. Who then hit the home run? In the accounting of the game, the seventh hitter gets all the credit, but does he deserve it?

Finding the places where the individual ends and the team begins in baseball is trickier than it is in other sports. On a baseball team, 25 grown men must learn to play a game together, even though most of the time they are only minimally interacting with one another. In sports where any of the players can score at any time, one or two players can carry the load. In baseball, the lineup dictates who will bat next and the calendar determines the day's starter. Anyone, however, might be thrust into a key situation. Everyone has to be ready. Baseball is a very democratic sport.

In baseball, if I can't be involved in the play because it's not my turn, I can at least help my teammates out mentally. I can share my knowledge about the opposing team, but there's a lot more mental space in the game than that. Major League teams spend months together, play daily games, and change cities twice a week. It's said that if you want to test how well your relationship is going with your significant other, you should take a long car trip together. Imagine taking a couple of long car trips each week with the same 24 significant others who also happen to be your coworkers. On top of that, you're a well-known millionaire, and there are plenty of people who will try to take advantage of you. Calling home to your family from the road is nice, but those 24 other guys might be the only points of trustworthy live human contact that you have. There's only so long that a human being can go without hearing a friendly voice.

Let's hope those 25 guys all get along, or at least tolerate each other. If they do, it can mean that when a player comes to bat with two out in the ninth and the tying run on third, he's not fighting back a sense of loneliness at the same time he's trying to fight off a 98 mph fastball. Those interpersonal connections on a baseball team might be one of the most powerful forces in the game, but since much of that happens behind the scenes, we don't have a good way of studying it.

That doesn't mean we shouldn't try.

When people talk about the importance of clubhouse chemistry in baseball, do me a favor. Believe them. It's easy to think about baseball players as individuals, because we have ways of measuring their individual performance. Rule 1.01 reminds us that they form a team, a team of nine people, picked to live together in a series of hotels, work together, and wear funny matching pajamas while they do it. A baseball team is its own little society, and just like any other society, the hows and whys of its functionality, whether harmonious or discordant, are important.

*　*　*

"...UNDER DIRECTION OF A MANAGER...."

I believe some hack writer said a few paragraphs ago that baseball was a very democratic sport and that everyone has to rally together for the good of the team. This is true, although within this "democracy," there is a dictator.

The manager is given some pretty impressive powers by the rulebook. There are only nine men who get to play at any one time and the manager gets to decide which of the 25 available players will get the call. He may remove them at will (though not bring them back) and decide when and where they play. The manager is the only person involved in the game (other than the umpire) given *any* sort of power to force someone to do something that he does not want to do. If the starter doesn't want to come out of the game, it doesn't matter. Once the manager performs the ceremonial touching of his left wrist, the move is binding. The starter can throw a tantrum all he wants, but if he tries to throw another pitch, it will not be recognized as valid.

That power of substitution turns out to be enough to make the manager the *de facto* strategic leader for his team. A good amount of strategy in baseball comes down to inserting one of the 16 players who don't start the game into a specific situation where he might do the most good. Because the manager not only has the power of *who* will play, but also *when*, he also gets to make strategic decisions on what times in a ball game are the most important. For example, a manager could use his closer in the eighth inning against the heart of the other team's lineup or save him for the ninth because it's the last inning. That might cause a debate among people watching at home or even the players in the dugout, but it's only the manager's opinion that actually matters. In fact, the most important word in the prepositional phrase "under direction of a manager" is "a." In theory, a baseball team could be managed by a committee, but the rules gently nudge it toward a dictatorship of one man.

If a manager is going to have substitution powers, he's already got his hand on the majority of the tactical levers. He might as well be the guy who thinks about tactics more generally. "He pushed all the right buttons tonight" is perhaps the highest praise that a manager can receive for his work in a game, and in its early days, much of the sabermetric movement focused on picking apart a manager's performance *as a tactician*. Those strategic gambits are part of the job. It's just not the whole job. It might not even be the lion's share of the job.

Other than substitution policy, the manager is given no other power. He does not pitch or bat. He just touches various body parts to relay the "steal" sign through his third-base coach. There's no rule saying that after stealing second, a runner has to produce a permission slip signed by his manager, but it's agreed that the manager gets to make those calls anyway. Still, the manager can only do his job if his players go along with his orders. The dictator must become a leader.

To become a successful leader, a manager needs enough of his 25 charges to be happy and healthy enough to win the game, while trusting him enough to follow his orders. He needs to do this over the course of a daily, grinding season. Like anyone who has a job title containing the word "manager," his job is to keep his employees motivated to do their best and to put them in situations where they can succeed. That's tough. Over a six-month season, it's easy for a player to give in to that grind of being constantly on the road and having to do treatments for that ankle issue each day and the endless meetings to go over.... *What are we even meeting about?*

The four most toxic words in baseball are "Why should I bother?" Some players wake up and think of nothing but baseball. Pete Rose was quoted as saying that he would walk through hell in a gasoline suit to play baseball. For those who don't own a gasoline suit, the manager's job is to keep them engaged. Those meetings might be a drag, but they are important. You might pick up something about the day's starter that helps you lay off that 2-1 curveball and turn what would have been a 2-2 count into a 3-1 count. What happens if you decide to mentally check out during that two minutes and miss that insight? Baseball is filled with ways to bleed away tiny bits of value around the edges, mostly in ways that the untrained eye would never perceive. Eventually those little bits add up. I'd argue that the most important job of a manager has nothing to do with calling for the hit-and-run. It's answering the question, "Why should I bother?"

This is where the one power that the manager does have—substitution power—comes into play. Consider the modern bullpen. The manager picks the moment that a reliever comes into a game, but he also sets the general structure of how the bullpen is used. Since the 1980s, most teams have followed the same pattern. There is an ace reliever, also known as "the closer," who protects leads in the ninth inning, and his lieutenant "the set-up guy" take the next juiciest set of morsels.

Those plum assignments also come with perks. The ninth inning, being the end of the game, is often more *emotionally* than mathematically relevant to the outcome of a game, but it's nice to be the guy who "saved" the game by locking down a one-run lead in the ninth, rather than the guy who "just" did the exact same thing in the seventh inning. There's a hierarchy, and hierarchies, especially among young males, promote competition to reach the top. In other words, the manager creates a natural answer to the question of "Why should I bother?" If you want to make it to the top of the chart, young man, go to those meetings and watch the tape and do your training work.

This is a manager's challenge. He only has the powers of substitution to work with, but those powers allow him the ability to carve out different roles and niches for the 25 players whom he has in his dugout. All he has to do is figure out a system that has 25 roles that give each of those 25 players a way to feel useful and at the same time, 25 roles that are useful in winning a game. If a manager can get all of the players to buy in to that system, there will be a clubhouse of 25 guys who are, at the very least, not whining. Maybe they'll even be happy. That takes someone who can come up with a vision of that system and can sell it. That's leadership.

Let's stop for a moment here. This is a book about baseball. Why are we talking about feelings? Why does it matter if players are *feeling* valued or *feeling* that they're contributing? Rule 1.01 is again telling us something if we stop to listen carefully. To understand baseball, we have to think about issues like motivation and leadership, not in the "Rah! Rah! Coach is never wrong!" sort of way, but in a real, measured—dare I say scientific—way. We lose the plot if we think of the manager as just a button pusher. He's also a leader of men. That matters.

*   *   *

"...PLAYED ON AN ENCLOSED FIELD IN ACCORDANCE WITH THESE RULES...."

In the 1930s, the pioneering psychologist B.F. Skinner introduced the operant conditioning chamber, or as it became better known, the "Skinner Box." Skinner believed that human behavior was primarily a response to the external environment, a philosophy known as behaviorism. In this view, people respond to whatever brings them pleasure and avoid what brings them pain. If you change the incentives, then you change the behavior.

A classic Skinner Box consists of an enclosed environment, usually a Plexiglas box with an animal test subject inside. The box is designed to elicit some behavior from the animal (pushing a lever is common) and then to provide some sort of reward for doing so. It's nice because lever presses can be counted and timed for nice, neat data points, and more importantly, the experimenter has near-complete control of the environment. There is a box, there are rules that apply within that box, and Skinner could manipulate the rules to see what happened.

Skinner was not the first behaviorist, but he was one of the first scientists to take a largely empirical approach to behavior. The genius of the Skinner Box was that it was a *recording device* for behavioral data, and those data were observable and impartial. The rat either pressed the lever or it did not. That might seem obvious nearly a century later, but the idea of observational, quantifiable data as a way to understand behavior was a break-through at the time. Prior to Skinner, much of what passed for the science of "Why did you do that?" was influenced by the practice of introspection. In an introspective study, scientists would ask trained test subjects to perform some action and then to speak, stream of consciousness style, about what they were doing. There was no way to validate whether the person was providing an accurate report, nor (as a Freudian theorist might suggest) whether they were suppressing something. In fact, later experimentation showed obvious flaws in the idea that humans are accurate reporters on their own mental states.

In 1977, researchers Richard Nisbett and Timothy Wilson asked volunteers to memorize several pairs of unrelated words. For example, "lion" and "yarn" might be paired together. Nisbett and Wilson introduced a small wrinkle into the method. For some volunteers, they included the word pair "moon-ocean." For others, "moon-ocean" was replaced with another set of words. After giving the research participants some time to memorize the words, they were then asked to do something seemingly strange, which was to name a brand of laundry detergent. Puzzled, the volunteers dutifully named one, but perhaps not surprisingly, the group which had memorized "moon-ocean" among its word pairs was twice as likely to name Tide laundry detergent. Nisbett and Wilson pointed out that the connection between "moon-ocean" and "Tide" was fairly obvious from the outside, but when the participants were asked why they had selected Tide, none of them were able to see the link.

Skinner didn't start with the question "Why did that happen?" It was more important that the behavior happened and that it might happen again, given the right circumstances. "Why?" could be explored later. The Skinnerian triumph, such as it was, was not his eponymous box. It was the idea that human behavior could be quantified and measured by observing it *from the outside* and that the insights gained from these data could reveal something about the human condition that, even if not fully correct, was more correct (or perhaps less wrong) than what came before it.

✳ ✳ ✳

THE OFFICIAL RULES OF MAJOR LEAGUE BASEBALL WOULD fill a small binder if printed out. Some of the rules are known to anyone with a cursory knowledge of the game (Section 5.08 is titled "How a Team Scores"), while some are arcane (Rule 3.06 governs the exact size of a fielding glove). Together, though, they create a standardized set of rules for our enclosed box—pardon me, baseball diamond.

From a data-collection perspective, baseball is a wonderland...at least for behavior within the box. The game unfolds in a linear fashion. The outcomes that we care about on the field are mostly sequential and easy to segment. The pitcher throws the ball to begin the sequence. We can measure the speed of the ball, how quickly it is spinning, and how much it moved in flight, but eventually it ends up near the plate, either in the strike zone or not in the strike zone. Somewhere during that flight, the batter must decide whether he'll swing or not. If he swings, he'll either hit it or not hit it. If he does hit it, it will either go fair or foul. If it goes fair, the fielders will either catch it or not. Then, the cycle starts again.

You can tell a fairly complete story of a baseball game using a simple scorecard on which you notate nine types of plays from which nearly all games are built: walk, strikeout, hit by pitch, single, double, triple, home run, groundout, or fly out. It's possible to go deeper than that (What was the count on each of those plays? Was the ball hit to left, center, or right?), but all of those things can be counted and measured, and we have literally decades of those data to draw from.

I'd argue that baseball is going through its Skinnerian moment. For a long time, the way in which the public learned about baseball was through the news media. While beat writers have written "gamers" recapping the actions of what happened in the game for ages, the game story has always included (and still does!) a quote or two from the game's hero (or goat) describing why he did what he did. It makes sense on the surface. People want to know "Why?" so let's ask the man himself! Introspect for me!

If our hero says that he hit that big home run because he "saw the ball differently today" it's entirely possible that he did. We have no way of directly knowing. Perhaps he's looking back fondly through the gauzy lens of a big emotional moment and it's distorting his memory. Perhaps the guy in the locker next to him who grounded out to second right before that big home run saw the ball differently too, *but no one ever thinks to ask him why he grounded out to second.* Baseball journalism might be fun to read, but it should never be mistaken for sound research methodology.

The ability to perform well, even in high-stress situations, has often been chalked up to some unobservable factor, such as "heart." A player who has "heart" will be able to hit that home run, even in the bottom of the ninth when all eyes are on him, and in a triumph of circular reasoning, the home run is taken as evidence that he has "heart." Maybe there is some sort of "heart" factor out there, but if we're really going to understand baseball, we should demand proof that is based on better methods than introspection and hero worship. Show me some data.

*   *   *

"...UNDER JURISDICTION OF ONE OR MORE UMPIRES."

The umpire is an anachronism in baseball. In any competition between two teams, some third party has to enforce the rules. At one point, umpires were necessary, but in a world where plenty of other workers have been replaced by machines, the umpire persists. Perhaps "under the jurisdiction of one or more robots" just doesn't have the same ring to it. The reality is that the technology to call balls and strikes automatically has existed for years. On most plays, out/safe calls aren't very close, but when they are, there are cameras all over the park and instant replay can adjudicate in slow motion and from multiple angles what the umpire, perhaps with an obstructed view, had to process at full game speed. There's no reason to think that the bases couldn't be "umpired" by someone just watching the slow-motion video feed at MLB Headquarters in New York. Technology always has its flaws, but it really only has to be better than the humans who normally wear the blue shirts. Yet, there are still umpires.

The arguments for and against umpires are well-worn, and they all boil down to an argument for baseball as a game that should be adjudicated with mechanical precision versus a game where the inevitable human error is a necessary thread in the fabric of the game. The primary argument for keeping umpires around seems to be that they make things less efficient, and people see that as a triumph. We want a game where one team can actually be better than the other and still get penalized because the home-plate umpire blinked at an inopportune time. We don't want everything to go exactly right. We don't want perfection...until a blown call goes against our favorite team in a key game in September.

Rule 1.01 says that we have to be okay with the thought that one person has the power to be extremely wrong and there's nothing we can do about it. In 2014, Major League Baseball allowed the use of instant replay during games, but in a way that preserved the umpires. There's still someone out at second base in a blue shirt who gets to make the initial safe/out call, and that call is considered the default. Replay evidence must be conclusive to the contrary to overturn it. The human hand still holds the leash of the machine.

In 2017, there were 1,338 plays where the umpire's call on the field was reviewed, either by a manager asking for a review or the umpires initiating one themselves. Forty-seven percent (627) of those were overturned. That makes it sound like umpires are doing a horrible job, but it's important to remember the sample that we're working with. If a play was challenged, it means that it was extremely close *and* at least one person watching thought it was called incorrectly, usually with the benefit of a second look on video replay. We don't have data on how many times there was a close play, but after watching it a second time everyone realized that Blue got it right. Still, 627 overturned calls means that there was a call every three or four games where we know that an umpire got it wrong. In the past, we let those go by. Why did it take baseball so long to do something so rational?

I think it's because baseball fans are used to tolerating irrational behavior. Being a fan of one specific team, often one randomly chosen for me by my place of birth, is an irrational act. I exercise no control over what happens to them on the field or in the front office. My emotional well-being is entirely at the mercy of people who might be geniuses or fools. That doesn't make sense either.

We aren't getting rid of Blue. Blue might not make sense, but Blue is in Rule 1.01 and everything about baseball is a tiny bit irrational anyway. Rule 1.01 isn't just the preamble to the MLB rulebook. It's a mission statement. It's a warning. It's a little essay on the nature of baseball. Baseball is a place where we have to understand the intersection of the individual and the group and authority and injustice and randomness. It's about the absurdity of trying to have rational rules and irrational people trying to follow those rules. Baseball is a game played by two teams that often act more like 18 individuals, under the direction of a manager who sometimes makes bad decisions, on an enclosed field in accordance with rules that sometimes aren't actually there, and which are administered by umpires who sometimes get it wrong. That's what Rule 1.01 is saying. Baseball is a messy and complicated game, played by imperfect people. To really understand the game, you have to understand the humans who play it. That's what we're going to study in this book. So, gather with 40,000 of your closest friends around the Skinner Box and let's see what happens.

Play ball!

- 1 -

The Most Dangerous Thing in the World

WHEN I WAS IN HIGH SCHOOL, THERE WAS A QUIZ-BOWL show on one of the local TV stations, which was hosted by the weatherman for their evening newscast. During my senior year, my high school was invited to send a team to compete on the show. I was the captain of that team. It was the closest I ever got to being varsity anything. Like any team, we felt the need to practice our craft, so we met a couple of days a week after school in Brother Dave's classroom and we watched old episodes of the show. It seemed like the thing to do. This was a show about trivia questions, so we sat around answering trivia questions. Cross-country runners ran around the neighborhood together. Chess-club members played chess against each other. I tried to be faster than my friends at remembering the chemical symbol for lead.

The show always started out with a rapid-fire round where Weatherman Guy asked 10 "buzz in to be called on" questions to the three teams on the stage. The game alternated between these rapid-play lightning rounds and more relaxed rounds in which each team got a chance to answer questions with no competition, but in the lightning rounds, every question that one team answered was a question that the other teams couldn't. At the end of the show, the winning team got to shake hands with Weatherman Guy, and maybe they got a spot in the playoffs.

The TV station taped a couple dozen episodes over the course of a year, so that a bunch of schools from the greater Cleveland area could have their one shining moment. According to the rules, the nine schools that scored the most points during these preliminary matches earned a playoff spot. Looking back, it probably meant that getting into the playoffs had more to do with the quality of the competition, rather than a team's own smarts, but that wasn't the way I thought of it at the time. On the day of taping for our preliminary round, I got on that stage, listened to Weatherman Guy ask questions, and hit that buzzer just like we practiced. We won! Not to brag, but we also finished with the seventh most points overall for that year. Turns out that knowing random pieces of information could take you places in Cleveland. We were headed to the playoffs!

A few weeks later, that first playoff match went according to the plan. Weatherman Guy asked us about minutiae. We buzzed in. We got it right. We squashed the other two teams. After our victory, I was exhausted, but pleased with the thought that at some point in the future, we'd be coming back down to Channel 5 to tape the final. What I didn't know was that "some point in the future" was scheduled for 10 minutes later. The station wanted to tape all the playoff shows in the same day. It seemed that Weatherman Guy had other plans for next weekend.

Despite the exhaustion, this is what we had practiced for, and adrenaline started kicking in. How often does one have the chance to win a championship in anything, even if it was the nerdiest thing possible? We got situated and the camera operators pointed their cameras at us. Weatherman Guy did his "Welcome to the show..." introduction that I was now hearing for the second time that day and informed us that the opening round of questions would be about geography. He would say the name of a famous landmark, and we had to identify the country in which it was located.

"Let's get started."

I was ready for this. Our team had already won twice. We were good. We were going to win this one too.

That's when things ran off the rails. Before Weatherman Guy even started asking the first question, someone from one of the other schools rang the buzzer. I knew we were going up against some smart people, but how could someone know the answer before Weatherman Guy had even said anything? That's when *it* happened. Weatherman Guy still read out the name of the land-mark, because even if it was technically a quiz bowl, it was also a television show, and the people who would eventually watch this at home needed to hear the question. Because the other team had technically buzzed in first, they got the chance to answer.

Hang on a second...

As soon as Weatherman Guy said "correct," I could again hear the sound of buzzer buttons being speed-pounded from the other two podiums, again all before Weatherman Guy even said anything. It took me until the fourth or fifth of these cycles until I realized what the other two teams were doing. To each side of the stage, there was a screen on which they showed the name of the landmark that Weatherman Guy was about to read, in text form. (It was also on the screen for the viewers at home.) As soon as the question appeared on the screen, the buzzer system went live. At that point, it was open season on those big red buttons. It still took a couple of seconds for Weatherman Guy to breathe in, read out the name of the landmark for the viewers at home, then look up to see which team's light was lit. That gave them enough time to formulate a response and have it ready when Weatherman Guy asked for it. The rest was a race to hit the button first.

We got wiped off the stage. I had practiced for a game in which there was a certain cadence of politeness. In the social norms that I grew up with, you didn't interrupt someone before they were done (or before they even started) talking. A quiz show was supposed to be about recalling pointless, but poignant, facts. Buzzing in was supposed to be the indicator that the buzzee had found the answer in their cerebral rolodex. Recall came first, then buzzing. For most of the half hour that we were on that stage, I couldn't move past those unwritten rules even when I realized that the other teams were gaming the system and racking up points because of it. It felt like I'd be breaking an honor code to copy their plan. Unfortunately, the scoreboard didn't care how I felt.

There was never actually a rule that said that we were required to wait for Weatherman Guy to finish—or even start—his sentence or that we had to know the answer before buzzing in. In fact, as part of his opening monologue, Weatherman Guy said that "*the team that buzzes in first* and gives the correct answer will get the points." The other teams had realized that buzzing in quickly was more important than figuring out the answer quickly. As long as someone on the team was able to pull up the answer within the three seconds that it took for the host to demand it, being a 10th of a second faster on recall than the other team didn't actually matter. In some sense, the other teams won the game before it even started. They didn't ask how the game had traditionally been played. They found a place where the rules were silent and an unenforceable social norm had filled in the gap. Then they found a way to exploit it to their advantage. I had spent my time solving one question—*How can I remember and quickly access more trivia answers?*—but it turns out my answer didn't matter, because I wasn't asking the right question.

"SMITH WAS 1-FOR-3, WITH A WALK."

Most baseball fans wouldn't blink at that sentence. We have a quick summary of Smith's day at the park. He came to the plate four times. In two of those times, he made an out. In one of them, he got some sort of hit. There was also that one time when he walked, but it doesn't *really* count. It happened, but we don't want to talk about it. We'll just append it to the back of the summary. Language is a powerful thing. Often, we can learn more by looking at *how* people talk about something, rather than what they say. In this case, relegating the walk to afterthought status shows a profound discomfort with ball four. Why does baseball get so freaked out about walks?

To understand why, we have to go back to the year 1887, still within the formative years of professional baseball. For the '87 season, the two major leagues at the time, the National League (which survives to this day) and the American Association (which eventually folded), came to a common agreement that the number of balls needed for a walk would be five, reducing the number from six (American Association) and seven balls (National League). By this time, batting average was already well-known as a statistic within the sport, and had been since the mid-1860s. In an era well before the modern power game (Billy O'Brien's 19 home runs led all of baseball in 1887), batting average was considered the main indicator of one's batting prowess.

In the years before 1887, as now, a walk didn't count toward a player's batting average. It was a non-event. In 1887, that changed. Both leagues agreed that for the purposes of calculating batting average, a walk would count the same as a hit. Apparently, things did not go well. There were reports that players started actively trying to walk to boost their batting average, and that led to slower, more passive games. Surely, baseball was dying! The data tell a somewhat different story. In 1886, the average game featured 2.64 walks per team. In 1887, there was a modest increase to 2.86 walks per team per game. We can't know how much of that increase was because players were trying to walk more often to boost their batting averages or because the new five-ball rule made it easier to walk than the old six- or seven-ball rules, but it's mostly pointless speculation. There was no epidemic of walks. The actual difference between 1886 and 1887 was about one extra walk for one of the teams every other game. As a point of comparison, between 2015 (2.90 walks per team per game) and 2016 (3.11 walks per team per game) there was a nearly identical jump in the raw rate of walks. While no one reading this book was around to witness the 1886 and 1887 seasons, I doubt that many people noticed the 2015 to 2016 jump in real time. Anyone who did probably only noticed it because they looked it up on the Internet. The Internet was much more primitive in 1887.

In 1888, the five-ball rule remained in effect, but walks were returned to their previous status as a non-event and removed from batting averages and have remained that way since then. The walk rate dropped that year to 2.18 per team per game. This likely had something to do with another rule change. In 1888, the strikeout rule changed from four strikes to its present "one-two-three strikes you're out" form. In 1889, both leagues changed the rules again and adopted the modern "four balls you walk" rule. That year, walk rates really did jump up, this time to 3.36 per team per game. If there was an outcry over having to write "BB" on the scorecard more often, it didn't result in a rule change back to five balls and never has. It doesn't seem like the walks themselves were the problem.

I think that the Great Walk Panic of 1887 was related to something else. I invite you, reader, to think of two people, Smith and Jones. Smith spends hours each day tinkering in the garage on a marvelous contraption that will solve a major social problem: reheating leftover pizza to the perfect temperature the next day.

Upon learning of Smith's invention, a company licenses Smith's work for mass production. Smith signs a contract that pays $1 million per year over the next 30 years. Jones, on the other hand, plays the lottery one day and happens to pick the correct six numbers. Jones will now be paid $1 million per year over the next 30 years. Which of the two is better off?

It's likely that the question "Which of the two is better off?" took you by surprise. Financially, they are equally well-off, but that's not the question that your brain started to answer. It started to answer the question "Which of them *deserves* it more?" with Smith being the obvious choice because Smith *worked for it.* In the United States' culture, there is a reflex to judge situations not on functional grounds, but on moral grounds. There is also a preference for Smith's industrious work over Jones's dumb luck. The inventor and the lottery winner, even if they end up with the same outcome, are viewed very differently. According to the cultural norms of the late 1800s, the walk was considered to be a lucky, lottery-winning event. The batter didn't *do* anything, at least in the sense that "doing something" involves physical action. He just stood there while the pitcher had a systems failure.

As things were put back to their rightful order after 1887, batting average once again completely ignored that walks ever happened. As baseball continued to develop and grow in popularity, batting average became *the* metric by which the "batting champion" was crowned. Lore developed around the ".300 hitter" and the nearly-mythical ".400 hitter." The numbers that we use to describe our world have their own cultural etymologies, and sometimes they have assumptions baked into them that we don't even realize. Sometimes those assumptions don't make sense. A walk and a single both end with the runner at first base, but our brains are too busy answering the question of whether the batter *deserves* first base or not.

If batting average had never existed, someone would have eventually invented something like it. The question, "How often has this guy done something positive with his at-bat in the past?" is a good one. The problem is that batting average isn't actually answering the question that we really want answered. It's answering the question, "How often has this guy done something positive *and socially acceptable according to the cultural norms of the late 1800s* with his at-bat?" The most dangerous thing in the world is the correct answer to the wrong question.

To state that Smith and Jones both had a batting average of .300 last year might be a true statement. To state that they were equally valuable to their teams based on those data alone is dubious. If Smith hits .300 *and* draws a lot of walks, but Jones does not, then Smith is clearly doing more to help his team win. Why not ask a better question if you have better data sitting there? Once you ask the right question, the rest is just long division to get a stat that already exists, on-base percentage (OBP).

If the sabermetric movement in baseball can be boiled down to one moment, it would be the moment when someone asked "Why are we pretending that walks never happened?" Perhaps the best-known piece of the book *Moneyball* was that the Oakland A's picked up on this very issue and began evaluating batters by virtue of their on-base percentage, rather than their batting average. To put it another way, the Oakland A's—more than a century after the Great Walk Panic of 1887—started asking, and then answering, the right question.

*　　*　　*

THERE ARE PLENTY OF PEOPLE WHO ARE SKEPTICAL OF THE sabermetric movement. Perhaps, reader, you are one of them. I've heard plenty of those objections. Some of them are just name-calling (Why thank you, I'm proud to be a nerd), but there's one that I think deserves some honest consideration. It's usually summarized in three words: You didn't play.

In my case, that's a true statement. I went to baseball camp when I was nine. I loved the game, but even the hubris and big league dreams that came with being in fourth grade eventually gave way to the realization that I couldn't hit a curveball. Or a fastball. Or a slow ball. I wasn't going to make it to the big leagues if I couldn't even make it in Little League. Years later, when I revived my major league dreams (and eventually achieved them—I've worked as a consultant to a couple of teams in MLB) by doing statistical research on baseball, I heard that a lot. How can someone who never played or managed professionally have something to say about Major League Baseball?

As someone who has been trained in psychotherapy, I'm painfully aware that it's not enough to just proclaim yourself an expert if you want real engagement with people. You have to be willing to both understand and address the other person's natural skepticism and to do so honestly and without resorting to "because I have more letters after my name than you do." At the same time, part of the job of being a therapist is helping people whose life stories I did not share. It's possible if you approach the work with an open mind, and sometimes, having an outsider's perspective gives a person the ability to see something in a way that they can't from the inside.

I've heard "You didn't play" in the therapy room, too. There, it's commonly said as "You haven't lived my life. You don't understand." That's a powerful statement that usually has the problem of being true. It can be a frustrating sentence. As a therapist, the correct response is generally, "Okay, help me to understand." I may not have walked the same path that you have, but I have my own experience and an open mind and I care about learning what you're trying to communicate. If I can understand how a person sees the world around them, I can usually work from there. There's another problem. "Help me understand" sounds great, but sometimes asking for an explanation doesn't work. There are times when people can't explain what exactly it is that they understand but you don't. That's not a fault; it's just hard to explain some things.

There are two different kinds of knowledge that humans have: declarative knowledge and implicit knowledge. Declarative knowledge covers what we might call the "facts" that we know (e.g., the capital of Wyoming is Cheyenne). Then there's implicit knowledge, which we don't often verbalize and sometimes don't even realize. It's mostly the product of experience rather than study. For example, if you've lived in your house or apartment for a while, you can probably navigate around even in the dark. When Uncle Larry comes to visit, he can't. The reason is that you have a mental map of where everything is based on more than just sight. You didn't set out to study that or learn it explicitly, it's just something that you've learned through repetition. How do you explain to Uncle Larry that when you hear the floorboard that makes the *eeeh-eh* sound, rather than the *eeeeeh-eh* sound, you are safely past the wall and can turn left without fear of crashing into it? That's implicit knowledge.

When I was learning to be a therapist, I worked mainly with African American children and families who lived in public housing communities in Chicago. I was a white guy from the suburbs of Cleveland. I tried my best to understand the families that I was working with, but I had a steep learning curve. I had never lived in a public housing community or even lived in Chicago that long. (At the time, I had no children of my own, and yet here I was giving parenting advice!) Sadly, there was a large amount of gang activity in the areas where I worked and there were invisible lines on certain streets that people dared not cross, for fear of their safety. Fool that I was, I would blithely propose meeting somewhere for a therapy session or enrolling in a great after-school program at a particular place where a family would have to cross one of those lines. I got a few well-deserved "No, you don't understand" comments along the way. They weren't dismissing me. They appreciated that I was trying to help their kids, but the truth was that I didn't understand. I was offering a suggestion that made no sense within the reality that they lived in, because I didn't understand their reality. It was probably annoying to have to listen to the "expert" say something so stupid.

In baseball (as in the therapy room), "You never played" can be used as a defense mechanism by people who want to shut down the conversation because they don't want to change. Those people are out there, but as a sabermetrician (and as a therapist), I've been guilty of being too quick to assume that stubbornness was the only reason that people would say it. Instead, I've come to realize that "You never played" often serves a different purpose. It's a way of saying there are things that players, managers, and baseball lifers know to look for *implicitly*, things that sometimes they themselves don't even realize they're picking up on. And I—like poor Uncle Larry feeling his way in the dark—have no idea these are even out there.

The experienced base stealer might say, "Sure your fancy regression model says that a stolen base attempt is a great idea here, but I've not been able to figure out this guy's move in three years of playing against him. I usually can read pitchers pretty well and that's why your model thinks I'm a great base stealer. This guy's different. I might guess right, but I'd be guessing and I'm not gonna be able to get a great jump. With that in mind, does your probability function still think an attempt is a good idea?" That's the full answer (and a good point), but sometimes it's hard to put that into words on three seconds of notice. Instead, it might come out as "You never played!"

When I hear "You never played," I've learned not to treat it as a dismissal, but as an invitation to collaboration. Tell me what I would know to look for if I had played that I'm not considering right now. After all, if I come up with a crazy everything-you-ever-thought-was-wrong idea about how baseball works and swear that no matter what anyone else thinks, I'm right, what I'm really saying is "You never calculated it!" If I'm using that as a defense mechanism to shut down conversation because I'm afraid I might be wrong, then I'm the idiot in the room.

IN 2012, THERE WAS A FLASHPOINT IN THE ONGOING CULtural battle around the sabermetric movement. Miguel Cabrera of the Detroit Tigers won the first Triple Crown that Major League Baseball has seen since Carl Yastrzemski accomplished the feat in 1967. Cabrera led the American League in batting average (.330), home runs (44), and runs batted in (139). After a season like that, surely he was a lock to win the league's Most Valuable Player Award. Twenty years earlier, this wouldn't have been a question, but in 2012, there was another contender: Angels center fielder Mike Trout.

Trout, who was a rookie in 2012 (indeed, he won Rookie of the Year honors), played the first month of the 2012 season with the Salt Lake Bees, the Angels' AAA affiliate. When he came up to the majors in late April, he was an instant success, and ended up leading the American League in runs scored and stolen bases, while hitting for a respectable .326 batting average with 30 home runs and 83 RBI. Trout was universally hailed as having a very good year...but Cabrera had won the Triple Crown.

That's when the "stateheads" went to WAR. Not the thing where people shoot guns and missiles at each other, but the statistic Wins Above Replacement. According to WAR, Trout's contributions had made the Angels around 10 wins better than they would have been without him. Cabrera undeniably had a good year, but according to WAR, his contributions were "only" worth about seven extra wins to the Tigers. Trout, screamed the statheads, was far and away the more valuable player to his team. Who then was the MVP?

Partisans for Cabrera pointed out both the historic nature of a Triple Crown and the fact that Cabrera's Tigers won the AL Central and made the playoffs (and eventually the World Series, where they lost to the San Francisco Giants). Trout's Angels finished in third place in the AL West and made golfing reservations for early October. Cabrera was therefore not only a good player, but a good player powering a winning team.

Trout's fans pointed out that batting average was a very flawed stat, and while it was nice that Mr. Cabrera led the league in it, Mr. Trout's on-base percentage (.399) for the year was superior to Mr. Cabrera's (.393). They also pointed out that while the Tigers made the playoffs, this was an accident of geography. The Angels (89 wins) had won more games than the Tigers (88), but the Angels had the misfortune of playing in a division which included west-of-the-Mississippi neighbors the Oakland A's (94 wins) and the Texas Rangers (93 wins). The Tigers, on the other hand, played in a division of fellow Midwesterners, the best of whom (the Chicago White Sox) had managed only 85 wins. Trout was therefore the best player on a team that was actually better than Cabrera's, but the victim of a map!

Cabrera eventually won the Most Valuable Player Award, garnering 22 of the 28 first-place votes cast, but the argument remained. Which of them was the more valuable player? Aside from pedantic nonsense about the ambiguity of "valuable," a more interesting word that emerged in the inevitable think pieces on the subject was "tradition." Batting average, home runs, and runs batted in were statistics that had been used for decades to mark a player's quality. They are still the ones that are shown on TV when a batter comes to the plate. Why did the nerds need to invent a bunch of new convoluted numbers?

The answer to that critique is already partially finished. Batting average is flawed mostly because, as we just discussed, it pretends that walks never happened. Home runs are wonderful and not a bad statistic to focus on, although they represent only one way to contribute to a team. Runs batted in have the flaw that a batter who comes up with more runners on base—something not in his control—is going to have more opportunities to rack up RBIs. Yes, it is undeniably good to have a higher, rather than a lower, batting average. Yes, it is better to drive a runner in than leave him stranded. Yes, a home run is the best possible outcome an at-bat can have. And yes, Miguel Cabrera was the best at all three in the American League in 2012. Fans of Cabrera were asking a question: "Who led the league in batting average, home runs, and RBI?" Historically, that question had always been answered: "the League MVP."

Fans of Trout were asking whether that was even the right question. In that sense, advocates on both sides ended up talking past each other, because they both had the right answer to their chosen question. Which side was asking the right one?

I think it's reasonable to say that the Triple Crown stats are a pretty good indicator of a player's value. I also think that there are other numbers that do a better job. In most other parts of life, "the old stuff works fine, but the new stuff works better" is a winning argument, but I also need to recognize that there's something else going on here. Baseball is a game awash in numbers. It's been that way for a long time. While baseball's numbers form a functional lexicon that can be used to describe a player (e.g., he's a ".280 hitter"), those numbers are also intimately tied to stories—sometimes legendary stories and cultural touchpoints—in the game. For those who are initiated, some of those numbers don't even need context to communicate their message.

56

61*

2,632

42

Immediately, we recognize the improbability of Joe DiMaggio's streak and the grandeur of the hitting ability that produced it. We see little-known Roger Maris, who became immortal by having a career season and controversially dethroning one of the game's first icons from one of its signature records. We see Cal Ripken's tenacity and perseverance showing up to work every day. We see the courage of Jackie Robinson as he crossed a barrier and succeeded even when some of the fans who came to see him wanted that barrier put back. These are powerful stories, communicated effortlessly and wordlessly through a vocabulary of numbers.

Storytelling is a quintessentially human endeavor. All societies have ways of passing down knowledge and traditions through generations. The fact that baseball has been measured using many of the same basic stats across time provides a language to tell these stories. This vocabulary which spans generations provides an *entrepot* for parents and grandparents to discuss the game with their (grand)children. There aren't any legendary stories in baseball that involve WAR.

To return to DiMaggio's 56-game hitting streak for a moment, it's a little surprising that the number 84 hasn't made its way into the pantheon of baseball numbers that need no explanation. In 1949, Ted Williams (himself the holder of a legendary story number, .406) reached base in 84 consecutive games. Some of Williams's games involved walks, but he was on base. There's no question that DiMaggio's achievement is worthy of praise, but why has it entered the realm of mythology while Williams's accomplishment is a trivia question? Even casual fans of the game know what 56 is.

DiMaggio's streak was a story as it was happening. When it ended, newspapers in cities where there weren't even Major League teams noted it on the front page. The number 56 doesn't hold a special place in baseball because it represents the best way to understand the inner workings of the game. Its focus on hits is an artifact of the same faulty assumption that brought us batting average. Fifty-six is special because it *came with a story* that was the talk of the time it existed in, and is now a way of communicating the glory of a bygone age.

There were plenty of sportswriters and fans alike who felt a certain tug at their heartstrings upon seeing Miguel Cabrera finish the 2012 season by winning the Triple Crown. Whether or not batting average, home runs, and RBI are the best metric to use, they grew up in a culture where those three stats were the measure of a hero. Maybe those numbers aren't the best ones available, but they are the ones that are the foundation of a story-telling tradition. The 2012 MVP debate wasn't just a mathematical argument. It was an argument about a piece of cultural heritage.

*   *   *

AS SOMEONE SEEKING GENUINE ENGAGEMENT, I NEED TO be upfront about my own baggage. In this book, I am approaching the game of baseball through a lens of dispassion. I'm a scientist, not a sportswriter. My starting point is the question, "What is the best way to win a baseball game?" I'm purposefully short-circuiting the impulse to judge things on anything other than functional grounds. I don't care whether a single is morally superior to a walk. I care that both lead to the batter standing on first base. Sabermetrics, as defined by Bill James, the man who coined the term, is the search for objective truth about baseball. Science, by its very nature, has to be fearless. It doesn't matter whether things have "always been that way." People can be wrong, and "tradition" sometimes just means that they've been wrong for a very long time. As a scientist, nothing is beyond questioning. Maybe "tradition" is hiding some deeper truth about the game, but I want to see the proof. That can rub some people the wrong way. Not everyone is in the mood to think about baseball or watch a game with their cultural assumptions thrown overboard.

There is research showing that high pitch counts in a single game put pitchers at a greater risk for injury. Teams are very aware of this fact. It's now rare to find a starting pitcher who is allowed to throw more than 110 pitches in a night. There have been critiques that the present generation of pitchers isn't tough enough to throw 150 pitches (or more) as their forerunners did and that pitch limits are ruining the game. "Tough enough" and "ruining the game" are moral judgments. If your belief is that the game is more aesthetically pleasing when pitchers regularly throw 150 pitches in a game, that is your prerogative. I would only reply that—aesthetic and moral opinions aside—teams are most interested in protecting their pitchers' health for the simple reason that it will win them more games in the long run.

If you are someone who is a skeptic of the sabermetric movement, it's possible that we just want two different things out of being baseball fans. I promise that I'm not out to destroy the game of baseball. I'm just approaching it in a different way. Even if that's not the vantage point that you usually take, I'd invite you to read this book with that thought in mind. This is a different way to look at the game. Maybe it will be fun.

But...the numbers. There are probably those reading right now who are nervous that this will involve algebra or calculus and it may have been a few years since you took algebra or calculus. I promise that the math won't be that hard, and honestly, the math itself isn't all that important. When we discussed the Great Walk Panic of 1887, we saw that batting average contained an outdated assumption that simply was passed along unquestioned into our modern box scores. The most important part of any number is understanding the logic that powers it. What question does this number answer? Is that the right question? The rest is nitpicking about minor methodological details. So, even if you don't understand all the math, understanding the shift in thought behind it is the real issue.

In 2012, proponents of Mike Trout for the MVP Award often referred to a statistic known as WAR or Wins Above Replacement, and for a large chunk of the baseball-loving public, 2012 was the first time that they had even heard of it. The backstory of WAR sounds a lot like the backstory of punk rock, only nerdier. Its foundations were laid down in the late 1990s on an obscure Usenet discussion group (*rec.sports.baseball*). Usenet itself was an early internet forum, segmented into topics, where anyone could post. The discussion group, populated by statistically curious baseball fans—some of whom found paths into Major League front offices—served as fertile ground for new ideas on evaluating baseball players. Every movement has its "I was there at the beginning" mark of credibility. This was the little club where all the bands who eventually got big played their first shows. These were the bands that asked tough questions of the establishment, and sometimes flouted those establishment traditions just because it made people angry. This time, they were wielding spreadsheets rather than guitars.

WAR, like the punk movement, was not a calculated moment. It was an outgrowth of a natural desire to ask questions of people who were not used to being asked questions. As a result, WAR initially lacked institutional approval. While batting average had been around for a century and had been stamped by the proper authorities as the good and respectable way to evaluate a player, WAR was a newcomer and it was...weird. For one, WAR bragged about comparing all players to some non-existent "replacement player." It claimed the ability to directly compare the value of pitchers and position players. Was Warren Spahn or Mickey Mantle more valuable to his team? Generations of bar arguments, which generally ended with, "Well, I guess there's no good way to compare the two," could now be solved, and what fun is an argument that has a correct answer?

I think it's worth considering WAR on its own merits. Like any other number, especially something that purports to be a single-number solution to everything, WAR has its strengths and its flaws and most importantly, its assumptions. Instead of walking through the gory mathematical details, I think it's more instructive to walk through the thought process of WAR. WAR is not a perfect measure, but I'd argue that it's irresponsible to disregard the places where something is correct simply because it is not *entirely* correct.

The word "value" is a slippery one. We're going to need a working definition. To get there, we are going to need to make some assumptions, and in some cases, those assumptions reveal weaknesses, and the first assumption of WAR is that we only include the things for which we have available data. Thankfully, in baseball, we have reasonably good data on most of the things that go on between the foul lines. We know who hit a single and when. We know who caught the ball and who let it drop. We know who swung and missed and who fouled off that 2-2 pitch to stay alive. We also have very little idea what happens *outside* those foul lines. If a 39-year-old veteran sits down with a 23-year-old kid and finally gets through to him that he *really* needs to work harder, then in theory, part of that kid's breakout season should be credited to the veteran. However, WAR has no idea that the conversation ever happened. It simply notes that the kid got better and gives no credit to his mentor. We are going to have to live with that weakness, and it's a big one.

LET'S BEGIN WITH THE MECHANICS OF HOW WAR WORKS. The "R" in WAR stands for "replacement," which is short for "replacement level" or "replacement player." It's said that you can tell how important your job is by what would happen if you decided not to show up. WAR begins defining "value" by asking a similar question "What would have happened if Mike Trout hadn't shown up for the 2012 season and had instead decided to become a cabbage farmer?"

Everyone would agree that the Angels would have been worse off, but how much worse? WAR assumes that they would have made do with the best that they already had on hand or what was freely available. That might mean promoting their fourth outfielder from the bench into a starting role. It might mean bringing up a kid from AAA to fill the spot. It might mean signing someone off the waiver wire. None of those are great options, but at the same time, the Angels would have gotten *something* out of their stopgap. Trout hit 30 home runs in 2012, but the Angels wouldn't be losing all 30 of them. His replacement would probably have hit a couple of dingers.

Here's where WAR gets a little abstract. The first instinct might be to go back and review the actual 2012 Angels roster. Trout debuted in late April that year, and before that point, Peter Bourjos got most of the playing time in center field for the Angels. After Trout made the majors, Bourjos was mostly relegated to fourth outfielder duties. It's reasonable to think that if Mike Trout had simply vanished before the 2012 season, Bourjos would have continued as the Angels starting center fielder, and thus would have gotten most of the playing time that Trout ended up with.

In a surprise, we're not going to compare Trout to Bourjos. Instead, WAR assumes that Trout would have been replaced by a composite of bench players from around the league. This might seem like a strange choice, but it comes with a benefit that might not be immediately obvious. One of the missions of WAR is to evaluate players only according to things that the player himself can control. The answer to "What was Mike Trout worth *to the Angels*?" is best answered by the distance from Trout to Bourjos, but that pegs Trout's value to the fact that the Angels' next best outfielder at the time happened to be Bourjos. Trout had no control over who else was on the Angels roster. If the Angels had a young Ken Griffey Jr., fresh out of a time machine from 1990, ready in their minor league system, then the Angels wouldn't have lost much if Trout had decided to go backpacking in Iceland rather than play baseball. We don't want to credit (or debit) a player for the greatness (or incompetence) of his teammates or his general manager. To do that, we need to set everyone against a common baseline.

How to form that baseline? Here we introduce another assumption of WAR, which is that *position matters*. In the 1980s, sabermetric pioneer Bill James introduced the idea of a "defensive spectrum." He noted that the average shortstop was a worse hitter than the average second baseman who was a worse hitter than the average left fielder who was a worse hitter than the average first baseman. The positions fell nicely in order from the defensive spots considered the easiest to play to the ones that required the most specialized skills.

Table 1. Aggregate Batting Average, On-Base Percentage, and Slugging Percentage for Players at Each Defensive Position During the 2017 Season

Position	AVG	OBP	SLG
1B	.265	.347	.487
RF	.264	.339	.458
3B	.258	.330	.445
CF	.264	.333	.431
2B	.269	.333	.422
LF	.256	.327	.427
SS	.264	.319	.416
C	.246	.315	.410

We can see that we expect less with the bat from a shortstop than we do from a first baseman. A player who hits like an average first baseman and plays first base is an average player. A player who has the exact same batting line *but can play a competent shortstop* is an All-Star. The fact that Mike Trout was able to play a premium defensive position, such as center field (and he played it quite well), rather than being consigned to an outfield corner, meant that the Angels were getting good value out of a spot on the field where teams normally don't get as much production. It also meant that the Angels, when shopping to fill out their outfield, could go digging for a player in those much more productive corner bins, rather than the center field one. The fact that the 2012 Angels were only able to come up with Vernon Wells (.230/.279/.403 in 2012) to be their left fielder is not Mike Trout's fault.

Replacement level or "the replacement player" is probably the hardest concept to understand in WAR, because it isn't an actual human being. Here's how it works. Take all 30 teams and identify the player who had the greatest amount of playing time at each position. For pitchers, identify the five starters and seven relievers on each team who pitched the most innings. Everyone *not* in that group is a "replacement player." That's going to mean bench players, utility guys, guys who bounced up and down between AAA and the majors, September call-ups, and even fringy guys who got 20 plate appearances when a team needed a warm body to fill a roster spot after a rash of July injuries. The nice thing is that even bench and fringe players get at-bats, so we have some idea how they would do against Major League pitching. That production probably isn't great (otherwise, they would be in the "starting" group), but it's something. For a center fielder like Mike Trout, we find all of these marginal players who showed that they could play center field in 2012. We mash all of those "replacement" center fielders into a big ball, and figure how often players in this group hit a home run. In 2012, these "replacement" center fielders hit a home run every 54 plate appearances.

In 2012, Mike Trout came to the plate 639 times at the major league level. He hit 30 home runs, one every 21.3 plate appearances. If Mike Trout were replaced by this ball of cast-offs and fourth outfielders and that mish-mash were given 639 plate appearances, they would have hit 11.8 home runs. (Yes, it's impossible to hit eight-tenths of a home run, but WAR and most of sabermetrics works in decimals.) Mike Trout was therefore 18.2 home runs better than replacement level. We can do this with his entire stat line, including all the singles and doubles and strike-outs, and we can do it for the stat line of every player in baseball. We can compare center fielders to replacement center fielders, third basemen to replacement third basemen, and shortstops to replacement shortstops.

NOW THAT WE'VE FIGURED OUT WHAT TO COMPARE MIKE Trout to, we need some way to calculate how much value he produced when he played. To that end, WAR makes another assumption, which is that *everything matters*. We will again read from the MLB rulebook, this time looking at two rules in particular.

Rule 1.02: The offensive team's objective is to have its batter become a runner, and its runners advance.

Rule 1.03: The defensive team's objective is to prevent offensive players from becoming runners, and to prevent their advance around the bases.

According to the rulebook, anything that increases the chances of a batter becoming a runner (hitting) and advancing on the bases (baserunning) and anything that decreases the chances of the other team doing those things (pitching and defense) has value. In 2012, Miguel Cabrera did win the Triple Crown, but the Triple Crown only contains statistics which describe hitting and provides no information about Cabrera's baserunning or fielding performance. Is it possible that the distance between Miguel Cabrera's superior performance with the bat could have been eclipsed when we consider Mike Trout's performance with his glove and legs?

Perhaps Mike Trout was better at going from first to third on a single, effectively "stealing" a base for his team. That has value. Perhaps he ran down a fly ball that a lesser center fielder wouldn't have gotten to. That has value. Can all of that value be converted into extra points on a batting average? Rule 1.05 tells us that "The objective of each team is to win by scoring more runs than the opponent," and so we're going to try to convert everything into the true measure of baseball goodness: runs.

HITTING

While hitting has the most well-known suite of statistics from which to draw, it's not as simple as "a double is worth half a run." It's true that a double brings you halfway around the circuit, but what a double really does is give a team a better chance to score a run than it had before. If, before the double, the bases were empty and there were two outs, the chances of the batting team scoring a run were low (say 10 percent—and here I'm making numbers up for ease of illustration). By reaching second, a batter improves his team's chances of scoring in the inning to 40 percent (again, a made-up number). Just by getting to second, he's added 30 percent of a run (0.3 runs). This gets credited to his account. Our batter—now our runner at second—might end up scoring. He might not. That will depend on what the batter behind him does, but again, we don't want to credit or debit a player for what his teammates do. He's increased his team's *chances* of scoring, and we will give him credit for that, no matter what else happens.

If there were runners on base, a double is also good because any runners on second or third go from being potential runs to actual, scored runs. If there's a guy on first, he might score too. The batter didn't put those ducks on the pond, so he doesn't get credit for them being there (which is exactly the mistake that RBIs make), but if a runner on second has a 40 percent chance of scoring before the double, he has a 100 percent chance of scoring after the double, and it's because of the batter. The batter just added 60 percent of a run. That gets deposited into his account as well. If our batter strikes out though, rather than doubling, his real crime is that he has reduced the team's chances of scoring runs. His account gets debited for that.

There's one other important assumption of WAR that we need to go over. Let's say that there are two players, Smith and Jones, who happen to be clones of each other. Smith plays on a team with a bunch of guys who can't hit. Smith hits a lot of doubles, but there's never anyone on to drive in, and no one hitting behind him who can drive him in. Jones also hits a lot of doubles, but he is lucky to be in a lineup filled with guys who are always getting on base in front of him and who can drive him in, so his RBI and runs scored totals are impressive. Jones's team scores more than Smith's. But Smith and Jones both hit the same double. Should we penalize Smith for the fact that his teammates are terrible? WAR says no. If they were traded for each other, they would still hit the same double, but now Smith would have the RBIs to show for it and Jones would be the hard-luck loser. This is the final assumption of WAR. We want to value a player's contributions paying no attention to what his teammates did around him. WAR gives the *exact same amount of credit* to Smith and Jones for the double that they hit, even if the end results for their teams were different.

BASERUNNING

We can look at baserunning in the same way that we look at the value of hitting events. Stealing a base, whether it's a stolen base in the usual sense or taking an "extra" base on a hit (e.g., going from first to third on a single) improves a team's chances of scoring. You get partial credit for a run that may or may not eventually score, but you deserve credit for making those odds better. Then again, you can also lose some value for your team by being thrown out on the basepaths or for being so slow that you don't even try to advance most of the time. When evaluating baserunning, we usually compare a player's performance to the rest of the league's. If the rest of the league goes from first to third on a single about 60 percent of the time, and you get to third 80 percent of the time, you are adding more value than average, and you should get credit for that.

DEFENSE

It's not easy to measure defense in baseball, but we have a decent idea how to do it. Suppose you're a shortstop, and there's a ball bounding up the middle in your general area. If you get to the ball and throw out the runner, you've decreased the other team's chances of scoring. There's now an extra out on the board, and there's no runner at first. If you can't get to the ball because you are slow, the ball trickles into center field. Because of your lead feet, a runner is now at first and your team didn't get that out that it wanted. Again, we can calculate how much your slowness has affected the chances of the batting team scoring a run, much like we did with baserunning. We'll add that to your tally.

No fielder will get to every ball. But there seem to be a lot more balls that trickle into center field with some shortstops than with others. If we see that the average shortstop gets to about 80 percent of the ground balls hit in his general area, and you are able to get to 90 percent, then you are providing more value than the average shortstop. Go you!

PITCHING

Neither Trout nor Cabrera pitched in 2012, but pitchers also provide value to their teams. We do need to be a little more careful with them. In fact, one of the first major findings to emerge from the sabermetric movement was that pitchers actually have less control over what happens in the game than we usually give them credit for. The findings, which were published by researcher Voros McCracken, noted that if you look at the percentage of hitters that a pitcher strikes out from year to year, the players at the top of the list tend to stay fairly consistent, as do the ones at the bottom of the list. (In statistical terms, we say that the year-to-year correlation is high.) Same with walks and hit batsmen. We see a slightly weaker correlation, but still "good enough" when it comes to home runs allowed.

Then there's everything else that happens. These are the balls that are "in play," since we've taken away everything where the batter either doesn't hit the ball or the batter hits it over the fence. It turns out that knowing what sort of batting average on balls in play (often abbreviated as BABIP) a pitcher allows in one year tells you little about how he'll do the next year on that stat. McCracken (and others) interpreted this finding as evidence that pitchers have little to no control over what happens once the ball is in the hands of the defense. Further research has found that "no control" is going too far, but we should be more forgiving of pitchers who allow a few bleeders through the infield. They induced the batter to hit a weak ground ball, which is the right idea, but the ball just happened to find a hole to scoot through. Or the shortstop was too slow.

For balls in play, there are a few work-arounds that we can use, including giving pitchers credit for the *type* of batted ball that they allowed. Research has shown that pitchers are far more consistent from year to year in their ground ball vs. fly ball rates. In 2017, 76 percent of all ground balls became outs, so we might give a pitcher credit for three-quarters of an out for inducing the grounder, and not penalize him if his teammate at shortstop is slow, something that he can't control. Similarly, we would look less favorably on a pitcher who gives up a line drive. In 2017, 69 percent of all line drives became *hits*, but we don't credit the pitcher for the fact that the batter was polite enough to hit the ball close to the shortstop who made an astonishingly beautiful catch.

At the end though, pitchers are given credit in much the same way that position players are, which is to say in runs. In the same way that we can credit Mike Trout for how many home runs he hits above what a replacement center fielder might hit, we can figure out how many extra strikeouts a pitcher collected above a replacement-level hurler. A hitter who strikes out surrenders a certain amount of probability that his team will score a run, and the pitcher who struck him out gathers that value unto himself.

ADDING IT ALL TOGETHER

We can keep a ledger of all of these contributions over the course of a year and add them together for any player. Because we've converted everything into runs, all of his contributions, whether at the plate, on the bases, in the field, or even on the mound all add together. We have a reasonable baseline to compare him to, which is our replacement level. The rest is simple math to create "runs above replacement level."

The final step is converting runs into wins. The easiest way to do that is simply divide by 10, which might seem like an arbitrary number, but there's a reason behind it. In the 1980s, Bill

James introduced the "Pythagorean Record." It's the idea that if you want to know how good a team *really* is, look at the number of runs they've scored versus the number of runs that they've given up. A team that wins five consecutive games by a score of 2–1 will have a 5–0 record to show for their work. A team that wins one game 10–1, then loses four straight 1–0 games will have a 1–4 record for their work, but the two teams have scored and given up the exact same number of runs. One of them just scored their runs at more opportune times. James created a formula which predicted what a team's record *should* have been given their runs scored and runs allowed. It might seem silly at first to judge a team on how many games we figure that they *should* have won rather than how many they *actually* won, but testing shows that if you want a better predictor of who will win *tomorrow's* game, their Pythagorean record works better than their actual record.

The idea of 10 runs being worth a win comes from the fact that if we start with a team that both scores and gives up runs at a league average rate, the Pythagorean method would estimate that they are an 81–81 team. It takes adding about 10 runs scored (or subtracting 10 runs allowed or five on each side) before their projected winning percentage goes up enough to equal one extra win over a 162-game season. So, when we say that a player is a two-win player, we're saying that on a team that was otherwise average, the things that player did over the course of a year were worth about 20 runs in expected value compared to what a team would have gotten from a replacement level player at his same position. Because of that, we believe that his team won two extra games because of his contributions. It's a mouthful, but that's WAR.

In sabermetric writing, it's common to read about something being worth "four-tenths of a run" or "seven-tenths of a win." To the fan who has watched the game for years and has never seen a decimal point on the scoreboard or in the standings, that might be a little unsettling. Teams do not win half games, nor do players score half runs, but outside of a home run, there aren't any events in baseball where a player generates a run entirely by himself, and certainly not a win by himself. However, if we're going to give (or take away from) each player the credit for the *probability* he added to (or subtracted from) his team's chances of scoring (or keeping the other team from scoring), that's going to require some decimals. Decimals don't mean that sabermetricians believe in half-wins, but simply that they acknowledge that creating a run or a win is a team effort, and one person is only entitled to some of that credit.

There are tweaks that other researchers have made to WAR. Some like to chop up credit for certain events a little differently. Some like to adjust for how friendly (or unfriendly) the hitter's (or pitcher's) home ballpark was. Some adjust for the position he played a little differently. All of those are worthy lines of research to pursue for those who are interested, but even without delving too deeply into those, you now know the basic idea behind WAR.

WAR answers the question, "Given the limits of our data, which ignore any value that a player might provide off the field, but include all the value that a player contributed in his hitting, fielding, baserunning, and pitching (ignoring what his teammates did around him), how many extra games do we estimate that a hypothetical 'league average' team (rather than his actual team) would have won because of a player's contributions, compared to what his team would have gotten from a bench/fringe player who would have been capable of playing his same position?"

This is not *the* perfect question and it's tempting to dismiss things that aren't perfect, but I'd argue that it is the best question that we are able to answer. If nothing else, it's better than what came before it. It includes everything that a player does on the field, including his baserunning and defense, rather than relying on just his hitting statistics. It addresses the reality that the position a player plays is important to figuring out how valuable he is. It gives a player credit for what he did, rather than what his teammates did or did not do around him. It compares everyone to the same baseline.

The real test is whether you buy in to the shift in thinking that WAR represents in defining "value." If you found yourself nodding and saying, "Yeah, that makes sense" as the explanation went along, then the math is simply an expression of that logic. If that's the case, then you may actually be a WAR believer and not even know it.

* * *

IN 2012, MIGUEL CABRERA WAS A BETTER HITTER THAN MIKE Trout, but Trout was the more valuable all-around player. Trout stole 49 bases (leading the American League) compared to Cabrera's four. That's 45 extra times that Trout effectively turned a single or a walk into a double. In 2012, Trout had 27 doubles and eight triples, for a total of 35 extra-base hits, while Cabrera had 40 doubles and no triples. While Cabrera had the edge in raw numbers of extra-base hits, Trout was standing on second base just the same after a single and a steal, and he was standing on second base more often than Cabrera. In addition, Trout was one of the best in baseball at adding value with his baserunning, "stealing" extra bases in other ways, while Cabrera's baserunning rated as below average. On defense, Mike Trout saved the Angels around 20 runs in the outfield, making him one of the most valuable defenders in the league, while Miguel Cabrera played an adequate, but slightly below average third base. Add it all together, and according to WAR it was Mike Trout by three lengths.

The most dangerous thing in the world is the correct answer to the wrong question, because it often stops further examination. A person can honestly say, "But I've got the right answer."

In 2012, Miguel Cabrera won the MVP Award, meaning that voters were asking a different question than the one that WAR answers. Perhaps they were answering, "Who led the league in three statistical categories that have traditionally been valued within baseball culture as the exemplars of hitting excellence?" In that case, they got the correct answer to their question. Were they asking the right one?

If we're to understand baseball—or anything—better, then the way to do that is with better questions. Before you answer any question, *question the question* first. If you want to understand sabermetrics, you don't need to fully understand the math. You just need to hold on to the moment of doubt that comes from wondering why batting average doesn't include walks. Why are we asking a question that pretends that something that really did happen never happened? If a question itself doesn't make sense, then the answer to that question isn't worth much. That's the real goal of sabermetrics. It's not creating Byzantine numbers for the sake of creating them. It's about asking better questions about baseball. The math works itself out.

– 2 –

How to Score Half a Run

I STOOD IN FRONT OF MY 8:30 AM "STATISTICS IN PSYCH-ology" class. It was the beginning of the school year, and I had just become a professor, in the loosest sense of the word "professor." I was still a 25-year-old graduate student, but the psychology department "politely encouraged" us to teach classes to the undergraduates, many of whom were only a few years my junior.

Some of my students were trembling in fear, if not of me, then of the class itself. Most psychology majors cite a desire to work with people, not numbers, and yet here they all were in a class about numbers. Psych Stats had the reputation for being a "major killer," in that it was a required course, but a hard class to pass. Some people solved the problem by switching majors. I was going to need a good opener.

"It's a good thing you all came to the first day of class, because today I'm going to teach you the only thing that you need to know about statistics." I hadn't even mentioned my name. "Can I borrow a quarter?"

The students, hearing that the graybeard at the front of the class was about to reveal the mysteries of the universe, had all grabbed their pens and notebooks and waited to write down the wisdom that I was about to impart. They all did a double-take when I asked for the quarter. Someone in the front row happened to have one, and I thanked her for it. I held it up to the class and said with the conviction of a magician who already has the second coin up his sleeve, "This is a fair coin. By a fair coin, I mean that it isn't a trick coin. It's not a two-headed coin. It's not weighted in any way. I don't have any skill in making it land on one side or the other. If I were to flip it, it is exactly a 50/50 chance that it would land on heads or tails." They nodded. A few of them started writing that down.

I then gave the first quiz of the class. "How many of you believe me?"

There were some puzzled looks throughout the room, but most of the hands went up, signaling that they believed the madman at the front of the class. They were humoring me.

"Why? Why do you believe me?" I already knew the answer to this one: because when there is a madman yelling things at you, you nod your head and hope that he will calm down. Also, I was the professor.

After some murmuring, some brave soul put up her hand and said the two words that I had hoped to hear. "Prove it." The game was afoot.

"How shall I prove it to you?"

"Well, I guess flip it a few times."

I obliged them. Heads. Tails. Tails. Tails. Heads. Tails.

"Four tails, two heads. That's not 50/50! So, am I a liar?"

More confused nodding for the madman.

Another brave soul, "Maybe flip it some more?" Not bad for 8:37 AM.

I suggested that they imagine that I had flipped the coin 100 more times and in those 100 flips, there had been 50 heads and 50 tails. I asked who now believed me that this coin was a fair one. This time, all the hands went into the air confidently. Alright, Socrates, time to throw a curveball.

"What if it had been 51/49, who still believes me? If you do, keep your hand up." They all stayed up.

"52/48?"

"53/47?"

"55/45?" Some hands started falling. A few other hands looked to be having an argument about probability with the arms supporting them.

"60/40?" There was a sound as of a small rushing wind as half of the hands in the class fell into the laps of the students who had brought them.

"65/35?" Only two or three brave souls remained.

"70/30?" The last of the resistance had fallen.

Then I said something only a clinical psychologist could say in a stats class. "Let's talk about how that made you feel." I summarized my observations to the students of what I had seen in their behavior. The quivering arms. The crisis of confidence in my truth-telling abilities when the split in those 100 coin flips hit 60/40. The fact that at one point, those arms had been raised with the confidence of the Statue of Liberty. "Think about the moment that you personally decided to put your hand down, when you went from believing that it was a fair coin to believing that it was not a fair coin. What was your thought process?"

They were into it. A few hands went up and I asked them to tell their stories of disbelief. I challenged them. "Is it *possible* that a fair coin could come up heads 70 percent of the time?" Everyone agreed that it was possible, but one student finally put it into words.

"Yeah, but there came a point where it just got *too* weird."

I paused for dramatic effect. "If you can hold on to *that* moment, the moment where you went from believing me to doubting me to not believing me, that moment where it got *too* weird, you can understand the entirety of statistics."

*   *   *

READERS WHO REMEMBER THEIR INTRO STATS CLASSES will recognize my live demonstration of null hypothesis testing, but readers who don't know what "null hypothesis testing" means will hopefully grasp the basic idea. Sure, sometimes weird things happen randomly, but there's a point where the line is crossed and we no longer give randomness the benefit of the doubt. Statistics is just a way of formally calculating where that line is.

I taught Psych Stats a few times, and each time, this demonstration with the borrowed quarter and the raised hands was my leadoff. After that, I switched from madman mode into acting like a proper professor. I took attendance, horribly mangled a few names, introduced myself, passed out the syllabus, told them when and where my office hours would be, and because this happened in all of my classes, assured them that they were allowed to bring in knitting to work on during class. It's amazing how much knitting goes on in American college classrooms. People need a way to manage anxiety. For some people, that's making a scarf while someone drones on about standard deviations.

Even after I assured them about the knitting, there was still plenty of anxiety hanging in the air. People's career plans were figuratively in my hands. I needed a second act. Thankfully, I had another question lined up that blessedly made me sound a little more normal. "Who here speaks a language other than English?" The hands started raising, again, some confidently, some tentatively. I clarified, "And before you put your hands up, I mean that you speak the language well enough that if I were to switch into that language, it might be five minutes before you even noticed." The tentative seemed relieved to be able to put their hands down.

I find bilingualism amazing, mostly because I've never been able to pick up another language for myself, a fact that my Russian-speaking wife gently reminds me of every now and then. Four years of high school Latin has left me well-equipped to translate state mottos and things that people say when they are trying to be pretentious, but not much else. In some sense, we all speak multiple languages, whether they are formal languages (French, Gujarati) or the technical "language" that goes along with a job or a hobby. Still, I always made it a point to ask the students who raised their hands what languages they knew, for no other reason that I think that it's neat.

Continuing on though, I relaxed my standards a little bit. I then asked how many people in the room knew a language well enough that if they were suddenly dropped into the middle of a country where that language was spoken, they could fake it for a week and not die. Most of the hands went up. I asked how many of them were counting on what they learned in their high school Spanish classes and most of them nodded. I told them that my class had much the same goal. The psychology department wasn't expecting these students to walk out of that class being able to discuss the finer points of a Type I vs. a Type III Sum of Squares. The department knew that I would be teaching them *ex nihilo*. The point of the class was to establish a base vocabulary around the subject.

If they wanted to major in psychology, they'd at least need to be able to pick up a scientific journal article and read it. Even if they didn't understand what hierarchical linear modeling was, they might at least understand the basics of a regression line or a t-test and why good research methodology was important. If nothing else, my belief was that if I stopped someone from blindly accepting some insane conspiracy theory they read on the internet before someone offered proof, I had done my job. I view this chapter much the same way.

This is...*The Math Chapter!*

Wait. Just hear me out before you start thumbing ahead to Chapter 3. I promise this won't hurt. (Though I say that in the same way the nurse promises you the shot won't hurt. It's a lie, but a helpful one. It hurts for a split second, but not nearly as much as you had imagined and not nearly as much as the flu it prevents you from getting.) My goal in this chapter is not that you'll be able to run park-adjustment calculations for Coors Field in your head. (No one has figured out Coors Field yet.) My goal is to introduce a few basic concepts. If you're the sort of person who wants to know more, there are plenty of options out there to pursue that. This chapter is meant as a starter course in some basic math concepts that are foundational to sabermetrics.

WARNING! GORY MATHEMATICAL DETAILS AHEAD!

IN THE LAST CHAPTER, WE TALKED ABOUT GIVING CREDIT to a player for the things that he did, with the odd idea that we were going to give him credit for fractions of runs, rather than whole runs. How can a player score half a run?

A baseball game is more like 18 (sometimes more!) mini-games called half-innings. Each team plays nine of them on offense and nine on defense. A half-inning—for the defense—is a race to get three outs before any (more) runners score. In a half-inning of baseball, there are two factors that most shape how many runs will be scored before the game resets: how many outs there are and where the runners are. Once the defense gets those three outs, the game resets itself and goes back to no outs and no runners.

Weird things do happen in baseball. There are cases where a team loads the bases with no outs and somehow doesn't score.

There are cases where a team is facing a two-outs, no-one-on-base scenario and somehow comes up with four runs before the third out is recorded. Given a choice between those two scenarios *before* I know the outcome though, I know which one I'd take. In statistical terms, we're talking about "expected value" and in baseball (and life) it's one of the most important concepts to understand.

Suppose I offered you a chance to bet on a coin flip. You lay a dollar down, and call the flip in the air. If you call it correctly, you walk away with three dollars. If you are wrong, you walk away with nothing. Should you pay the one dollar it costs to make that bet? At the moment that you are deciding whether to make that bet, you have no idea what the outcome will be. Assuming it really is a fair coin, you have a 50 percent chance of walking away with nothing, but you also have a 50 percent chance of walking away with three dollars. After you choose to make the bet, but before you know the outcome, expected value says that the bet is worth $1.50 (50 percent of three dollars).

Now, let's say that I change the rules. You still need to lay down a dollar to play the game, but to win you need to call *two* coin flips correctly and the prize is still only three dollars. The potential outcomes (no money or three dollars) haven't changed, but the chances of winning are now lower (25 percent). Your expected value is also lower (25 percent of $3.00 is 75 cents).

A statistician would call the first bet a good wager even though you might lose your money on an individual coin toss. The expected value ($1.50) is higher than the cost of the bet ($1.00). In an ideal world, you should sit there all day and bet dollar after dollar on my game. At the end of the day, you'd be rich. The second bet is a bad idea because the expected value of 75 cents is less than the dollar it costs to play the game. You might win one round, but if you played that game over and over again, you would eventually lose all your money.

This brings us to our first rule of probabilistic thinking: When you have to make a choice between two strategies *before* you know the outcome, pick the one with the highest (or the least negative) expected value. An individual decision might end up being wrong, but if you make a bunch of these probabilistic decisions over time, you will end up ahead.

In baseball, we see these sorts of probabilistic decisions all the time. Should the third-base coach send the runner or hold him? Should the shortstop fielding a ground ball take the sure out at first that allows the runner to get to third or should he take a chance on getting the lead runner? Should the manager pinch hit here? Should a general manager trade the three best prospects in the organization for an ace starter in the middle of a pennant race? Eventually the third-base coach, shortstop, manager, and general manager will have to make those decisions, and shortly thereafter, they'll find out whether their decisions "worked" or not.

While it's not always easy to figure out the expected value on a decision, expected value should always be the guiding principle. There's a small problem though, because while "always pick the highest expected value" is easy to say, there are all sorts of pitfalls in actually doing it. As an example, how would you approach this problem?

An outbreak of a particularly nasty infectious disease has been reported in a remote town in Oklahoma. The disease is highly contagious and deadly if left untreated, and it's likely that all 100 residents of the town are infected. The town is put under quarantine. There is a well-known medication for the disease that works in about 60 percent of cases. Unfortunately, 40 percent of the people who take the medication still die. It's not great, but it's the best that's available.

There is a second, experimental medication that has not yet been tested in humans, but has been developed by a well-respected pharmaceutical researcher. It cured 100 percent of the lab rats in tests, but there hasn't been time to study the drug's effects on humans. The researcher believes that there is a 50 percent chance that the experimental medication would work and cure everyone and a 50 percent chance that it would have no effect and everyone would die. When the public health workers parachute into this town in their hazmat suits, should they bring the well-known or the experimental medication with them? From an expected value point of view, there is no question. The well-known drug would save 60 lives. The experimental drug has an equal chance of curing everyone or killing everyone, so it has an expected value of 50 lives saved. Sixty is more than 50. Expected value would vote for the well-known drug.

Even knowing that, I'd wager that plenty of readers are still tempted to pick the experimental drug. The idea of saving *everyone* probably has some appeal. One could make the case that using the well-known drug means a 100 percent chance that *someone* will die, and the experimental drug drops those chances to 50 percent. The community will certainly never be the same again with the well-known drug. With the experimental drug, it might survive intact.

Flipping the question on its head for a moment, suppose that *you* were diagnosed with this same disease. The doctors present you with the same two options. The well-known drug gives you a 60 percent chance of survival, the experimental drug gives you a 50 percent chance. Which would you want? The answer there is fairly obvious. Either way, you're in a bad spot, but sometimes we must pick the least bad of two awful options (I like to call this "picking between messes") and the well-known drug gives you a better chance at living. Despite the same set of facts, your answer might depend on how you conceptualize the question.

Thankfully in baseball, no one is making life-or-death decisions, but the cultural frame through which we view these decisions can affect how we apply a seemingly cut-and-dried mathematical concept. Baseball—being a game played by humans—is tied up in many of those cultural values and cognitive biases that can lead to decisions that don't follow the rules of expected value. Sometimes, the mathematically correct decision is the one that feels the worst emotionally, but runs are runs and the scoreboard doesn't care about how you feel. That leads us to Rule 1A of probabilistic thinking: When you have to make a choice between two strategies before you know the outcome, pick the one with the highest expected value, *even if it feels icky.*

* * *

IN THE COURSE OF A HALF-INNING, THERE ARE THREE POS-sible numbers of outs that can be on the board (zero, one, or two) and there are eight possible configurations of baserunners (no runners, runner on first, runner on second, runner on third, runners on first and second, etc.). That gives us 24 possible combinations of runners and outs. At the end of every plate appearance, at least one of three things happens: an out is recorded, the configuration of runners changes, or a run scores. Sometimes all three happen on the same play.

Since the object of the game is to score runs, we can look back over a year (2017, in the table below) and calculate how many runs teams scored, on average, when they were in each of those 24 situations.

Table 2. Expected Runs Per Base-Out State, 2017 MLB

Situation	No outs	One out	Two outs
Bases empty	0.523	0.286	0.109
Runner on first	0.895	0.541	0.235
Runner on second	1.110	0.690	0.330
Runner on third	1.362	0.933	0.384
Runners on first and second	1.481	0.945	0.455
Runners on first and third	1.733	1.187	0.510
Runners on second and third	1.948	1.337	0.604
Bases loaded	2.320	1.592	0.730

We see that with the beginning of an inning scenario (bases empty and no one out) the average team scored about half a run (0.523). The scoreboard doesn't record half-runs, but at the beginning of an inning, we don't know what's going to happen yet. Now let's say that the leadoff hitter walks. On average, with no outs and a runner on first, MLB teams scored 0.895 runs. Again, we don't know what will happen to that runner. He might score. He might be erased on a double play. His team might score three runs. What we do know is that his walk took his team from a situation where we expect them to score 0.523 runs to one where we expect 0.895, for an increase of 0.372 runs to his team's expected value.

Using the expected-runs table to evaluate strategies was popularized by researchers John Thorn and Pete Palmer in their 1985 book *The Hidden Game of Baseball*. It led to at least one surprising conclusion. The sacrifice bunt was actually a bad idea. Bunting a runner over from first to second, usually with no one out, has been a staple of baseball strategy since the earliest days of the game. A team trades an out to get the runner into "scoring position" at second base. The run-expectancy matrix tells a different story.

Let's look at a team with a runner on first and no outs. They could let the batter swing away—we see on the chart that teams scored an average of 0.895 runs in these situations—or they could ask him to bunt the lead runner over, a play which, if it "works", would put a runner on second with one out. The problem is that looking on the chart for "runner on second, one out" we see that teams averaged only 0.690 runs in 2017. The "successful" sacrifice bunt has made a team 0.205 runs *worse off* than they had been.

Further research (both that I've done and by researcher Mitchel Lichtman, who co-authored *The Book: Playing the Percentages in Baseball*) found that when we account for the fact that a bunt might actually go for a hit or that the defense might make an error, bunting itself is actually neither a good nor a bad strategy. It's effectively the equivalent of betting a dollar on a coin flip for the chance to win two dollars, but it's only because these unexpected bonus outcomes happen occasionally.

There is no question that what is commonly hailed as a success (a sacrifice bunt that retires the batter, but moves the runner) is a failure in the eyes of expected value. The out is more valuable than pushing the runner up a base. Some readers may be having one of those *icky* moments right now. The sacrifice has long been seen as a noble play in the game. The word "sacrifice" suggests putting the team above individual needs. The rules of the game even carve out an exemption such that even though you made an out, because you made a *noble* out, the sacrifice doesn't count as an at-bat (and thus, it doesn't penalize your batting average). The sacrifice may very well be a noble play, but chivalry points can't be put on the scoreboard.

*   *   *

THE EXPECTED-RUNS TABLE ALSO PROVIDES GUIDANCE ON another decision. Let's put our runner back on first base with no outs. Since bunting him over to second is a bad play, perhaps we could have him try to steal second base. Steal attempts are risky. Our runner might make it. He might not. Where is that dividing line between a good and a bad bet?

With a runner on first and no one out, the runner might be safe on his steal attempt, which puts him on second with no outs (run expectancy: 1.110). If we knew for sure that he'd make it, we'd certainly send him, but he might also get caught, which would erase him from the basepaths *and* put an out on the board (run expectancy: 0.286). Or the third-base coach could communicate the "stay put" sign by touching his head, shoulders, knees, and toes, and lock in a run expectancy of 0.895. How sure do we have to be before it makes sense to send the runner?

We're going to call that boundary line "p" for the probability that the batter will be safe on his steal attempt. Since there are only two outcomes (safe or out), and we know that the probabilities must add up to 100 percent, we can mathematically express the probability that he will be out as $(1-p)$. A lot of decisions in baseball are yes/no decisions, and so we often use this sort of analysis to figure out where the line between "yes" and "no" should be.

Since we don't know what p is yet, we'll have to solve for it using algebra. (I warned you that there would be math!) We can write the problem as:

$$0.895 = 1.110 * p + 0.286 * (1-p)$$

We see the expected value for holding the runner at first (0.895) on one side. The other side is the expected runs value for a runner on second and no outs (1.110) times the probability of being safe (p), plus the expected runs value for no runners and one out (0.286) times the probability *that* would happen $(1-p)$.

Just in case you aren't reading this with a calculator at your side, solving for p gives us 0.7391, or 73.91 percent. If the manager believes that the runner has a better than 73.91 percent chance of stealing, even if he believes that it's a 73.92 percent chance, then a steal attempt is a good bet. The runner may get caught this time; he may not, but since we don't get to know the outcome of the decision before we make it, we have to do the next best thing and pick the strategy with the highest expected value (even if it feels icky). If we do that over and over again, we'll eventually end up ahead.

*   *   *

IN 2008, MAJOR LEAGUE BASEBALL INSTALLED A SYSTEM IN every big league ballpark that logged the velocity, spin, break, and eventual landing place of every pitch thrown during every game. They put the data on the internet for anyone to use. It's hard to overstate how valuable this was to the baseball research community. Before the advent of the Pitch F/X system, there were data on whether pitches had been called a ball or a strike by the umpire, but now there was a public way to check whether the umpire really did need a vision exam.

Naturally, researchers began looking at the strike zone and found that for the most part, umpires did a pretty good job. Eventually, they moved past just looking at the strike zone, and even more interesting things started to come from the data set. Researchers noticed that the strike zone—as it was actually called—was not always a black-and-white proposition for Blue. Balls down the middle were always strikes and balls two feet off the plate were not, but there were gray zones where one umpire might call a ball and another a strike. But eventually, researchers noticed another player in the equation who seemed to be making a big difference: the catcher.

Research by some talented analysts, chief among them Mike Fast and Dan Turkenkopf (both of whom were eventually hired as on-staff researchers by MLB teams), found that certain catchers seemed to be better at getting these edge calls than others.

The effect of this skill, which would come to be called "pitch framing," was something that might affect one pitch out of a hundred, but the implications for it were rather big. Consider a 1–1 pitch that ends up on the edge of the strike zone. If it's a ball, the count goes to 2-1 and the batter is ahead in the count. If it's a strike, the batter is behind. In 2017, when a batter faced a 2-1 count at some point during his time in the batter's box, he hit .254/.398/.437 during those plate appearances. If he faced a 1-2 count, his performance dropped to .173/.227/.278. That's a pretty big drop, and through some additional math, we can estimate that turning a ball into a strike is worth about .15 runs to a team.

In 2017, the average Major League game featured 145 pitches per team. That means that over the course of 120 games caught (catchers generally do not play every day), a starting catcher might handle 17,400 pitches. If he can turn 1 percent of those from balls into strikes by catching the ball in such a way as to fool the umpire into calling "strike" rather than "ball," he has affected 174 pitches. If each is worth 0.15 runs, he has effectively "saved" 26 runs. The key is volume. Because catchers handle so many pitches during the course of a game, even a small effect is going to add up over time, or as my oldest daughter likes to say, "A little plus a little plus a little eventually equals a lot." Saving 20

extra runs is the equivalent of adding *two wins* to a team, and it
could be done just on this framing skill alone.

It's helpful here to take a look at some data on how often certain
events happen during a season. They represent an "average" team,
and can be read either as offensive or defensive opportunities. (For
instance, an "average team" has 23,444 pitches that are thrown to
their hitters and 23,444 pitches that are thrown by their pitchers.)

Table 3. Seasonal Frequency of Various Events, "Average" Team, 2017 Data

Event	How often it happens
Pitches	23,444
Team plate appearances	6,176
Balls hit into play	4,253
Plate appearances by leadoff hitters	756

Often, when we think about how a team can make itself better,
we think about replacing a bad player with an All-Star. That's one
way to get better, but it's an expensive one. Signing an All-Star
free agent can cost more than the annual gross national product
of a small island nation. Even if a hitter played all 162 games and
hit in the leadoff spot (the spot in the lineup that comes up most
often), he would only affect 12.2 percent of an average team's
plate appearances. He might hit 30 more home runs than the
player he replaced, but that's not the only way to find 30 more
home runs. What if it were possible to do something that would
make all of the hitters on the team just a little bit better? Maybe
each of the nine starters hit one extra home run every other
month during a season. That's 27 home runs right there.

Our second rule of probabilistic thinking is that a small effect, repeated over and over again, can be as important as a large change that happens once. If we find something that affects players in something that they do regularly, we can generate significant value, sometimes without having to spend a dime more than we had been.

I STARTED HIGH SCHOOL IN 1994, THE SAME YEAR THAT THE Cleveland Indians opened Jacobs Field. That year, the Indians introduced their new acrobatic, charismatic, Venezuelan shortstop. Omar Vizquel was a joy to watch on the field for the decade that he called Cleveland home. He had a penchant for grabbing bounding balls with his bare hand and throwing to first to nab a disbelieving runner who thought he had a hit. There were double plays that he turned worthy of a Cleveland Ballet audition tape, if only the Nutcracker were allowed to throw baseballs to the Sugarplum Fairy. Vizquel gained a reputation as one of the best fielding shortstops in the game during his time in Cleveland and perhaps as one of the best of all-time, and for years, I assumed that I had been witness to history back in my high school days. Vizquel spun a highlight reel like no one else could.

To my horror, I eventually discovered that he was merely an above-average defender during the years in which I watched him. It's an odd curse to call someone "merely above average." It means, by definition, that there are more people who are worse than you than are better, but in United States culture, it's come to be a synonym for "entirely forgettable." There was no forgetting Vizquel. How could a man with a reputation as the Hank Aaron of shortstop defense be anything less than the best? Perhaps an imprecise but instructive analogy would be helpful here.

I went to an all-male, Catholic high school. For reasons that have never been fully explained to me, the school, despite having a female enrollment of zero, had a yearly election of a Homecoming Queen. The candidates were all from one of the three local all-female Catholic high schools. During the school year, the young women from these "sister schools" were welcome to be part of the St. Edward marching band, plays, pit orchestra, and cheerleading squad. There were also community service projects and retreats that the schools would jointly sponsor. The Homecoming Queen was supposed to be the young woman who had contributed the most to the school, presumably through these avenues. The voters for the honor were the members of the senior class (read: a bunch of 17-year-old boys). Let's just say I don't believe that "contributed the most to the St. Edward community" was always the deciding factor for who ended up as Homecoming Queen. Perhaps other, less noble, concerns were taken into account.

If we had wanted to get a good idea of which young woman had really contributed the most to the school, we might measure things like how many hours she spent on activities sponsored by the school or how many leadership positions she had taken in those organizations in the past four years. We'd need a record of everything that she did and didn't do during her time in high school, the way that we have a record of just about everything done on a baseball field, strecthing back for several decades. The creepily obsessive nature with which data about baseball games are collected only becomes apparent when you imagine the same level of detail being applied to other areas of life.

Because of that obsessive data collection, we have a pretty good record of what happened when Omar Vizquel was on the field throughout his career, including data about how many ground balls (and pop-ups and line drives) were hit in his general direction and how many of those eventually turned into outs. While Vizquel made plenty of plays that are fun to watch again and again, those highlights were worth the same as any routine looking 6-3 groundout. His actual job was not to create content for *SportsCenter*, but to log as many of those 6-3 groundouts as possible. If Vizquel converted grounders (and pop-ups and line drives) into outs at a higher rate than the rest of the league, then he could be considered above average for that season. We can even put a run expectancy value on that.

The website Baseball Reference keeps a statistic, based on the work of researcher Sean Smith, that does this very calculation. Prior to coming to the Indians, Vizquel spent five seasons (ages 22–26) with the Seattle Mariners, and had posted "runs saved" totals (where zero is average) that rated him as "pretty good." But once Vizquel came to Cleveland in 1994, his performance was... well, merely above average. He manned the shortstop spot for 11 years in Cleveland (in what were his ages 27–37 seasons), where he gained a reputation as the second coming of the other noted paragon of shortstop defense, Ozzie Smith. Except that the data tell a different story.

Here are Vizquel's numbers from Baseball Reference during his years as a shortstop, compared to the same aged seasons for Smith and another well-known shortstop (though not for his defense) from that era, Cal Ripken.

Table 4. Omar Vizquel vs. Ozzie Smith and Cal Ripken, Runs Saved on Defense

Age	Vizquel	Smith	Ripken
22	6	N/A	11
23	13	3	23
24	14	14	0
25	12	21	16
26	16	4	0
27	4	21	–6
28	1	12	20
29	1	14	22
30	2	20	22
31	9	16	12
32	14	14	11
33	–1	18	17
34	–8	32	22
35	–2	14	N/A
36	10	3	N/A
37	2	13	N/A
38	1	4	N/A
39	7	12	N/A
40	16	0	N/A
41	9	4	N/A
Total	**126**	**239**	**170**

(Note: Smith did not make his MLB debut until age 23 and retired after his age 41 season; Ripken moved to third base in his age 35 season; Vizquel became a utility player at age 42)

A clear-eyed look at the data shows that Omar Vizquel, over his career, was barely half of Ozzie Smith defensively. He wasn't even the equal of Cal Ripken, and had more seasons at shortstop than Ripken in which to make his mark. Vizquel should be credited for the fact that he played a non-embarrassing version of shortstop into his forties, and his full body of work in the field was good, but it wasn't Hall of Fame–level special. How can a man who was magic with a ball in his hand not actually be an elite defender? That can be summarized in our third rule of probabilistic thinking in baseball: When making an evaluation, we need to pay attention both to what happens and what *doesn't* happen.

Vizquel had a weakness, or at least a relative weakness. While he really was a magician once he snared the ball, first he had to get to the ball. In 2017, 87.8 percent of ground balls that a shortstop managed to field were eventually converted into outs (some turned into infield hits, some into errors), which suggests that just "getting there" is most of a shortstop's job. What the data show are that when a ground ball was hit in Vizquel's area, he was merely above average in getting over to it before it went into either left or center field. Vizquel was often compared to Smith on the basis of his ability to make acrobatic plays, but the Wizard of Oz covered more ground and *that*—not the high-flying jumps and did-you-see-that throws—is what made him an elite defender.

We don't often think of defense in this way because it's hard to think of the plays that a fielder *doesn't* make. It's common to see a ground ball that is smacked through the left side that the shortstop can't quite catch up with. We don't instinctively fault him for not getting there because no one gets to all of them. What if he had moved a little more quickly and had gotten to that ball? The difference between an elite shortstop and a merely above-average one might be one extra ball out of perhaps 15 or 20 that he converts into an out, perhaps a ball or two per week. Even if you watch all the games it's hard to pick out *the* ball that the elite shortstop fields successfully that would have been out of range of the merely above-average shortstop. It's much easier to count the amazing dives and leaps.

A lot of the problem has to do with the way that baseball is shown on television. By the time the camera switches to the shortstop on a ball where he might have a play, we see the last few steps of his run and either the ball bounding into his glove or skipping past him. We don't see where he started from, nor how quickly he reacted, so we have no reference point to see how much ground he was able to cover. We *do* see it if he boots the ball or botches the throw or if he makes an astounding diving stop, and we instinctively fault or credit him for those. Those are things that he *did*. It's hard to see the groundout that *didn't* happen, but over the course of a season, those base hits that could have been outs can add up.

While Vizquel may have excelled in making shortstop play fun to watch, he was merely good at the most important job of a shortstop, which was the boring work of preventing balls from getting into the outfield. It's ranging over and making a routine-looking play on a ball that another shortstop might have to dive for, because he wasn't quick enough to get there other-wise. (The lesser shortstop will be on the highlight reel *because of his weakness*.) Like my high school classmates, we should have been paying attention to the routine things that were hard to see instead of voting for what looked the prettiest.

BASEBALL IS A GAME OF INCHES PLAYED AT INSANE SPEEDS. It takes a 90 mph fastball roughly 400 milliseconds (four tenths of a second) to go from the pitcher's hand to home plate. It generally takes the human brain about 200 milliseconds to respond to a stimulus, and sometimes even longer. Psychologists who study cognitive processing know that *within the same person*, it's possible to see variation. Sometimes, people are a little faster and sometimes a little slower. Sometimes there's no discernible reason. Even a lag of 50 extra milliseconds—something that is literally less than the blink of an eye—takes away a quarter of the actionable time that a hitter has to produce the correct response to that fastball.

Baseball is a game with an asymmetry not found in many other sports. In games like football and basketball, both teams are trying to win possession of the ball, because it's the only way that they are able to accomplish their goal of scoring. In games like volleyball or tennis, both teams or players are trying to *dispose* of the ball in an approved manner (e.g., over the net, inside the lines). But in baseball, we have one player (the batter) who is actively trying to dispose of the ball while another team (the defense) is actively trying to gain possession of the ball as quickly as they can.

Baseball is a game of brute strength. Consider the incentives inherent in hitting a baseball. If the batter hits the ball far enough, he will exceed the boundaries of the field, and his reward is a home run. In other games where balls are hit or thrown, propelling the ball beyond the edge of the field is usually a foul or a turnover or results in a point for the other team. Tennis players do not simply smack the ball as hard as they can. They must try to place the ball so that it falls within the lines on the other side. In baseball, even if you don't hit the ball over the wall, the batter still wants to hit the ball far away from the area where he will do the next part of his job, the running of the bases. The further that he can move the ball away from that area, the better. If the ball falls outside the other set of boundaries, the foul lines, the penalty is relatively minor, and sometimes nothing. In baseball, there is little incentive to steer the ball to a specific place or even a specific area. It's not that hitters don't try to pull the ball, but the resolution that they have in mind is much more "leftward third of the field" rather than "this one specific spot, about 80 feet away from where the left fielder is standing."

Baseball is a game of colliding objects. There are plenty of games which essentially come down to collision physics, although in many of them (billiards, golf), the ball has the courtesy to stand still while the human playing the game tries to hit it with a stick. In baseball, hitters are trying to play billiards, only the cue ball is traveling fast enough to be charged with reckless driving. More than that, for a ball traveling that fast, the baseball itself is comparatively small, as is the circumference of the stick used to hit it. With a small bat, a small ball, and the pitcher trying to make the ball move in ways that surprise the batter, it means that there's a lot of room for error in trying to predict the angle at which the ball meets the bat. A matter of inches in where ball and bat collide separates a line drive from a pop-up.

Baseball is a game where the inches matter in strange ways. Inches do matter in other sports. A basketball player's job is to place the ball in the approved cylinder and if he is off by a couple of inches, it's the difference between making and missing his shot, but in basketball, the player's entire job is to *aim* the ball correctly. Baseball is one of the few games in which aiming—at least when hitting—isn't a valued skill. The physics and neuropsychology of the act don't permit much of it. As a result, teams have, since the beginning of the game, used a defensive strategy of spreading out the defenders and spacing them some distance apart so as to cover as much room on the field as they can. This means that there will be portions of the field that aren't covered (the field is too big for nine men to cover the whole thing), but those pockets of safety are at random intervals. If hitters could aim better, they would of course try to drop the ball into those safe zones, but for the most part, they can't. They can only try to make solid contact, followed by hope. The fundamental unfairness of baseball is that there is a great deal of uncontrolled variation in where the ball lands, and that randomness can be the difference between a base hit and a pop-out.

Baseball is a game where sometimes you do everything right and it doesn't work. (My mother likes to say this about life more generally.) We recognize that the rules of the game incentivize solid contact. We realize that when Smith hits a line drive right at the shortstop, he did exactly what he was supposed to do and that his bad aim was mostly bad luck. We realize that when Jones hits a weak flare that just happened to find one of those Swiss cheese holes, he is standing on first only because he got a bit lucky. But the numbers that we usually use to describe the game don't tell that story and the scoreboard doesn't care. Smith is 0-for-1 and Jones is 1-for-1. Before I knew the outcome, I'd rather have Smith's line drive than Jones's pop-up, but sometimes randomness turns all notions of fairness upside down.

Baseball is a game where it pays to understand the difference between process and outcome and between talent and luck. There's a taboo in sporting culture around acknowledging the role that luck plays in the outcome of a play or a game or a season. Teams whose players suffer freak injuries "don't want to use the injuries as an excuse." Perplexed sportscasters looking at an event that was improbable—though entirely possible—will often resort to clichés about a player or a team that "wanted it more" that sound silly if we would take but five seconds to reflect on them. Apparently, there are players who have dedicated their entire lives to the pursuit of one thing, and when given the chance to achieve it, they decide not to give 100 percent effort.

Why fear the truth? There are a lot of things that can happen on a baseball field. The worst teams in the league routinely win 40 percent of their games. Things happen because sometimes the dice just come up the wrong way. The most you can do in baseball (and life) is to understand what things make it more *likely* that the outcome will end up in your favor, but then live with the reality that "more likely" is not a guarantee of anything. In baseball, we have to live with the fourth rule of probabilistic thinking. Sometimes you do everything right and it doesn't work.

- 3 -

Why Does It Feel So Icky?

FOR 40 YEARS, MY FATHER WAS IN THE BUSINESS OF RUN-
ning parking lots in downtown Cleveland. He had one of those
jobs that someone has to do, but you never really think about a
person actually doing it. He was, at various points, President of
the Cleveland Parking Association, on the Board of Governors for
the National Parking Association, and a contributing columnist
to *Parking* magazine. I swear that I'm not making that last part up.

His office uncomfortably resembled a bunker beneath the
Cuyahoga County courthouse, but it was right across the bridge
from Cleveland Municipal Stadium, home of the Indians before
they moved to Jacobs (later Progressive) Field. It meant that we
got free parking when we went down to see a game when I was
a kid. On a day-to-day basis, his job included managing the ca-
shiers and dealing with irate customers who had forgotten where
they had parked, along with filing reports on how business was
going. He liked to call himself the "Parking Czar."

Our family had dinner together every night at about 6:00. Dad did most of the cooking, since he got home first. He once told me that if I ever planned to live by myself, I had to know how to cook. He also told me that if I ever planned to live with someone else, I had to know how to cook. I told him that this covered every possible situation. He looked me in the eye and said, "Exactly."

Dinner was pretty ritualistic, but then all human gatherings have rituals associated with them, especially food rituals. After my mother got home and had a moment to decompress from her drive, my father would literally call us to dinner by blowing on a wooden train whistle. My brother and I would emerge from wherever we happened to be in the house and gather at the table. We all sat down in our assigned spots and the ritual began. My mother would ask how everyone's day had gone. We all understood that this was just a formality, so we all just mumbled "fine" in anticipation that Mom would ask the question that everyone wanted both to answer and to hear the answers to: "Who did something stupid today?"

For a man whose job mostly involved looking at cars that were empty and not moving, my father was a surprisingly endless font of anecdotes in which someone did something exceptionally stupid. Maybe it was because many of the cars in his parking lot belonged to county politicians. Sometimes, the "someone" was a customer, sometimes an employee, and sometimes it was my father himself. There were the garden variety stories of people who couldn't remember what color their car was, and the employees who had laughably flimsy stories on why they were late for work. Then there were the bigger ones that took on legendary status.

Dinnertime at the Carleton household was a master class in bad decision making, held over 18 years.

One of his most memorable stories—which I admit might have been apocryphal—was retold from a conversation with another parking lot operator. Apparently, the lot was installing new ticket spitters in their entrance lanes. The machines are obviously meant to be placed just to the left of the lane so that the driver can roll down the window, grab a ticket, and trigger the entrance gate to go up. Because these particular machines had to be anchored in the concrete itself, replacing them involved jackhammering around the old ones to get them out and then installing and setting the new ones in new concrete. It was a serious undertaking.

The workers who were doing the installation were given a schematic of the garage that showed where the new machines should be placed. That seemed a little silly even to my civilian ears because the answer was most likely "where the old ones were." But still, this was written down for them. On this particular drawing though, there was a mistake and it showed the new ticket spitters placed in the middle of the entrance lane, meaning they would block the path of the cars trying to enter the garage. The obvious conclusion would have been to either recognize that this must be a mistake and to install the new machines where the old ones were, or at the very least, to call someone to ask the question that was probably on everyone's mind: "Really?"

Undaunted though, the workers began digging a hole right in the middle of the lane to install the new machine. Fortunately, someone from the garage management saw what was going on and stopped the workers before they got too deep into their work and the concrete.

When asked why they had done something so obviously stupid, the workers protested that this was what the schematic called for. And then one of them unleashed the four most powerful words in the English language.

"It's not my fault!"

IN GAME 7 OF THE 2014 WORLD SERIES, THE KANSAS CITY Royals were in a tough spot. They were down 3–2 to the San Francisco Giants in the bottom of the ninth. Giants pitcher Madison Bumgarner, who three days earlier had pitched a four-hit shutout to win Game 5 of the Series, was at it again. Following only two days of rest, he had entered the game in the bottom of the fifth inning, given up a single to Royals second baseman Omar Infante, and promptly dismissed the next 14 Royals batters who came to the plate. With two outs, Royals left fielder Alex Gordon stepped to the plate, representing the Royals' last line of defense for keeping their world championship hopes alive.

Bumgarner's 0-1 pitch to Gordon got a little too much of the plate and Gordon poked it into left-center field, where it fell for a clean hit in front of center fielder Gregor Blanco. Blanco had charged the ball, and as he tried to play the bounce off the grass, it handcuffed him and scooted past him to the left-center-field wall. Gordon had been running hard. He took second after Blanco's miscue, and when left fielder Juan Perez had trouble picking the ball up at the wall, Gordon kept his motor running and headed for third. As the throw from Perez came in to Giants shortstop

Brandon Crawford, acting as the cutoff man for the play, all of Kansas City learned something new: the name of their team's third-base coach, Mike Jirschele.

Jirschele, who had been a minor league manager in the Royals system for two decades, was in his first season as a third-base coach with the big club. On that play, he held the charging Gordon at third base, igniting a "what if?" debate that raged for the rest of that off-season. Gordon had a full head of steam coming in to third base and Brandon Crawford had received the throw from Juan Perez a little beyond the infield dirt. If Gordon had tried to score, Crawford would have been forced to make an accurate turn and throw home to Giants catcher Buster Posey, who would have had to tag Gordon and perhaps withstand a collision as Gordon tried to touch the plate. Gordon was fairly fleet of foot, having stolen 12 bases that season, but Crawford was well-known as one of the best defensive shortstops in the game and had a good arm. We'll never know whether Gordon would have made it, but we do know what happened next. With Gordon still 90 feet away from tying the game, Bumgarner got ahead of Royals catcher Salvador Perez and induced a pop-up to Giants third baseman Pablo Sandoval to end the game and the Royals' season.

Had Jirschele been too cautious in not waving Gordon home? At the moment he made the decision, he had no idea what would become of Salvador Perez's at-bat, but he also had been given a front-row seat to the magic that Bumgarner had been working since the fifth inning. There were two outs in that ninth inning, so if Gordon was going to have any chance to score from third, Salvador Perez, at the very least, would have to avoid making the third out with his at-bat. Perez had an OBP of .289 during the 2014 regular season (and an OBP of .233 for the playoffs) suggesting that he was a less than 30 percent chance to avoid making that out, and that was before factoring in that he was facing Bumgarner, who had been near unhittable all night. It's very likely that Gordon would have been thrown out, but if he had a better than 30 percent chance of making it, it would have been the best chance that the Royals had of scoring the tying run. Neither was a great option, but sometimes you have to pick between messes.

*　　*　　*

THERE'S A FAMOUS PROBLEM IN THE FIELD OF ETHICAL philosophy (and experimental psychology) known as The Trolley Problem. There are several variations, but the general form goes like this. A train (or trolley) is barreling down the tracks at a rate of speed that will not allow it to stop quickly. You are observing this train when you notice that there are five people who are trapped on the tracks ahead who will all surely be run over and killed before anyone can get to them. However, you happen to be standing next to a lever that could divert the train onto another set of tracks, saving those five people. The problem is that on the other set of tracks, there is one person working who will not have time to get out of the way and will surely die. Do you pull the lever?

From a rational standpoint, this is a quick calculation. It is always sad when someone loses their life, but one death is a better outcome than five. From that perspective, the correct choice is for you to pull the lever. There's an important word in that sentence: *you*. While most people recognize that *someone else* pulling the lever results in fewer deaths and that this represents a better outcome, they hesitate to pull the lever themselves when put into a similar situation in a lab. The problem is that pulling the lever means that they have to *do something* that causes a death. While one could certainly argue that by *inaction*, our railyard worker was effectively sentencing five people to die who could otherwise have been saved, humans do not process information that way. It feels different when it's our fault.

In the last chapter, I proposed the first rule of probabilistic thinking in baseball: When you have to make a choice about two strategies before you know the outcome, pick the one with the highest (or least negative) expected value, *even if it feels icky*. There's a pleasant myth that people tend to believe about themselves that they "look at all the facts and decide from there." We are fond of thinking of ourselves as logical. This is, without question, not true.

While the railyard example may have seemed rather far-fetched at first, it maps nicely onto that Game 7 situation, with Alex Gordon playing the part of the barreling trolley and Mike Jirschele as the railyard employee trying to decide whether to pull the switch. There are plenty of fans who don't even know the name of the third-base coach for their favorite team, and most of the ones who do would struggle to name even one of the other 29 people who hold that job, but the third-base coach is a surprisingly important person to study. He's got a job that sometimes feels icky.

Let's reset our Trolley Problem to something a little less grue-some. There's a runner on third with one out and the batter hits a fly ball to medium-deep left field. The runner on third retreats back to the base and assumes a sprinter's pose as his third-base coach watches the ball fall into the left fielder's glove. Our run-ner is waiting to hear one of two words: "Stay!" or "Go!" Which one should our third-base coach yell?

In his head, our third-base coach should be sizing up the probability of the runner scoring, given the runner's speed, the left fielder's arm, and how deep the ball was hit. He doesn't have the benefit of a laptop out there to estimate those odds, but if he's done his homework, he should at least know the break-even point for that decision. In Chapter 2, we learned how to calculate that break-even point using the run expectancy matrix. As the left fielder squeezes the fly ball into his glove, there are now two outs and a runner on third. The third-base coach could yell "Stay" and accept a run expectancy of 0.384 runs (using 2017 numbers). Or he could yell, "Go!" and risk the runner being thrown out, which will take his team's run expectancy to 0.000 runs (that would be the third out). He might be rewarded a no-runners, two-outs situation (run expectancy = 0.109 runs), but also an actual run, for a total expected value of 1.109 runs. Using the break-even point formula on this one, we get an answer of about 34 percent. That's it.

If our third-base coach thinks that his runner has a slightly better than one-third shot at making it, he should throw the switch. It's entirely possible that the third-base coach could size up the situation and think, "He has a less than 50 percent chance of making it" and it would still make sense to send the runner. The thought of sending a guy when the most likely outcome is that he'll be thrown out might sound insane on the surface, but the correct question to ask in this situation is not "How do I *feel* about the runner's chances of scoring?" Instead, it's "What are the runner's chances of scoring if I send him versus the other option, which is hoping the next batter knocks him in?" You're going to *feel* icky, but you should send him anyway.

Between 2013 and 2017, there were 7,760 potential sacrifice flies (less than two outs, runner on third) hit to an outfielder. Most of the time (81 percent), the runner did try to score, but the rest of the time, he held at third. Of those who tried to score, 97 percent made it home safely. This next sentence may sound strange, but third-base coaches should have a *lower* success rate than that. If the runners were successful 97 percent of the time, third-base coaches were only sending the ones who seemed sure to make it. Let's make up a number and assume that of the 1,520 runners who stayed on third, they all would have had a 50/50 shot of making it if they had been sent. That means 760 would have made it and 760 would have been out. This would have lowered the overall "success rate" for our third-base coaches to 88 percent.

We'll never know whether those held runners would have scored or not if they had tested the outfielder's arm. We do know that among that same group, only 39 percent of them (599 in total) eventually made it home. Even if the runner had a 50/50 shot at making it, it was probably still the best chance he was going to have to score.

*   *   *

I THINK THAT ALL THIRD-BASE COACHES SHOULD BE FIRED and replaced with a sign on a stick that points to the left and says "RUN!" The reason is that signs don't have ears and sticks don't have feelings. If a runner gets thrown out at the plate, Ed from Lakewood will call in to the local sports yakker and complain that the third-base coach was being "too aggressive." If the third-base coach is made of plywood, he won't care. Unfairly, if the runner scores, it's usually the *runner* who gets the credit for scoring because he's so fast.

If the third-base coach holds the runner and the runner doesn't score because the next batter strikes out, the third-base coach can say the four most powerful words in the English language: "It's not my fault." People would likely believe him. He didn't *do* anything, so there's nothing to blame him for. All of the emotional incentives line up for the third-base coach to be extremely conservative and to yell "Stay!" even when expected value tells him to yell "Go!"

We can look into the numbers and see exactly how squeamish third-base coaches are. Data are publicly available for the exact distance from home plate for all fly balls that were caught by an outfielder and hit with fewer than two outs and a runner on third (that is, a potential sacrifice fly situation) from 2015 to 2017. We can see how often third-base coaches yelled "Go!" and how often the umpire yelled "Safe!" about five seconds later, based on how deep the ball was hit.

Table 5. Potential Sacrifice Fly Send and Safe Rates, 2015–2017

Distance	Send rate	Safe rate
226–250 ft.	13.4%	97.8%
251–275 ft.	50.4%	94.4%
276–300 ft.	89.5%	97.4%
More than 301 ft.	99.5%	98.8%

Third-base coaches are hesitant to send runners until the ball gets past 275 feet from home plate, and they aren't universal in their send decisions until the ball reaches the 300 foot mark. However, they're getting near universal success even at 225 feet away.

We can do a more sophisticated analysis and control for additional pieces of information like the speed of the runner on third. Using a technique known as logistic regression, we can estimate how likely it is that a runner would score from third if he tried, given his speed and the distance that the outfielder (and cutoff man) would have to cover with their throws. We can also use the run expectancy matrix to determine the "break even" point for each potential sacrifice fly opportunity in our data set.

What's amazing is that in 98 percent of cases—and 90 percent of the cases where the runner *wasn't* sent—the regression suggests that the chances that the runner had of scoring were better than the break-even point. Just about all of the runners in our data set *should* have made a mad dash from third, according to expected value, but only a little more than 80 percent tried. Those 20 percent who stayed on third cost their teams runs. Looking a little deeper into the data, it turns out that the average team routinely gave away about three runs per season by not being more aggressive on sacrifice flies, or to put it another way, because it felt icky. By "more aggressive," I mean sending absolutely anyone any time there was a sacrifice fly situation. Replacing the third-base coach with a sign on a stick would have netted a team a few extra runs each year. *And that's just on sacrifice flies.*

The third-base coach also gets to make a few other potentially icky calls on the basepaths, including the decision to wave runners from second to home on a single and first to home on a double. If he's giving away three runs on the potential sacrifice flies, how many is he giving up in the other situations?

Here are data on how often third-base coaches have to make that call per season, how often they throw the lever, and how often they succeed.

Table 6. Frequency of Third-Base Coach Decisions, per Team, 2017

Event	Frequency	Send rate	Safe rate
Potential sacrifice flies (third to home)	49.5	79.6%	97.1%
Potential advancement second to third on a fly ball	39.7	32.2%	97.1%
Potential first to third on a single	173.0	30.6%	97.0%
Potential second to home on a single	138.0	69.7%	95.3%
Potential first to home on a double	81.3	46.3%	94.4%

We see the same pattern over and over. "Safe" rates are nearly perfect, and that's again probably an indicator that third-base coaches are only sending the runners who they are pretty sure will make it. There are still a lot of unsent runners, and there's still some room to grab extra value. I'd argue that a third-base coach should have such a windmill arm that he's occasionally mistaken for part of a miniature golf course. He'll get a few more runners thrown out, but if he can overcome that icky feeling that comes with sending a runner into danger's way, he'll make his team several runs better.

SPORTSWRITER JEROME HOLTZMAN IS WIDELY CREDITED with inventing the "save," coining the term to refer to a reliever who finished a game and preserved a lead for his team. Holtzman felt that this was a better indicator of whether a reliever was doing his job than relying on a reliever's win-loss record. A win for a reliever could mean that he had come into a tight game and had *given up* the tying or go-ahead runs, only to be bailed out by his team's offense. In that sense, the save really was better than what came before it.

MLB adopted the save rule formally in 1969. The rule specifies that a save can only be awarded to the final pitcher of the day, and that he must enter a game where his team is leading (usually by three runs or fewer), and protect that lead. At the time, the rule made sense. Teams who found themselves with a very good reliever out behind the left-field fence would—not surprisingly—reserve him for games which required the most delicate diplomacy, using him in the now all-but-forgotten "fireman" role. His job would be to enter into the seventh or eighth inning of a tight contest and "put out the fire," often by finishing off the game. The save rule recognized his valiant efforts, though we now hardly recognize a reliever pitching for two or three innings to get a save outside of the playoffs.

Tony La Russa, then manager of the Oakland A's, is credited with the invention of the modern closer, through his use of Dennis Eckersley in the late 1980s. Eck, who had been a decent starter from 1975 to 1986 (he even pitched a no-hitter in 1977), had transitioned into a bullpen role with the A's and still had the ability to pitch well, but seemingly only in short bursts. La Russa began to deploy Eckersley in one-inning stints, eventually giving him responsibility for handling the ninth inning of close games. Eckersley thrived in the new role, and the one-inning job meant that La Russa could bring in Eckersley in back-to-back (and sometimes back-to-back-to-back) games, when needed, rather than having to rest Eckersley between appearances. It meant that La Russa could set up his bullpen around the idea that the ninth inning was taken care of. He just needed to get the game there. The reliable sidewinder Eckersley amassed 45 saves in 1988.

A look at the evidence shows that La Russa didn't actually invent the one-inning closer. The trend away from multi-inning saves was clear in the data over the years, and researcher Rob Mains has noted that Cincinnati Reds reliever John Franco had recorded 32 saves in 1987, with 26 of them lasting an inning or less, but Eckersley became the mustachioed face of that particular shift in the game.

Table 7. Outs Recorded by Pitchers in Saves

Year	Average number of outs per save	Percentage of saves with four or more outs	Percentage of saves with seven or more outs
2017	3.22	13.6%	2.5%
2007	3.13	11.7%	1.6%
1997	3.35	20.4%	4.7%
1987	5.00	60.0%	23.0%
1977	5.33	62.1%	31.5%

The Eckersley (or perhaps more correctly, the Franco) experiment begat a wave of copycats. Where a manager had once asked one reliever to throw both the eighth and ninth innings, he could now ask two relievers to throw one each, and likely still have them available for the next day. Freed of the obligation of throwing multiple frames and able to throw at maximum effort, a new type of pitcher emerged, built for the short-burst format. It wasn't necessary to have the endurance to last two or three innings in the bullpen. Teams realized that two or three of these one-inning specialists could provide the same (or better) service as one fireman did, and still come back the next night to do it again. It was a brave new world in how bullpens were designed.

A funny thing happened though. The save rule itself wasn't designed for this new world. In the old fireman system, there was usually no doubt which pitcher deserved the save that day. With all the one-inning specialists, though, a great deal of that clarity was lost. If one reliever pitched a scoreless eighth and another a scoreless ninth to seal a 3–2 victory, why did the ninth-inning pitcher get a gold star while his friend got nothing? Sure, pitching in the ninth is psychologically different than pitching in the eighth, but both men still had to get three Major League hitters out in a tight spot. Surely, the eighth-inning reliever deserves *something* for his efforts. Eventually, MLB introduced the "hold," which was supposed to be a junior varsity version of the save, but few people paid attention to it.

The save was still seen as the primary indicator of a reliever's abilities. With the dawn of a new role that allowed a reliever to collect 40 saves in a season if he pitched well and at the correct time in the game, a new class of closers got paid for their save-collecting ways and also demanded to be inserted into those situations in which they could collect the magical amulet. Managers started making bullpen assignments based on the save rule itself. They forgot to ask whether the save rule was actually prioritizing the correct situations. Was this the best way to get one anointed reliever a lot of saves or was it the best way to win a ballgame?

Ideally, the best reliever on a team should pitch in the situations which are most important to winning a game, but what are those situations? There is a concept in sabermetrics, developed by researcher Tom Tango, known as leverage. Leverage starts with the idea that from any point in a baseball game, we can look at the score, the inning, the number of outs, and the configuration of runners, and determine the state of the game. For example, let's take a game in the bottom of the third inning, with the visiting team leading by one, one out, and a runner on first. Between 1993 and 2017, this situation has happened 2,737 times, and in those games, the home team won 46.9 percent of them. That's the home team's win probability.

In this situation, a number of things could happen. The batter could hit into a double play, ending his team's chances of scoring for the inning (his team's win probability would drop to 40.1 percent). He could hit a home run, moving his team from being down a run to up a run (win probability would increase to 67.8 percent). He could single and chase the runner from first to third and increase his team's chances of scoring a run (and their win probability to 59.0 percent), even though no actual runs have scored. What we do know is that by the time the batter is done, some new situation will have emerged.

In the third inning, those win probability numbers do change, but not wildly because there's still a lot of baseball to play. Even a home run is not a death blow. If the batter hits that same home run in the bottom of the *ninth* inning though, the game is over and his team has won. If he hits into that double play in the ninth, his team has lost. The same home run or double play is worth more—in terms of win probability—the later in the game that we get. This is the essence of leverage, that there are certain situations where a team's chances of winning move up and down more rapidly than others.

We can do this leverage calculation on a plate-appearance-by-plate-appearance basis, but relievers, especially closers, tend to enter the game at the start of an inning—when there are no outs and no runners—with the intent to stay there for the whole inning. We can simplify our leverage calculations to look for which inning/score combinations are the most important ones in the game, based again on how much they affect the only outcome we really care about, who will win the game. Leverage numbers are given in what's known mathematically as a "scalar value." They don't represent any specific events or measurements (e.g., 1 foot or 1 home run). In this case, an inning with a value of 1.00 is an "average" situation. An inning with a value of 2.00 is twice as important as that average and a value of 0.50 is half as important.

Table 8. Highest Inning Leverage Values, Score Relative to the Pitching Team, 2003–2017

Top of an inning	Leverage	Bottom of an inning	Leverage
Ninth inning, up one	2.29	Ninth inning, up one	2.87
Ninth inning, tie	2.03	Eighth inning, up one	2.26
Eighth inning, up one	1.92	Ninth inning, up two	2.05
Eighth inning, tie	1.65	Seventh inning, up one	1.87
Ninth inning, up two	1.59	Ninth inning, tie	1.85
Seventh inning, up one	1.53	Eighth inning, up two	1.74
Seventh inning, tie	1.41	Seventh inning, up two	1.57
Eighth inning, up two	1.40	Sixth inning, up one	1.56
Sixth inning, up one	1.37	Eighth inning, tie	1.53
Seventh inning, up two	1.35	Sixth inning, up two	1.45

(Note: extra innings are functionally the same as the ninth inning for these calculations)

There are a couple of important lessons to take from this chart. The first is that one particular situation in which the closer routinely enters the game, with his team up by three in the ninth, is not *nearly* as important as another ninth-inning situation in which he does *not* often enter, the tied game. In fact, "up three" in the ninth isn't even on the chart of the Top 10 most important innings. It matters more who's pitching the *sixth* inning with a one-run lead! While the save rule recognizes protecting a three-run ninth-inning lead as an act of valor, the actual math of winning a baseball game is less impressed.

The second lesson is that a one-run lead in the seventh or eighth inning is (nearly) as important as a ninth-inning two-run lead. The two most important runs in baseball are the run that ties a game and the run that unties a game, and so the most important pitching situations are the ones in which a team is at risk of giving up one or both of those runs. The save rule has subtly trained fans (and perhaps managers) to view a game not through the lens of the score, but of the inning. The ninth inning. As a result, as fans, we don't obsess over the seventh or eighth inning as much as we do the ninth. We should. The job that the seventh-inning guy does can be as important as the job that the closer does.

If they are playing according to the numbers, managers should use their best relievers in situations where the danger is greatest, no matter what the save rule says. In an era of one-inning relievers, it's not likely that the multi-inning fireman is coming back, but there is a simple adjustment that could make bullpens more effective. Managers could farm out their three-run ninth-inning leads to one of the middle-of-the-pack bullpen guys and swap in the closer for those ninth-inning *tie* situations instead. The closer won't get a save for pitching in a tie situation and some middling middle reliever will officially pick up a dozen or so saves for his work. That's okay. The point of baseball isn't to get one guy to 40 saves. It's to win games.

Why don't managers protect ties the same way they protect three-run leads? The answer again lies in the fact that it feels icky. *Loss aversion* is a concept that has emerged from the field of behavioral economics. It was originally popularized by researchers Amos Tversky and Daniel Kahneman, to explain some odd human behavior. People tend to react more strongly to losing something that they already have than they do to gaining something that they don't have, even if those things are of the same value. In baseball, a team which is holding a three-run lead has the most important thing that a team can have in a game that is not yet finished: *the lead*. If the reliever can do his job, his team wins.

A tied game doesn't feel so emotionally salient because the pitching team does not, by definition, have the lead. Even if everything goes right, a team can't take the lead back while pitching. The reliever can only preserve the fact that his team isn't currently losing. This is a case where the fact that the English language (and baseball lexicon) doesn't contain a word that means "the fact that his team isn't currently losing" becomes key. *The lead* is a thing. *The lead* is something that can be lost. In contrast, it almost sounds grammatically improper to say "The Braves have the tie, and they're trying to protect it here in the ninth" and yet protecting a tie is one of the most important things that a pitcher can do.

Sometimes people make bad decisions because they don't have a word that allows them to conceptualize the problem in the correct way. If there was a word that meant "the fact that his team isn't losing" we could say things like "The Braves have sent him out there to protect the *groffle*." Alas, we lack the word. The words that we do have tell the same story of loss aversion.

Losing a three-run lead in the ninth is usually described as a "gut punch." We lack a similar painful metaphor to describe a game that was tied in the ninth, but was lost. Those games "slipped away." The harsh reality is that the standings page doesn't care about emotional reactions. They both go in the same column.

*   *   *

THE UNDERVALUING OF TIE GAMES LEADS TO ONE OTHER way that managers aren't optimizing their bullpen, although for a slightly different reason. Imagine being the manager of the visiting team, headed into the bottom of the ninth with the game tied. It's not a great situation to be in, because to win that night's game, your pitcher will have to prevent the home team from scoring in the bottom of the ninth (otherwise, the home team gets to jump up and down and throw things at the guy who got the walk-off hit), your offense must score in the top of the 10th, and you must hold the lead in the bottom of the 10th. That's a best-case scenario. If you make it to the 10th inning and your offense doesn't score, you are back in the same situation, again faced with needing to get two more innings out of the bullpen, likely both of them needing to be shutout innings.

What's strange is that managers don't normally bring their closer into the tied bottom of the ninth inning. The most common explanation is that the manager is saving his closer for what he hopes will be a 10th-inning *save situation*. At first, it might seem like the manager has a point. Looking back on the inning leverage table from earlier, we see that a one-run lead in the ninth inning or later is *the* most important situation that a team faces. A ninth-inning tie is important, but if the closer can only go one inning, then the manager is simply saving this scarce resource for the more important situation. There's a problem. That save situation might never come.

In the 2016 American League Wild Card game, Orioles manager Buck Showalter faced exactly this decision. During the regular season, Orioles reliever Zach Britton had posted one of the finest seasons a reliever ever had, finishing the year with an ERA of 0.54 in 67 innings. As the visiting Orioles entered the bottom of the ninth tied 2–2 against the Blue Jays, Showalter could have called on Britton to take the hill. Instead, he summoned reliever Brad Brach. Brach had also had a good season in 2016, though not one like Britton's. Still, Brach did his job and held the Blue Jays scoreless in the ninth, but the Orioles were not able to break through in the top of the 10th.

Headed into the bottom of the 10th, Showalter summoned to the hill...Darren O'Day. O'Day had made the All-Star team in 2015, but he had been hurt and only managed to throw 31 Major League innings in 2016. Fortunately, O'Day got the Orioles through the 10th unscathed. In the top of the 11th, the Orioles offense sputtered again. Surely Showalter would go to his closer, figuring that in a do-or-die game, Britton was available to pitch multiple innings. Out from the bullpen trotted...Brian Duensing? Duensing had spent more time pitching for the Royals' AAA affiliate in 2016 than with the Orioles. In a game that literally meant the season to the Orioles, Zach Britton was sitting in the bullpen wondering what he had to do to get a phone call.

Duensing did his job though, striking out Blue Jays left fielder Ezequiel Carrera, before giving way to Ubaldo Jimenez. Jimenez had been terrible in 2016, posting a 5.44 ERA, mostly in a starting role. Yet here he was thrust into the biggest game of the year at one of its biggest moments. He promptly gave up two singles and the three-run home run to Edwin Encarnacion that sent the Toronto Blue Jays to the next round of the playoffs. Britton never got to pitch.

Let's do this one logically first, and then do the math. In the bottom of the ninth inning of a tied game, if the pitcher on the mound gives up a run, the game is over and his team loses. In the bottom of the 10th with his team leading (the situation that the manager is "saving him" for), if the pitcher on the mound gives up one run, the worst that happens is that the game is retied. That's not a great outcome, but it's better than losing outright. There is more margin for error with the lead than there is in a tie game, so if you have to pick, you want your better pitcher on the mound when there is no margin for error. Even if Zach Britton had only been available for one inning that night, he would have been better served pitching the ninth. Someone else might have had to notch the save, but you have to get to the save situation first.

Mathematically, we see that, going into the bottom of the ninth (or later) tied, the inning leverage is 1.85, while the value for a 10th-inning one-run lead is 2.87. (Careful readers will note that the visitors might score seven runs in the top of the 10th, which renders all of this pointless, but for a moment, we will assume that our visitors can only be counted on to score one run.) We have another situation where the manager has to make a decision before he knows the outcome, and in that situation, he should pick the one that has the greatest expected value.

Buck Showalter could have put Zach Britton into the tie game in the ninth (or 10th or 11th), and guaranteed that his closer would face a situation with a leverage of 1.85 or he could have held Britton out for the possibility of facing a situation with a leverage of 2.87, but he also risked a situation in which Britton faced a leverage of zero, because the game had ended and the Orioles had already lost. Showalter held Britton back and lost the bet.

Using the expected value method from Chapter 2, we find that if a manager believes that his team has a greater than 64.4 percent chance of grabbing the lead first, he *should* save his closer for that potential 10th-inning (or later) save situation. That 64.4 percent chance seems optimistic, though. If nothing else, at the time the manager is making that decision, the home team has the first shot at taking the lead (and winning the game). Managers are showing the effects of something called Optimism Bias, which is exactly what it sounds like. People are overly invested in the idea that things will work out in their favor, even when there is no logical reason for them to believe this. Buck Showalter was playing in a way that suggested that he was overly confident that his team would score first. That optimism bias may have cost the Orioles a chance to advance in the 2016 playoffs.

* * *

WHEN I WAS 14, MY FAMILY TOOK A VACATION TO THE northernmost reaches of Michigan. We rented a small cabin by a lake and spent a week or so in family togetherness. I think by the end of the week, we were all ready to not be so together anymore. As we drove back to Ohio, we stopped off for lunch in a town called Mount Pleasant, Michigan, which I remember being a misstatement on both counts, but it had a casino. I suppose my parents were just as sick of me and my younger brother as we were of them. They decided to stop in to play a few minutes of slots, while my brother and I browsed the gift shop. I bought a local paper and looked through the box scores.

I wasn't old enough to enter the casino floor, but the idea of gambling intrigued the teenage version of myself. I hatched a plan whereby I gave my father a dollar out of my wallet. I instructed him to find a quarter slot machine, insert the dollar, hit the button four times, and bring me whatever was left. When he came back, he told me that the first three spins came up with nothing, but the fourth spin won me five quarters, which he placed in my hand. I was 25 cents up on the gambling industry. I still am.

Casinos are monuments to mathematical and psychological illiteracy. Psychologists have known for a long time that when a behavior consistently produces a reward, it quickly becomes boring and the behavior goes away. If you want to train an animal (or a person) to do something—for example, stick money into a machine—you don't reward them every time. You reward them some of the time and at random intervals. Psychologists call this an intermittent reinforcement schedule. You sometimes win while playing slots and the win comes without warning. When you "win" a spin, there are lights and cute little animations on the screen. Perhaps there's the lovely clinking sound of quarters dropping into the tray below. Pair winning with a little shot of the neurotransmitter dopamine and you've got them hooked. As someone trained in psychology and statistics, I find slot machines to be terrifying. Expected value theory says that casinos should be empty. Expected value theory does not work on actual human beings.

If there is one taboo that Major League Baseball holds on to dearly, it's the taboo against anyone associated with the game being involved in gambling. Part of what MLB is selling is the idea of a good, clean competition between two teams, and baseball has its scars on the subject. In 1919, the Black Sox scandal saw eight members of the Chicago White Sox, most famously "Shoeless" Joe Jackson, banned for life from baseball when the league ruled that they had thrown games in that year's World Series after taking money from gamblers who then bet on the eventual—deserving or not—champion Cincinnati Reds. In 1989, Major League Baseball ruled that Pete Rose had bet on baseball while he was managing the Reds, a charge that Rose publicly confessed to in 2004. The charge was considered serious enough that despite a playing career worthy of the Hall of Fame by any measure, Rose was ruled ineligible for election to that honor.

Despite the prohibition on actual wagering, we still see managers act like gamblers. They're not gambling on games, but they are acting like gamblers in the strategic decisions that they make. In theory, a manager should look at the situation in front of him and decide a strategy based on whatever information he has available at the time. What happened on the last spin should make no difference. My father likes to point out that everything works "in theory."

Suppose for a moment that in the second inning of a game, a manager finds himself with a runner on first and no one out. The runner on first is fast, so the manager tells the third-base coach to put his left arm in and take his left arm out. The runner nods, takes his lead off first, and then is off with the pitch. The problem is that he didn't get a good jump, and the catcher fires on target to nab the runner red-handed in his act of thievery.

Fast forward to the sixth inning. The manager has another runner on first with no one out. What should he do? Should he call for a steal again? That's a complicated question. It will depend on the speed of the runner, the abilities of the catcher, the score, and maybe a few other factors. It might even depend on whether the manager is the sort of chap who likes to hit the "steal" button or who prefers less aggressive baseball. All of those are reasonable things to factor in the decision, but one thing that *shouldn't* be involved is the caught stealing that happened in the second inning.

The data, however, show that it *does* influence the decision. But in which direction: for or against?

I found all situations from 2013 to 2017 where a team had a runner on first and no runner on second. I wanted to know what factors would help to explain whether the manager sent the runner. I controlled for all of the game situation factors, and not surprisingly, all of these helped to predict whether the manager gave it a go. Then, I added a variable to the mix: whether the manager had one of his runners caught earlier in the game. While this shouldn't have made a difference, the regression *clearly* showed that it did.

Managers called for the steal *more* after an earlier unsuccessful attempt. It's not that managers try to steal every single time after they get caught, but the chances that you'll see the runner break from first go up.

Why are managers doing something that they shouldn't? One possibility is that they are trying to "get back" the steal that they "lost," as if they must restore some balance to the universe or get rid of that icky feeling of failure. Maybe that's masculine pride at being "defeated" and needing to even the score. They might also be falling victim to something known as the Gambler's Fallacy. If a fair coin has come up heads five times in a row, what is the chance that the next flip will be tails? If your answer was anything other than 50 percent, you just committed the Gambler's Fallacy, because you assumed that the five tosses before had anything to do with the sixth. Don't worry. Managers do it too. It's as if managers believe that since the last runner was out, that this next runner is somehow more likely to be safe, and so they feel more comfortable sending the runner. That makes no logical sense, but the data show that it happens anyway.

*   *   *

HUMANS AREN'T VERY GOOD AT LOGICAL DECISION-MAK-
ing. There's probably an entire book to be written just using
baseball examples on ways that baseball's players and coaches
and managers and general managers and owners and fans defy
logic. I don't blame them. Sometimes doing the logical thing
feels icky. If there's one major cognitive bias to rule them all, it's
that humans base their decisions and their emotional reactions
not on expected value, but on the desire for certainty.

Suppose I were to offer you the services of a starting pitcher
who was guaranteed to start every fifth game, and to go six innings, giving up four runs every time he went out there. How big
of a contract would you give to that pitcher?

Now, consider a starter who will have an ERA somewhere
around 5.50. How much would you give that guy? Probably less.
The hitch? That's the same pitcher. A pitcher who gives up runs
at a rate of four per six innings will give up six runs every nine
innings, and assuming that a few of them are unearned, that
means his ERA would be around 5.50. In 2017, among starting
pitchers who threw at least 100 innings, an ERA of 5.50 would
have been good for 115th place in the majors. That's 200 innings of
fifth starter–level quality pitching. Locking in consistency is nice,
but locking in "consistently bad" isn't.

When I framed the offer as a guaranteed performance and
asked how much you'd pay that guy, there were a lot of zeroes in
that number, weren't there? That pitcher may still belong on a

Major League roster, and perhaps at the right price, he'd be a bargain, but go back to the number that you originally thought of for his salary. Do you think you could take that money and do better with it? You could probably concoct a strategy that if things went well, would do better, but you wouldn't have a guarantee of that. The allure of certainty, even "certainly awful," probably ended up being worth a lot of money in your mind. You're not alone.

There's a similar emotional problem that goes along in explaining baseball (and life in general). Andy Rooney, longtime reporter for the television show *60 Minutes*, called it "the 50-50-90 Rule." If you have a 50-50 chance of getting something right, you will get it wrong 90 percent of the time. That doesn't make sense numerically, but it describes human behavior all too well. People fixate on the times that they faced an uncertain situation and the result did not go their way far more than they remember the times where it worked out nicely. Faced with another uncertain situation, they will dread that 90 percent more than they should. Uncertainty feels icky and people will go to great lengths and do irrational things to get rid of uncertainty.

Looking back to Mike Jirschele's decision to stop Alex Gordon at third base, we could mathematically put together a decent estimate of Gordon's chances of scoring on that play, given the information that Jirschele had when making his decision. His chances were better than zero. Maybe Brandon Crawford makes a bad throw home in a pressure-packed situation. Maybe Buster Posey drops the ball when trying to tag Gordon at the plate. The answer would not be "he was certain to score" either. That's not as emotionally satisfying as claiming "He definitely would have made it" or "He was certainly a dead duck." We like things that are denominated in "definitely" and "certainly." It's why humans tend to judge things by their outcomes. At least we know with certainty after the fact what happened, and we can tell ourselves that it was always "destined" to happen that way.

In baseball, there are *a lot* of decisions that have to be made well before we know some very critical information. Free agents are guaranteed a salary years in advance of when they will play the games that earn them that salary. Teams sign international free agents at age 16—before they even finish puberty—with an eye to having a serviceable Major Leaguer in eight years. Veterans are traded for prospects who've yet to achieve Major League success. There's uncertainty all over the place.

Along comes a guy with a spreadsheet, who says, "I can show you methods that will produce the right answer 60 percent of the time, rather than 50 percent." We can all recognize that 60 percent is better than 50 percent, but it still means being wrong 40 percent of the time. "Doing the numbers" might make for better decisions, but it doesn't make for perfect decisions or emotionally easier ones. There's no certainty in that spreadsheet, and that's what people are *really* craving. That's the emotional shift you have to realize to make better decisions in baseball (and the rest of life).

That's why it feels icky.

- *4* -

The-Perfect-Team

IN SEPTEMBER 1999, I BEGAN MY SOPHOMORE YEAR AT Kenyon College. I was part of a campus Christian group and had done some work organizing a welcoming committee for the new kids on campus. Through that work, I had gotten to know a couple of first-year students in the incoming Class of 2003. One of them mentioned that he and several other people would be hanging out later that night in Room 315 of McBride Residence Hall. "Come by whenever," he said. That night, when I got to Room 315, I happened to sit down (perhaps not accidentally) near a tall, gorgeous Russian woman. Her name was Tanya and she remains the most interesting person I have ever met.

She was born in Moscow, but had moved to Atlanta when she was 11. We started talking in 315 and later in the exit stairwell that, at two in the morning, led a very smitten 19-year-old me down to the path back to my dorm. She thought my nerdy jokes were funny. She didn't know anything about baseball, but we ended up bonding over babysitting. My summer job in college was working at a day care center, and she had spent the previous summer babysitting two little girls who were six and two. A few years later, they were the flower girls in our wedding, but we're getting ahead of the story.

At first, we were just two people. I'd see Tanya around campus quite a bit. Kenyon was a small school in the middle of nowhere Ohio. It's hard *not* to run in to someone, even if you're trying to avoid them, and I didn't mind running in to her. We had several friends in common, we ate breakfast around the same time, and she was fun to hang out with. In February of each year, the school held an annual formal dance for everyone on campus. The school's founder was an Episcopal bishop named Philander Chase, so the dance was Philander's Phebruary Phling, and that year, it phell on Valentine's Day.

Phling was supposed to be the highlight of the Kenyon social calendar, although I had gone the year before and it was mostly just the same people I saw in class, obscenely drunk and dancing in the dining hall. In formalwear.

A few days before Phling, Tanya sent me an instant message (hello, 2000!) asking if I was planning to go. This was silly because everyone knew that everyone went to Phling. It was really the only thing to do on campus that weekend, but Tanya had something in mind. She said that she had always wanted to go to a formal dance wearing a suit and with her date in a dress. She had asked a few of her friends from her hall, and none of them would take her up on the idea. Then, she thought to ask me. I typed back two words that changed the entire course of my life. "Why not?" Thankfully, she had a dress that fit me "well enough."

We told no one of our plans and simply showed up together. That night the legend of *Tanya-and-Russell* was born.

Except that we weren't dating. We were *that* couple, the ones who are the last two people in the world who realize that they are dating each other. By this point, we were regularly having breakfast together. Over the next summer, we wrote each other letters (on paper!) and I even called her on her birthday to sing the birthday song. My mother likes to tell the story of the next September, when everyone was getting back to campus for the new school year. After a summer apart, I saw Tanya and ran over to her and at the same time, she saw me and ran toward me. My mother told me several years later that in that moment, she had turned to my father and said, "Explain to me again how they're *not* dating." We weren't. Really.

Well, by that point we were having breakfast together, usually lunch, and most of the time, dinner. We would rent kids movies on VHS (hello again, 2000!) from the Village Market and watch them together. We would study together in the library even though we were in completely different majors, because we were nerds. Sometime in October, one of our mutual friends asked, "Is it just me or does everyone think you two are dating?" We swore that we weren't. Tanya was my friend with whom I just happened to spend nearly every waking hour. It wasn't until that December that we admitted to ourselves that we were dating. We were apparently not the most aware people in the world.

There's a beautiful and subtle vocal shift that takes place when any serious romantic relationship forms, and it took place in ours. We became *Tanya-and-Russell*. Yes, we were still two people, but we also formed a unit that was somehow more than just the two of us. I started noticing that when friends said our names, they ran them together a lot more closely than they did when they spoke the names of any two other people in sequence. Tanya and I had a deep discussion about this one night. She'd noticed it too. She notices things like that. It's something I love about her.

The word "couple" is often used to refer collectively to people in romantic relationships, but I think there's a relationship status that's more than a "couple." It's the one where you get the hyphens and the ever-so-shorter pauses between your names, because the two of you are more than just two people now. Those are the good relationships. Tanya told me after we "started" dating that if we made it to three weeks together, we would probably end up getting married. Like most things in life, she was right.

In May of 2002, I graduated from Kenyon, but Tanya still had her senior year left. I moved to Chicago to start graduate school, which meant that we had a year of a long-distance relationship ahead of us. This time though, I didn't miss the obvious cue when she started talking about graduate programs in the Windy City. For my part, I spent a lot of weekends that year on U.S. Route 30, which runs through the middle of rural Indiana and nowhere Ohio, driving back to Kenyon to see the woman whose name and soul had become intertwined with mine. In June of 2004, I dropped to one knee and asked Tanya to make those hyphens permanent. She said yes.

*   *   *

I WAS NOT AN ART MAJOR. KIND OF LIKE MY DREAMS OF
being a major leaguer, my artistic abilities peaked in fourth
grade, when the art class assignments went beyond pasting construction paper shapes on top of each other in some prespecified
order. However, I was and still am handy with the collage, which
is the big-kid version of pasting shapes on top of each other. The
important task is to get all of the important stuff onto the page.
How it's arranged is secondary.

I think there's a common assumption that baseball teams are
put together the same way. Just put 25 really good players onto
the approved list and you'll be fine. It doesn't matter whether
they fit together or not. It's one of those things that seems intuitively true. Of course, a team with 25 All-Stars has a better shot
than a team with 25 guys who all belong in Triple-A. Talent is a
huge part of the game; but is that all there is?

There is a concept in science known as *emergence* or *emergent
behavior,* which is better known as the whole of an organism
being greater than the sum of its parts. Human consciousness
itself is an emergent property. The fact that you are currently
awake and aware cannot be fully explained by the physical
structures of the human brain, and yet here you are reading
this book. Emergence can be a wonderful thing. It can take two
goofy, nerdy college students and make them a couple. The
problem with emergence is that it isn't always good. It can take
a group of people and make them an angry mob. Worse, it can
make them do The Wave.

We are hardwired to see emergence in ways that we don't fully appreciate. A series of small lights next to each other on a marquee that flash in a serial sequence become a set of "moving" lights. There is, of course, no motion, nor would the brain perceive them as "moving" if they were to flash in a random sequence, but by the way that they interact with each other, they become something more than just blinking lights. When talking about baseball, people often discuss players who "play together as a team." A lineup where the "pieces complement each other." A clubhouse where good chemistry is said to be the driving force behind a surprising run toward a playoff spot. Is it possible that in baseball, there are ways for a team to be more than the sum of its parts?

For baseball fans, it can be a fun game to play "pick the perfect team," although it can quickly turn sour when you realize that it's just a game of "recite last year's All-Star roster" or "which inner-circle Hall of Famers do I have a strange fascination with?" Sure, your team of All-Stars would be better than any team currently playing, but this is not actually a team-building exercise. It's like having nine separate discussions. One about the best first baseman in the league, followed by a discussion of the best second baseman, and on and on.

I recommend a different challenge. Let's play "pick the-perfect-team" (with hyphens!). Imagine that for some reason, Major League Baseball has hired you and 29 other folks to helm each of the 30 teams. On top of that, MLB has just declared everyone a free agent! You get to start from scratch and your job is to put together a team that will win the World Series. There's always a catch, though. As a condition of your getting this dream job, you have agreed to be bopped on the head (MLB will provide some aspirin, if you like) and have your knowledge of the actual players in Major League Baseball erased. You retain the knowledge that there are infielders and outfielders and starters and relievers and good players and bad players and all-hit-no-glove-players and no-hit-all-glove players. Thankfully, MLB is willing to bop you on the head again and restore your knowledge, but only after you submit a plan detailing how you will go about your job.

While we're at it, let's pay some amount of respect to the realities of team construction. You'll need to actually find 25 guys and you'll be given a salary limit. If you sign Mike Trout to a mega-deal, it will probably mean no mega-deal for Bryce Harper, even though it would be *so much fun* to see the two of them in the same outfield. You do, however, have the freedom to sign any 25 players in any configuration that you like. With that in mind, what would be your strategy? Would it still be "grab the best 25 players available"?

WRITING IN THE *HARVARD BUSINESS REVIEW* IN 2015, AUTHOR Roger L. Martin laid out an astonishingly simple business maxim that can provide us a great deal of guidance here: "If the opposite of your core strategy choices looks stupid, then every competitor is going to have more or less the exact same strategy as you." In his article, Martin lamented the fact that in the world of mutual fund management, many firms had stated that one of their key strategies was "great customer service." At first this seems reasonable, because no business would survive if they provided poor customer service, but it's also not a strategy. It's a goal. No one would ever choose the opposite.

A real strategy forces you to make choices between options when it's not obvious what the answer is. In other words, a strategic choice is one where you might be wrong. Providing good customer service is a reasonable goal, but should our mutual fund company do so by hiring more account managers (which will cost them more money) so that each manager has a smaller caseload and more time per client to provide customer service? Should they not hire as many, leaving account managers with bigger caseloads, but saving on salary and benefits? How big can a caseload get before customer service suffers? If it does, how likely are customers to start taking their business elsewhere? I don't know the answer to any of these questions so I will use a phrase which means "I have no idea, but I still want to sound smart."

It depends.

I love "It depends" because it has the benefit of being a true statement that tells us absolutely nothing. It's true because the answer to just about every question in life really does depend on several complicated factors. If the answer were easy and obvious, then we wouldn't have asked the question in the first place. "It depends" tells us nothing unless it's followed by an answer to "On what?" Otherwise, "It depends" is mostly just a culturally acceptable way of saying "It's complicated and I have no idea." It's always telling to see what things a culture is unwilling to admit out loud to the point where they must create a code phrase.

If I'm going to do something other than guess, I need to know a few things. What do we know about our customers? Are they willing to pay more for an account manager who is more dedicated to their specific needs? Will they really take their business elsewhere if they don't get a call back within five minutes? Could we push our average time to 10 minutes? What's the company's current budget situation? If I knew the answer to those questions, I would be able to render a more qualified opinion (or any opinion at all), but the truth is that everything I know about mutual fund management can be written on the back of a dime with a crayon. If I want to answer this question, I'm going to have to dive in to the complexity to figure it all out. I will need real deep knowledge. I will need to know how all the parts work together.

Ah, but why do all the hard work of obtaining deep knowledge and understanding complexity when you can instead have a slogan! "Cut costs at all costs!" has the benefit of being easy to repeat, easy to follow, and sometimes might even be the right answer, or at least the right direction. Sentences with some variant of the word "always" in them are nice for the fact that they require minimal thought. Politicians love slogans. The engineer, on the other hand, answers questions like these often with complicated discussions about the details. Details are boring, but they run the world.

Baseball is full of cheap slogans too, some of which have even acquired enough mold to be considered wisdom. You can never have enough pitching! Defense wins championships! Power in the corners, speed up the middle! It's true that I'd rather have plenty of pitching than not enough, but at some point, I might want to sign a hitter or two, especially if I already have 24 pitchers on my roster.

*   *   *

THERE ARE TWO WAYS TO BUILD VALUE ON A BASEBALL team. One is to have better players. This is hardly revolutionary and immediately fails the Martin Test, but there's always room for being able to identify what makes a player "better" in ways that competitors do not see. In Chapter 2, we saw that in the early part of the 2010s, only a few teams appeared aware of the effect that catcher framing could have in providing value to a team, but those who did snapped up the catchers who were good at it, and benefitted from the extra talent that no one else saw. Eventually though, when the league caught on to the catcher framing effect, the market simply began pricing that value into the cost of a catcher's contract. It's hard to keep a secret in baseball.

I'm much more interested in the second way that a team can build value, which is value generated through understanding how players fit together within the structure known as a baseball team. I'm interested in going beyond the parts and engineering a better way for those parts to work together. I'm interested in emergence. Unfortunately, emergence is another one of those concepts for which we lack words in baseball. We are used to assigning credit for events to an individual player ("Barry Bonds hit 73 home runs in 2001"), but what happens when two players interact with one another to create value?

For example, if a team has a fantastic set of defensively skilled infielders, a pitcher who induces a lot of ground balls will be worth more than that same pitcher in front of a more average group of fielders. The pitcher hasn't changed, but he gets better results in front of the Gold Glovers. The Gold Glovers get to shine ever brighter when they play behind a pitcher who feeds them more ground balls. The team clearly benefits by generating more outs on defense, but to whom should we give the credit? The real fun of the "build the-perfect-team" game isn't in the final roster. I'd submit that the game is actually at its best when it serves as a way to have a deeper discussion about the guts of how baseball works.

Let's begin with the one advantage that we have been given in this exercise. We know that everyone is a free agent. That's helpful because it means that we don't have to make decisions about our team based on the fact that we already have 17 guys signed and we're pretty much stuck with them. It also means that we can try some new things. We've been given *carte blanche* to construct a team in any way we prefer. It has to function as a baseball team over 162 games, but perhaps we can move away from the tyranny of how rosters are currently constructed and try a few new ideas. Most people would begin this exercise by assuming that we will need five starters, a few garbage-time relievers, a right-handed specialist, a left-handed specialist, a set-up man, and a closer, and then eight position player starters, a spare catcher, a couple of utility infielders and outfielders, and maybe a designated hitter. Perhaps we could even rethink whether those categories make sense. Not only have we cleared the roster, but we can destroy and rebuild its scaffolding if we want. We have total freedom on this canvas.

Let's use it!

*   *   *

ONE OF THE MOST TELLING PIECES OF INFORMATION ABOUT baseball is that teams may employ 25 people on a given day, with nine of them playing at any one time. Half of those roster spots are routinely dedicated to staffing just one of those positions, with the other half used to staff the remaining eight. The pitcher is the most important person on the field, because no matter what else happens, he is the only player who is guaranteed to touch the ball during a play.

We will begin with a simple multiplication problem. Over 162 nine-inning games, a team will need to have enough pitching to cover 1,458 innings. Some of those innings will be in games where the score is already 10–2, and some will be the ninth inning of a one-run game. There will be days where the game will go 16 innings. There will be days when we don't need to bother with the ninth inning. Even more fun, a team goes to the ballpark every day having no idea which one of those will happen. A manager has to be ready for anything and there is probably going to be a game tomorrow night to think about as well.

It's also telling that baseball games are often subtitled by the names of the two *starting* pitchers ("It's Kershaw vs. Bumgarner! And oh yeah, the Dodgers are playing the Giants."). In fact, if a sportscaster gives *any* information about a forthcoming game other than the time it starts, it's almost exclusively the names of the two starters. It's for good reason. If the pitcher is the most important person on the field, then the pitcher who figures to be out there for the majority of the game would be the most important player on his team for that game.

Major League teams routinely carry five starting pitchers, and hope that they go six to seven innings in each game. I call this the 5-6-7 rotation. These five starters are generally backed up by a squadron of six to eight relievers who most commonly throw one inning at a time. (In 2017, 51 percent of relief appearances were cases where the reliever got exactly three outs.) Therefore, most teams follow the 5-6-7-1-1-1 model when filling out the pitching side of the roster.

Of course, it wasn't always this way. There was a time in baseball history where teams routinely used a four-man rotation and, while contrary to popular belief, the majority of starts *did not* take place on three days' rest.

Table 9. Percentage of Regular Season Starts Made on Three Days' Rest

Year	Percentage
2017	0.1%
2007	0.5%
1997	2.3%
1987	7.4%
1977	24.3%
1967	30.2%
1957	23.1%

There are those who long for the days of the four-man rotation, for the simple reason that it's hard to find five good starters. Why not make the task 20 percent easier? Research that I have done suggests that this is not likely to happen. While we don't have reliable injury information for pitchers going back into the 1950s and 1960s, we can use playing time data to find pitchers who were pitching for an extended period of time and then seemed to disappear for a while. Using a statistical technique known as Cox regression, I found that when I limited my data set to only the 1950s, the number of times that a pitcher started on three days' rest actually predicted a lower risk of one of these "mysterious disappearances." This was also the case in the 1960s.

In the 1970s and 1980s, the link broke, with pitchers who had a lot of starts on three days' rest being no more or less likely to have one of these absences. By the 1990s and 2000s, the effect was clearly pointing toward starters who had three days of rest more often suffering more "injuries." The decreased use of three days' rest in MLB and the increase in the risk of injury associated with it seem to track each other. It's not clear which one came first, but it seems that either pitchers are no longer conditioned to be able to throw on three days' rest or teams have slowly realized that it was a bad idea as they have gotten better at diagnosing what might have previously been "hidden" injuries.

We will not have a four-man rotation any time soon, but what if we had a four-and-a-half-man rotation? In this model, teams assemble five starters, but the fifth guy pitches only when his team plays five games in a row. If there's an off-day, he gets bumped. In 2017, 49 percent of starts were made on four days of rest and 40 percent were made on five or six days of rest. Again, research that I have done shows that pitchers perform neither better nor worse than their overall stats suggest they would when they pitch on four days of rest or five. So, if you have a pitcher who is fully rested, and he doesn't gain anything from having an extra day of rest, why give the ball to someone who is, by definition, worse than him?

Teams don't have to be dogmatic about it, but skipping the fifth starter once in a while could give an extra start or two to each of the other four in the rotation. During weeks where he is not needed, the fifth starter could be used in relief or he can be shuttled off to the minors so that his team can instead have an extra specialist reliever or a bench bat. It's the sort of strategy that can prevent a few extra runs per year, not based on who's on the team, but on how we use those players.

Here's another, more radical, idea to chew on. What if there weren't *any* starting pitchers? Yes, someone would be on the mound as the game started, and he would technically be "the starter," but what if he had a very different job description than we were used to. A starting pitcher is expected to begin the game and to pitch the majority of the team's innings for that day. In 2017, the starting pitcher averaged less than $5\frac{2}{3}$ innings. That's quite low by historical standards (in 1917, the average starter went more than seven innings per outing), but it still accounts for almost two-thirds of the game. The MLB rulebook even requires that for a starter to be awarded a win, he must pitch at least five innings. If he doesn't, the "winning pitcher" is at the discretion of the official scorer. It's supposed to be given to the most effective reliever for the day, but it may *not* be given to the starter, even if he pitched 4 ⅔ perfect innings.

In 1993, then–Oakland A's manager Tony La Russa (hello again!) tried an experiment in real time with an A's team that eventually lost 94 games. Instead of tasking one pitcher with throwing 100 pitches and six or seven innings (something that his staff struggled mightily with that year), he instead created three groups of three pitchers and asked them each to throw 40–60 pitches and hopefully three innings. The starting groups would take their turn every third day. La Russa reasoned that if his pitchers were having trouble making it through the mid-section of the game, why ask them to do something that they weren't good at. On Monday, July 19, 1993, Todd Van Poppel threw four innings and 49 pitches to the Cleveland Indians and was relieved by career-starter Ron Darling, who also threw four frames. The A's lost. Undaunted, on Tuesday night, La Russa "started" Mike Mohler, who struggled through an inning and two-thirds. Eventually, Bobby Witt, making only his second career appearance in relief, pitched four reasonable innings. The A's lost that one too. It's probably most telling that by the following Monday, the A's started Darling and he threw 94 pitches and went six innings against the Angels. The experiment was over a week after it began.

During the La Russa rotation experiment, the A's went 1–5, but even despite their poor showing, maybe La Russa was on to something. What if part of the reason why it's so hard to find five good starters is because there aren't 150 pitchers who have the tools to consistently make it through six innings? What if, instead of a mad search for those who can, teams upcycled the parts that they already had on hand?

If there's one nice thing to be said for the 5-6-7 model of starting, it's that it has the ability to provide a lot of innings from only five roster spots, but if we're to scrap the 5-6-7 model, we need some idea of what we need to replace. Let's look at how deep into games starters actually went in 2017.

Table 10. Number of Outs Recorded by Starters, 2017

Recorded 0–9 outs	7.1%
Recoded 10–15 outs	32.1%
Recorded 16–18 outs	34.1%
Recorded 19–21 outs	20.7%
Recorded 22–24 outs	4.6%
Recorded 25 or more outs	1.4%

We'll need to replace an average of just under six innings each night. Let's say that instead of asking one pitcher to throw 100 pitches, we ask two pitchers to throw 50 each. How many outs can a pitcher tally in 50 pitches?

Table 11. Number of Outs Recorded by Starters by Their 50th Pitch, 2017

Recorded 0–3 outs	0.8%
Recorded 4–6 outs	9.2%
Recorded 7–9 outs	42.2%
Recorded 10–12 outs	39.6%
Recorded 13 or more outs	8.2%

The average starter recorded just shy of 18 outs in 2017. By his 50th pitch, the average starter recorded 9.4 outs. Even if the starters changed nothing about themselves, we can feel confident that two starters throwing 50 pitches would likely record 18 or 19 outs, on average. Those are averages, so night-to-night the number would vary, but at least we know it would balance out in the long-term. If all went well, we could probably replace the bulk innings that the 5-6-7 model provides.

We're going to run in to a couple problems though. For one, the best-case scenario here is that our pitchers would throw 50 pitches and then have two days of rest. We'd need three sets of two pitchers, for a total of six "starters." That means that we've spent an extra roster spot and gained nothing in terms of innings covered. There's also a problem of variance. Starting pitchers have better stuff in some outings than in others. Some are more consistent, but in the 5-6-7 system, we accept that on some nights, the starter is going to flame out after pitching $2\frac{1}{3}$ horrible innings. There will also be a night a month later where that same starter will pitch eight strong innings.

With paired starters, one guy might be having a *really* good day and get you four innings in his allotted 50 pitches. The problem is that his tandem buddy is most likely to be having an average day and he'll get you $9\frac{1}{2}$ outs, or three innings. On the flip side, it's possible that the first guy will flame out and only get through one inning, but his tandem buddy will come in and again, he is most likely to be having an average day and will get you $9\frac{1}{2}$ outs. The tandem model limits the risk of the type of outing where the starter(s) don't get out of the third inning, but it also limits the chances of the starter(s) stretching into the eighth. It's not that either can't happen, it's just going to be rarer. The tandem system is lower risk, but it's also lower reward.

Here we run in to a quirk of how the rules governing an MLB roster inadvertently shape that roster. The 5-6-7 model compensates for this risk nicely. If the starter goes eight innings, that's wonderful. If he flames out early though, teams usually have a designated long reliever. He's usually an expendable "arm" who's trying to prove that he's not expendable, and if the starter has flamed out, it usually means that the score is 14–2 and the game is effectively over, barring a minor miracle—and when has one of those ever happened? It doesn't really matter who the long reliever is or what he does as long as he gets the team through the sixth with his arm still attached. If he has to pitch four innings, his team has the option of sending him back to Triple-A and some other fresh expendable arm can be called up to take his place the next night. Because teams can get another long reliever on short notice, they can afford to use a starting pitching strategy that is higher risk in terms of filling innings. It's remarkable to think that one of the reasons that the five-man rotation exists is because it's so easy to find and replace bad pitchers.

There are other ways to do the tandem model. Obviously, if a team has a Cy Young contender already in its rotation, they wouldn't want to restrict that guy to 50-pitch outings. If a team had two "real" starters (1, 2) and then two tandem pairs (3/4 and 5/6), the starters could rotate 1, 3/4, 2, 5/6, 3/4, 1, 5/6, 2, 3/4, 5/6, but again, we sacrifice a roster spot.

Then there's a practical problem: spare parts. Pitchers tend to get injured a lot. The way that rosters are currently constructed, there are two main roles on a pitching staff. The starter throws 100 pitches. The reliever throws 20. Our tandem starters would theoretically be throwing 50, even though the idea of a 50-pitch outing doesn't currently exist in MLB.

Table 12. Percentage of Outings within Pitch Count Ranges, 2017

Pitch count	Starters	Relievers
0–9	0.1%	19.4%
10–19	0.2%	47.5%
20–29	0.4%	22.1%
30–39	0.6%	7.3%
40–49	1.0%	2.2%
50–59	1.9%	0.8%
60–69	4.2%	0.4%
70–79	9.5%	0.1%
80–89	19.0%	0.1%
90–99	32.7%	0.0%
100+	30.3%	0.0%

We see that it's rare that anyone, starter or reliever, has an outing in the 40–70 pitch range. If a team loses a starter to injury, they can easily find someone in their minor league system or in the discard bin who is at least trained to throw 100 pitches (even if those pitches aren't all that great). If one of the tandem starters broke, how would a team replace him? There's almost no one in the league trained to do that, meaning that a team would need to find nine or 10 of these 50-pitch guys and have them in-house just to make the system work. They'd also need spare parts for their bullpen and for their "regular" starters.

It turns out that the five-man rotation, much like democracy, is the worst system in the world, except for all the other ones that we might try. The four-man rotation might have its advantages, but we've reached a point of no return on that one. Systems involving tandem starters require exactly the right roster, and rely on types of pitchers who may not exist in enough abundance for even one team to make it work. So, despite the freedom that we have to choose any type of crazy starting rotation that we want, we find that the boring 5-6-7 model seems the best suited to the realities of baseball, because it provides bulk innings with a minimal commitment of roster spots.

Before we leave the tandem starters though, perhaps we have learned something useful that we can take with us into the bullpen. There is another word that is lacking in our baseball vocabulary. This time, it's a word for a pitcher whose job is to throw 50 pitches. He's not a starter, nor does he fit into the usual mold of a reliever. Indeed, if a team tried to sign a player to fill such a role, what should they tell him his job is? But in that lack of a word is the presence of an opportunity. There once was the word "fireman," although that had a specific meaning of a pitcher who could be counted on specifically in high-leverage situations.

What would we call someone who was capable of throwing three innings, but who didn't need to be the best reliever in the bullpen? What if he were simply average?

Right now, there are probably pitchers who would excel in a three-inning role. The thing is that because there are so few pitchers who can pitch six good innings on a consistent basis, if a pitcher shows the ability to go three solid frames, he is likely to keep being pushed out there for the fourth and fifth inning, in the vain hope that he will become a "good" starter. When he doesn't, he will bear the label (and perhaps the price tag) of a "failed starter." There might be other guys out there who have already been converted into bullpen roles, but who could be so much more than a one-inning guy. What if there was a half-way point for those guys where they could do what they are actually good at?

I looked in the data to see if there were guys who fit this mold. In 2017, the average reliever had an ERA of 4.15 and the average starter had an ERA of 4.49. What if we could find a starter who had a better ERA than the average reliever in his first three innings, but was awful from the fourth inning onward, perhaps because he didn't have the stuff to turn over a lineup more than once? It would mean that—doing nothing differently from what he has already done in the past—he has the ability to go three innings at a time and to pitch like a league average reliever.

Table 13. Starters with First Three Innings ERA under 4.10, but ERA over 5.00 Past That, 2017 (min 100 IP)

Pitcher	ERA, first three innings	ERA, fourth inning and past
Brad Peacock	1.29	5.36
Lance McCullers Jr.	2.45	5.81
Dan Straily	3.09	5.66
Michael Wacha	3.20	5.11
Tyler Chatwood	3.61	5.77
German Marquez	3.93	5.04
Jason Hammel	3.94	5.55
Matt Garza	3.97	6.22
Robert Gsellman	4.09	5.62

These are just the cases that jump out of the MLB data set. There might be other pitchers knocking around in the minors who haven't made the leap to the majors because they are not "real" starters yet. The problem is that baseball's language only has two words to describe pitchers ("starters" and "relievers"), and if you don't fit into one of those two boxes, you are described as a "failure," and "failed" is a powerful word. Sometimes when there is no word for something, we don't realize not only that something exists, but that it's sitting in front of us.

Our reliever wouldn't even need to be a particularly noteworthy performer. His performance could be average, which means there's a place for him on a Major League roster. His ability to fill multiple innings from one roster spot with league average results could be very valuable in a bullpen world where everyone else is trained to go one inning. There are certain games during a season which are won because one team had more capacity to throw not-awful relievers for longer. There are certain games where a starter exits in the fourth or fifth inning though the game is still winnable. It's too early to bring in the late-inning corps, but the traditional long-man is likely a below-average reliever who is a poor choice for a game that calls for someone who knows what he's doing. If nothing else, his ability to soak up a few innings means that a team might not have to lean so heavily on one of its other relievers who is *below* average. So, we will be on the lookout for "failed starters." If we look at them from a different angle, we might see treasure in another man's trash. All that we needed to do was to reinvent a word to describe them.

IN CHAPTER 3, WE SAW THAT DESPITE THE OBSESSION WITH the ninth inning and the "closer," the most important innings that a team faces in a year are in games that are *close* rather than late. A one-run lead in the seventh inning is a more important situation than a three-run lead in the ninth. There's a message in there for roster construction. A team would do well to make sure that they have *three* very good relievers, rather than just one. The reason is simple. If the most important situations that a team will face all year can happen in the seventh, eighth, *and* ninth innings, there will be games in which *all three* of those situations happen, and a team will need three good relievers (or some combination of good relievers capable of handling three innings) to staff them.

Table 14. Percentage of Games in Which Teams Faced a High-Leverage Inning, 2013–2017

Situation	Percentage of Games
Ninth inning, tied or up by one or two runs	37.0%
Eighth inning, tied or up by one run	22.2%
Seventh inning, tied or up by one run	24.6%
At least two of these in the same game	23.2%
All three in the same game	13.4%

(Note: all cases represent the game state at the beginning of the inning)

In 13.4 percent of games (22 over a 162-game season), the average team is going to face three of these critical-situation innings. That might not seem like much, but these are the specific situations where the game could go either way. Being 12–10 in them versus being 10–12 in them could make a huge difference at the end of the season in making the playoffs.

In constructing our bullpen, we will prioritize our top three relievers over the rest of the crew. If a closer is worth obsessing over, the seventh- and eighth-inning guys, who are sometimes afterthoughts on a roster, are just as important. We will treat them as such in allocating our scarce resources. In our seven-man unit, we will have three ace relievers who will be tasked with pitching in high-leverage situations in the seventh, eighth, and ninth innings (and will cover a few other innings here and there as the need arises). We will hopefully have our three-inning specialist that we have reclaimed from the scrap heap, and we will have three other pitchers who will sop up garbage time innings. "Garbage time," oddly enough, includes three-run, ninth-inning save situations.

*   *   *

NOW THAT WE HAVE SOME IDEA OF WHAT ROLES OUR pitchers will fill, what sort of pitchers should we chase? The answer to that question might depend somewhat on who will be standing behind him. Among pitchers, we know there are grounder guys and fly-ball guys. What if we put a ground-ball pitcher in front of a really good infield? We have discussed that he would likely get better results than if he was standing in front of four lead-footed lads. How much value can we expect?

In 2017, the best fielding team on ground balls was the Toronto Blue Jays, with 78.6 percent of grounders turned into outs. The worst was the Washington Nationals checking in at 73.1 percent. In 10th place (a third of the way down the list), we see the Los Angeles Dodgers, and in 20th place, the San Diego Padres. This gives us some realistic boundaries of what a "good" and a "bad" infield defense might look like. In 2017, among pitchers who threw at least 150 innings, the highest ground-ball rate belonged to Marcus Stroman, with 62.1 percent of his balls rolling along the grass. The lowest belonged to Marco Estrada, with a 30.3 percent rate. Our one-third of the way down guy was Trevor Williams and two-thirds of the way down, we find Chris Archer. This again is meant to give us some idea of what the bounds of a high, medium, and low ground-ball rate are.

Now, let's make a nice grid. Let's assume that our starter gives up 600 balls in play (about average) during a season. We can estimate how many ground-ball *outs* a pitcher would record standing in front of each of the four defenses.

Table 15. Expected Ground-Ball Outs, 2017 Data

	Blue Jays **(78.6%)**	**Dodgers** **(76.3%)**	**Padres** **(75.5%)**	**Nationals** **(73.1%)**
Marcus Stroman (62.1% GBs)	293	284	281	272
Trevor Williams (48.0%)	226	220	217	210
Chris Archer (42.0%)	198	192	190	184
Marco Estrada (30.3%)	143	139	137	133

We can see that for the same pitcher, standing in front of a good defense means more of their balls in play will turn into outs. To take the extreme ground baller (Stroman) as an example, we expect him to generate about 373 ground balls over 600 balls in play. Moving him from the best ground-ball defense (the Blue Jays, in this example) in the league to one that is merely above average (the Dodgers), would cost him about nine extra balls that *weren't* turned into outs, and instead, go as "hits allowed" on his record. Again, that might not sound like much, but the value of turning a ground ball from a single into an out is roughly three-quarters of a run, which will make Stroman's results more than *half of a win* worse, just based on the four men standing behind him, even if he does nothing differently. Baseball's lexicon again lacks a word for this sort of intersectional effect.

A team doesn't even need to go to the extreme cases to generate a good amount of value. We project that when Trevor Williams, who has a medium-high ground-ball rate, is placed in front of an elite infield, his team gains about five extra ground-outs compared to the merely good infield. Chris Archer, with the medium-low ground-ball rate, would gain an extra four outs. Williams himself might only be worth one extra ground-ball out compared to Archer, but if a team can get one extra ground-ball out from each of its pitchers over the course of a season by being cognizant of how all its pieces fit together and signing more Williamses than Archers, then they may be able to prevent a few extra runs. If you have good infielders, sign pitchers who will feed them more ground balls.

NOW THAT WE'VE DESIGNED SOME STRUCTURAL PRIN-ciples for a pitching staff, we need to think about the other half of the roster. With eight fielding positions and, depending on the league, a designated hitter to find, and only 12 or 13 roster spots to use, we're going to need to be economical. Most teams follow the model that they have a designated regular starter at each of the positions, with the remaining spots going to lesser players who will fill in now and then.

Since we are starting from nothing, we may stop to ask whether we should prioritize a certain position over others. Perhaps teams should focus on signing a center fielder over a third baseman? The answer to this one isn't quite as interesting as one might hope. A lot will depend on which players are available at which position.

For instance, imagine a league where there are 30 center fielders. One of them is amazing and the other 29 are dreadful. That one All-Star is going to have a lot of suitors, because you're not just paying for his services, but you're also paying for the fact that you get to avoid all of the other bad options. The problem is that the other GMs in the league are going to notice his talent as well, and will bid up his price accordingly. If you end up with the amazing center fielder on your roster, it'll probably be because you were willing to pay *a lot* of money.

In economics, this is known as the Winner's Curse. You "win" an auction because you were the person willing to spend the most money. If you are at an auction with a bunch of fools who don't know what they're bidding on, there's room for being the person who is willing to spend the most. Unfortunately, there are no fools in front offices. About the best you can hope for is to find little bits of value that other people don't realize are there and the market is underpricing.

The more interesting question is whether a team should build its position player suite around power or speed or defense or maybe a little from each column. Suppose we had three players, all of whom we rate as "three-win" types, but who draw their value from very different areas.

Table 16. Completely Made-Up Players

Made-up player	Offense	Defense	Baserunning
Gleeman	3	0	0
Miller	1	1	1
Lindbergh	0	2	1

Lindbergh is obviously the best defender, but will probably need to hit eighth. Gleeman has a bat that he uses to hit long home runs *and* field ground balls. Miller has a more well-rounded game without much of a weakness. So, who's it going to be? Recall that one of the strengths (and weaknesses) of Wins Above Replacement (WAR) is that it evaluates a player by stripping out the context of who a player plays with. WAR would see all three of these players as equals, but now that we are creating the-perfect-team, we want to know how each player's talents might interact with those of the rest of his teammates. We need more than just WAR to make this decision.

If we take Lindbergh for his defense and can hit him eighth or ninth, then we can bury his bat, but the more all-glove guys we have, the higher in the order he will have to hit. If we take Gleeman, we can hit him near the top of the lineup, but we'll have to live with the defense. Which is more valuable?

Let's start with some numbers from 2017. The first set is how many times each spot in the batting order came up to bat over the course of the season (average for each team) and the second is how many chances each fielding position had to make a play on defense. (Catchers were excluded because their primary defensive duties are much different than those of the other fielders.)

Table 17. Plate Appearances by Batting Order Position and Chances by Position, 2017

Batting Order	PA	Position	Chances
1	756	1B	352
2	738	2B	595
3	721	3B	491
4	705	SS	671
5	687	LF	526
6	670	CF	615
7	652	RF	541
8	633	DH	0
9	614		

The defensive numbers line up with the conventional wisdom that it's best to have better defenders up the middle, because they handle the most chances. There are only so many corners in which to hide a bad glove. We also see that for each spot that a player gets pushed up (or down) in the lineup, he will gain (or lose) between 15 and 20 PA over the course of a year.

To go back to our three create-a-players above, suppose that we are considering replacing Miller, the all-around balanced player, with Lindbergh, the more talented defender. Lindbergh's defense is an upgrade over Miller's, though Lindbergh's hitting is, in a vacuum, an equal amount worse than Miller's. Miller hits sixth in the lineup currently, but Lindbergh will have to hit eighth and the current seventh and eighth hitters would have to bump up a notch. Trading Miller for Lindbergh therefore makes three spots in the lineup a little bit weaker, but perhaps the defensive upgrade that Lindbergh provides can make things worth it.

There's a fundamental difference between how these team-mate-interaction effects work on offense and on defense. The ability of a lineup to produce runs essentially relies on emergence. The only way that a batter can produce a run all by himself is to hit a home run. In 2017, there were 22,582 runs scored and 6,105 home runs hit, meaning that 73 percent of runs scored in 2017 involved one batter getting on base followed by another batter somehow knocking him in. We also know that batters do not come up in random order. If we have a leadoff hitter who is good at getting on base, the hitters who will have the most say as to whether or not he scores are the second and third hitters in the lineup. For a lineup to succeed in its mission, it needs good hitters who are *bunched together* so that they can get their hits in sequence. In addition, when a batter either walks or gets a hit, he not only adds value to his team, but he *doesn't make an out*, and that means another plate appearance for someone else. The more good hitters a team has, the more valuable those extra plate appearances are.

Conversely, if a team has several bad hitters, they will make outs more often and that will deprive the better hitters of a few extra turns at bat. Offense in baseball is structured so that a team with a critical mass of good offensive players will see *compounding* benefits. A team with a critical mass of bad hitters will see a similar compounding effect, but in a negative direction.

On defense, the story is different. In theory, having a good-fielding second baseman and a good-fielding shortstop should provide good value for the team. At the very least, we assume that the two of them won't get in each other's way, but that's not what happens. I've done research where I've found that a shortstop playing next to a good-fielding second baseman is *less* likely than we would expect to make a play on a ball than when he's playing next to a bad defender, even controlling for how hard of a play he had to make. (The effect also shows up for a second baseman playing next to a good shortstop.)

In psychology, there is a concept called the "diffusion of responsibility" that applies here. In an emergency situation, people are quicker to respond when they are the only person in the room. They hesitate when around others, because someone else might call for help. The shortstop, seeing a ground ball headed up the middle, but knowing that his keystone partner has some range, might hesitate just enough to let a ball or two go through now and then. When playing next to a lead-footed fielder, he might feel that everything depends on him and react a bit faster. Installing a good-fielding second baseman doesn't end up as a net negative, but the effect on the shortstop takes away a little bit of the value that the team thought it was getting. On defense, having a critical mass of good fielders actually *diminishes* the value that each provides. The effect sizes are not large, but they are not zero either.

In an ideal world, we would find a player who is good on both offense and defense, but again, "find someone who is good at everything" is not a strategy. It's a goal. Given the choice between two otherwise equal players, one of whom specializes in offense and the other in defense, we will have a preference for the better batter.

*   *   *

THERE'S ONE OTHER CHEAT CODE THAT WE HAVEN'T talked about yet. There are players in baseball who have the ability to competently play more than one position on the diamond. They hit well enough to be regulars, but don't mind shifting around in the field to fill whatever gap is needed. With apologies to 1980s and 1990s super-utility player Tony Phillips, the modern patron saint of these multi-instrumentalists is Ben Zobrist, who came into the league with the Tampa Bay (Devil) Rays in 2006 as a shortstop, but quickly found a home in not having a home on the diamond. He was a good hitter and had the athleticism to play some tough defensive positions reasonably well. The nice thing about his versatility was that by being willing to pack several different gloves in his suitcase, he allowed other value to emerge.

There are a few things that a Zobrist allows a team to do. He can allow a team to build a mixed-position platoon. He can allow his team to shift guys around in the late innings and replace a poor-fielding player in one position with an all-glove no-hit player at another (with our super-utility guy bridging the gap). He can enable a team to be much more efficient when it comes to giving players days off. The Zobrist Effect turns out to be meaningful.

Platoons are a well-known strategy for making one good player out of two flawed ones. In 2017, right-handed batters overall had an on-base percentage of .314 against right-handed pitchers, but .332 (18 points more) against lefties. Flipping that around, lefties had better outcomes (.336 vs. .310) when they faced a right-handed hurler than a left-handed one. Some individual hitters have more extreme splits than that, but if a team can find two guys who are both good hitters against one sort of pitcher *and* they both play the same position, they've got themselves a platoon. What happens if you have a right fielder who feasts on righties and a second baseman who loves hitting against lefties? If you have a Zobrist who can bridge that gap, you have a mixed-position platoon!

Having a Zobrist on the roster means that a team can expand the universe of platoon-eligible players that it can draw from, making it easier to construct platoons and construct better ones. If we assume that the platoon effect is worth about 20 points of on-base percentage and that our Zobrist allows his team to gain a platoon advantage that they otherwise wouldn't have gotten in an extra 100 plate appearances per year, that's two additional on-base events that they can grab. Remember that turning an out into a single is worth roughly three-quarters of a run. That's an extra run and a half of value that our Zobrist's versatility adds to the team's ledger, just by having an extra glove in his locker.

Teams can similarly use their Zobrist to facilitate a cross-positional defensive replacement. Assuming that our Zobrist plays average defense anywhere on the field, it means that late in the game, a team might be able to pull a poor defender from one position, say a bat-first second baseman, slide their Zobrist into that spot, and put their glove-first center fielder into the game in the eighth and ninth inning. A poor defender will cost his team about 20 runs in the field compared to an average fielder over the course of a season. A very good defender will save his team about 20 runs. What if a team could effectively replace a bad defender with a good one for 100 innings out of a season? That change would be worth about two and a half runs. Again, that's not going to turn a bad team into a pennant winner, but it's free value that can be had and is easier to grab if you have someone who can bridge those gaps.

Finally, a Zobrist allows a team to be more efficient when it gives days off to players or when it deals with injuries. If your second baseman gets hurt and will be out for two weeks, someone from the bench must take his place. The problem is that your team carries only one player on the bench who even has a clue at second base, and he is the worst hitter of the bench mob. Oh, if only your fourth outfielder could play second. He's not a great hitter, but he sure is better than the utility infielder. What if we could shift our Zobrist back to second and have the fourth outfielder take over in right?

Hitters who ride the pine do so for a reason. Either no one has yet recognized their brilliance, or there isn't any brilliance there to recognize. There are still differences between the best guy on the bench and the worst. Using data from 2013 to 2017, we can look at how often a team's 10th most used hitter (by plate appearances) came to bat and the average OBP that he provided. We can do the same for the 11th most used hitter and the 12th and on down to the end of the bench.

Table 18. Bench Production, 2013–2017

Player	Average PA	OBP
10th most used	274	.312
11th most used	236	.306
12th most used	202	.306
13th most used	173	.299
14th most used	138	.289

Being able to use the first guy on the bench to replace a guy who is hurt is worth 23 points of OBP over the last guy on the bench. Yet how often does the light-hitting utility infielder play because he's the only one who can fill in at shortstop? What if we could shift some of those plate appearances from number 13 and number 14 to number 10 and number 11 on that list? A Zobrist might be able to make that happen. If we were able to divert even

100 PA away from those bottom-of-the-bench players to our top hitter, it could be worth a couple of extra runs to his team. Every little bit helps.

One Zobrist is not going to be able to facilitate *all* of these tricks, but he might enable one or two. The more flexible the Zobrist (and the more Zobrists on a team), the more opportunities to realize some of this extra value around the edges. It's value that a Zobrist adds, not because of what he does with a bat or a glove, but because he's willing to change his glove. It's value that should be recognized.

*   *   *

LET'S COME BACK TO REALITY. REAL MAJOR LEAGUE TEAMS are never actually in this sort of "original position" (and yes, philosophy majors, this is a shameless baseball adaptation of philosopher John Rawls's work), where they are constructing a team from the ground up. They have to work within the constraints of what their farm system has produced and what free agents are available when they are out shopping. No one is going to build a team exactly like this, but they might be able to use some of these principles.

Talent is still going to be the primary driving factor in how well a team does, but there's a place for understanding emergent value as well. Baseball teams and fans alike have spent the last century and a half trying to figure out and measure "talent" in baseball. There aren't many hidden needles in haystacks when everyone has a metal detector. On the other hand, there's a painful lack of a statistic or even a word that describes the value that teams gather from these emergent sources, in which players provide value by the ways that they fit together. It's hard to think about things that don't have a word to describe them. How does one search for something that doesn't have a name?

So, if you're an enterprising researcher who wants to discover something new in baseball, this is a good place to start. Think like an engineer—a baseball engineer. It's a lot more fun than just reciting a list of All-Stars.

- 5 -

Why Didn't David Ortiz Just Bunt?

I TOOK MY OLDEST DAUGHTER TO HER FIRST BASEBALL game on Memorial Day of 2014 at Turner Field in Atlanta. When the day itself arrived, I told my wife that I'd been planning this for six months. She looked at me and said, "Don't kid yourself. You've been planning this day since the plus sign appeared on the pregnancy test." My wife is a very smart woman.

The Braves were playing the Red Sox that day in an inter-league game, something that didn't even exist when I was a kid. Interleague play allows MLB a chance to stage marquee intra-city matchups, where the Yankees play the Mets and the Cubs play the White Sox. In fact, each team is paired an official "natural rival." The Chicago and New York pairings (and the nearly intra-city A's-Giants and Dodgers-Angels matchups) made sense, although some of the other games on the schedule sounded more like geographic puns. The Cleveland Indians were paired with the Cincinnati Reds in the "Ohio Cup," despite the fact that Cleveland is much closer geographically to the city of Pittsburgh and its Pirates.

Technically, the Braves and the Red Sox were each other's designated rivals. It might go back to the fact that the Braves began their existence in Boston in 1876 (as the Boston Red Stockings!) and remained there through a few name changes (Beaneaters, Doves, Rustlers, Braves, Bees, and then back to Braves) until 1952 when they moved to Milwaukee and then moved again to Atlanta in 1966. In any case, I was inducting my daughter into the heated rivalry that was a Red Sox–Braves game. It was heated alright. Memorial Day weekend marks the unofficial beginning of summer and the game itself was played in a tureen of humidity soup. We eventually experienced a short mid-game rain delay, due to the fact that the air above Turner Field felt the need to sweat as much as everyone else.

I had picked Memorial Day in part because I knew my father would be in town. It was my dad who took me to my first baseball game in 1986 at Cleveland Municipal Stadium in honor of my kindergarten graduation. The Indians played the California Angels and lost 8–2. I remember that day as the first time I ever ate a foot-long hot dog, which, as my father reminds me every time we go to a game together, kept me quiet for two innings. Bringing my dad along seemed right. I learned to be a dad from my father. I learned about baseball from my father. I wanted my dad to be there the first time I took my daughter to a game. Plus, the mechanics of taking a soon-to-be-five-year-old (as well as my six-year-old Godnephew) to a baseball game were complicated. It was nice to have another adult there as backup.

I had bought tickets in the upper level, just offset of home plate to the third-base side. You can see the whole field from there, even if the players look like little dots. That's where I always sat with Dad when I was a kid. Of course, that also meant hauling our way up to the upper deck while making sure that the kids didn't wander off into the crowd. There were bathroom breaks along the way and we stopped off for lunch at one of the concession stands. My dad suggested that we get my daughter a foot-long, because it would keep her quiet for two innings. Nothing keeps my daughter quiet for that long.

I like getting to a game about half an hour early to spend a little bit of alone time with the ballpark and the grounds crew as they water down the infield dirt. There's a certain rhythm that goes with a day at the ballpark. For me, the first high point comes after working my way through the concourse and heading up the tunnel into my section, because that's when I get the first glimpse of the field. I always well up with emotion at that moment—that joy in seeing a long-lost friend. I wanted my daughter to have that experience too. When we finally got to our section, she wasn't impressed.

My daughter had a million questions about what was going on. She selected Braves first baseman Freddie Freeman as her favorite player, because he wore No. 5 and she was about to turn five. She politely applauded as Red Sox starter Clay Buchholz provided free passes to first base for any of the Atlanta Braves who were interested. In between questions and walks and water breaks, I did get a few precious minutes to have a small conversation with my dad.

Hitting fourth for the Red Sox that day was David Ortiz. Ortiz, who retired after the 2016 season, may hold the record for the number of baseball hot-button issues that could be conjured simply by speaking his name. The young Ortiz played in parts of six seasons with the Minnesota Twins, but was then *released* after the 2002 season. He signed with the Red Sox at the beginning of 2003 and in his first year with the team, finished fifth in MVP voting. In 2003, Ortiz also failed a test for a performance-enhancing drug. At the time, baseball did not have a fully-fledged policy on PEDs, and the results of the testing program in 2003 were not supposed to be released to the public. (Ortiz has maintained his innocence.) As a result though, "Ortiz" became a code word for the ongoing tension in baseball on how to properly credit (or perhaps discredit) players who hit a lot of home runs, but may have done so with a chemical advantage.

Ortiz's mystique grew beyond that. He developed a reputation as a "clutch" hitter, punctuated by his home run to win Game 4 of the 2004 American League Championship Series over the Yankees. The home run began a run of four straight wins for the Red Sox, erasing the three-games-to-none deficit that the Yankees had put them in, and then four more over the Cardinals in the World Series, notching Boston's first World Series title in 86 years. Ortiz became The Face of the Red Sox that night, but he also became the code word for discussions of whether "clutch hitting" was a real talent or a psychological mirage.

But if there's one thing that David Ortiz did that most changed the game of baseball, it might have just been that he was left-handed. It was well-known during Ortiz's career that he was a pull hitter, especially when he hit the ball on the ground. In fact, his pull tendencies were so well-known that in the mid-2000s, teams would routinely shift their infield defense when he came to the plate. Instead of lining up in a traditional formation with two infielders to the right of second base and two to the left of second base, Ortiz would often see three infielders on the right side of the infield, while the lone left-sided infielder would play in the space normally occupied by the shortstop.

It made sense. If Ortiz was going to hit his ground balls mostly to the right side, why not put an extra defender over there? This Sicilian defense had originally been deployed in the 1940s on another iconic left-handed Red Sox hitter, Ted Williams, but it left an obvious hole. The third-base line was completely unguarded. The nearest defender was playing 40 feet off the chalk. A ground ball hit anywhere near the line would have no trouble scooting through to left field for a hit. In fact, even if it didn't make it out of the infield, by the time a fielder got to it, even the slow-hoofed Ortiz would have been standing on first, the proud owner of a single. Everyone in the ballpark, including Ortiz himself, could see that.

So as David Ortiz strode to bat on this memorable Memorial Day in Atlanta and saw that once again, no one was bothering with the third-base line, my father leaned over to me and asked a question that had probably occurred to everyone else in the ballpark. "Why doesn't he just bunt?"

"Why doesn't he just bunt?" is the kind of question that seems easy to answer, but isn't. It's a good exercise in thinking a question all the way through. The most commonly given answer was that Ortiz was a power hitter paid to hit home runs, something that he did 541 times over his career. Bunting was for the weak.

Bunting was something that pitchers did when they had to bat. No matter what else bunting meant, ordering Ortiz to drop a little tapper toward third meant that he wouldn't be hitting a home run in that plate appearance.

There's a bit of masculine pride on the line. Most baseball players grew up in a culture where the "good players" were the ones who hit a lot of home runs. Even more than that, they grew up in a culture where masculinity is intimately linked to physical strength. A home run is a feat of might. A well-executed bunt might travel 60 feet and is a feat of restraint. Perhaps it was as simple as that?

BETWEEN 2010 AND 2017, THE NUMBER OF INFIELD SHIFTS by Major League teams increased by a factor of 10. This isn't surprising. We live in an age in which hitter spray charts are available to anyone with an internet connection. The rest is a little bit of back-of-the-envelope math. Once one team started shifting, it wasn't hard to figure out what they were doing and it's not like teams can secretly deploy the shift and not have the other 29 notice. (Hey, there are three guys over there!) The surprising thing was that not all teams jumped onto the bandwagon at the same time, despite the fact that they were all facing the same set of batters.

If it made sense for the Rays to shift against David Ortiz, then it probably also made sense for the Orioles and Blue Jays and Yankees to do the same. It's the same David Ortiz that they all faced. If everyone was behaving rationally, it shouldn't have taken more than a couple of years before teams had identified all of the shift-able hitters and set their strategy accordingly. Within a short period of time, teams should have had total numbers of shifts that were close to equal. That's not how it happened.

Table 19. Number of Shifts Employed, by Year

Year	No. 1 in shifts	No. 16 in shifts	Ratio of No. 1 to No. 16	No. 30 in shifts	Ratio of No. 1 to No. 30
2010	Rays (261)	Nationals (93)	2.80	Brewers (59)	13.05
2011	Rays (271)	Mariners (86)	3.15	Phillies (20)	13.55
2012	Rays (517)	Angels (159)	3.25	White Sox (46)	11.23
2013	Orioles (555)	Blue Jays (252)	2.20	Nationals (75)	7.40
2014	Astros (1,408)	Cardinals (433)	3.25	Rockies (191)	7.37
2015	Astros (1,697)	Royals (747)	2.27	Nationals (416)	4.08
2016	Astros (2,052)	Diamondbacks (1,078)	1.90	Cubs (603)	3.40
2017	Brewers (1,578)	Diamondbacks (749)	2.11	Cubs (302)	5.23

(Note: Only shifts that resulted in a ball put into play were counted)

In 2010, the league leader in shifts (the ever-tinkering Tampa Bay Rays and their forward-thinking manager Joe Maddon) employed the strategy about three times as often as the team in the middle of the pack and 13 times as often as the team at the low end of the scale. By 2017, the gaps were not so large. Even the non-believers were shifting. The 30th place team in 2017 (the Chicago Cubs and their hyper-reactionary manager Joe Maddon) would have led the league in shifts as late as 2011, and the team at the top (the Milwaukee Brewers) shifted a little more than five times as much as the last place team. Things were getting closer, but even after seven years, there were still significant differences between teams that fully embraced the strategy and those who were more tentative.

There was plenty of initial resistance to the shift for the same reason that there's opposition to any shift in thinking: it was weird. Pitchers grew up in a world where defenses lined up in a two left–two right formation. Consciously and unconsciously, over years of repetition, they had tailored their strategies to this set of assumptions. Sure, teams had a long history of moving their fielders a jump to the left or a step to the right depending on the hitter, but moving a fielder 30 or 40 feet is a very different proposition.

There was psychological resistance too. Loss aversion, which we discussed in Chapter 3, rears its head again. The shift inevitably produces a ground ball hit directly at a fielder who is playing in an odd place. It would have been a base hit if the team had lined up in a traditional formation, but with the shift on, it's an out. Success! The problem is that the shift also produces a few ground balls that scoot through into left field exactly past the place where the third baseman would "normally" have been playing. Mathematically, as long as the shift is producing more outs-that-would-have-been-hits than it does hits-that-would-have-been-outs, then it's a net winner. Unfortunately, that's not how the human mind works. Humans are more disturbed by "losing" an out that they could have had than they are by gaining one that they otherwise wouldn't have gotten. The shift felt icky, but baseball eventually embraced it.

*   *   *

NOW THAT THE SHIFT HAS BECOME A PART OF DAILY LIFE, with even the least shifty team using the strategy a couple of times per game, why hasn't bunting against the shift developed as a countermeasure?

Table 20. Bunts Against the Shift, by Year, 2010–2017

Year	Total shifts	Bunts against shift	Bunt against shift percentage	Percentage of bunts that resulted in hits
2010	2,463	23	0.9%	82.6%
2011	2,350	18	0.8%	72.2%
2012	4,576	42	0.9%	69.0%
2013	6,881	57	0.8%	54.4%
2014	13,298	91	0.7%	56.0%
2015	17,633	120	0.7%	63.3%
2016	27,924	184	0.6%	56.0%
2017	26,700	161	0.6%	51.6%
Total	**101,825**	**696**	**0.7%**	**58.2%**

The data show that bunting against the shift has never been popular. Less than 1 percent of balls that are hit into play against the shift are bunts (and the trend line suggests that the strategy is getting *less* popular, percentage-wise), but when the strategy is employed, it has a fairly good success rate. Most of the hits were singles, but it's a play that's had a nearly .600 batting average!

It could be that teams tend to shift against a certain type of hitter. David Ortiz was a power hitter who was not often called on to bunt during his career (he somehow tallied two sacrifice bunts over 20 seasons in Major League Baseball), and perhaps teams are simply shifting against players whom they know have limited bunting skills. Still, all baseball players need to have some familiarity with bunting. From 2013 to 2017, I looked for hitters who logged at least 250 plate appearances in a season and attempted to bunt exactly once that year. It turns out that these attempts by our out-of-practice bunters went into fair territory and on the ground 43 percent of the time. These guys might not be ace bunters, but they don't need to be. If they bunt and miss or if the bunt goes foul, it's just a strike. They can try again if they want.

SO WE RETURN TO THE QUESTION OF WHETHER IT MAKES sense for Ortiz to bunt and give up the chance at a home run. In Chapter 2, we learned the importance of picking the strategy that has the best *expected* value. Before a batter goes up to the plate, he has no idea what will happen in this particular encounter, but we can make some decent guesses. We have the benefit of knowing that Ortiz had a good year in 2014, with a AVG/OBP/SLG line of .263/.355/.517.

Framed another way, in 2014 when David Ortiz came to bat (something he did 602 times that year), he made an out 64.5 percent of the time. He made it to first base (by singling, walking, or being hit by the pitch) 25.2 percent of the time. He made it to second on a double 4.5 percent of the time. He hit a home run in 5.8 percent of his trips to the plate. (He had no triples.) There's no question that a home run or a double is better than a single, but Ortiz only did that once every 10 times to the plate. Is it worth giving up that one-in-10 chance?

In Chapter 2, we introduced the idea of the run expectancy matrix. Here's part of the matrix for 2014. Because Ortiz was leading off in the second inning in that Memorial Day game, we know that there were no runners and no outs, and that Ortiz cannot make more than one out by himself, nor can he put more than one runner on base, and since we can pretty much rule out a triple, we'll ignore that possibility as well.

Table 21. Runs per Base-Out State, 2014 MLB

	No outs	One out
Bases empty	0.455	0.239
Runner on first	0.818	N/A
Runner on second	1.039	N/A

If Ortiz makes an out, Boston's run expectancy for the inning falls from 0.455 runs to 0.239 runs. In that case, Ortiz has cost his team 0.216 runs. A single or walk or hit batsman, on the other hand, raises Boston's run expectancy by 0.363 runs. A home run increases Boston's run expectancy by 1.000 runs, the run that Ortiz himself scores (at which point he bequeaths the same no runners/no outs situation to the next batter).

Table 22. Ortiz's Expected Value Swinging Away

Event	Chance of happening	Run expectancy change	Expected value
Out	64.5%	(.216)	(.139)
Single/Walk/HBP	25.2%	.363	.091
Double	4.5%	.584	.026
HR	5.8%	1.000	.058
Total	**100.0%**	**N/A**	**.036**

If David Ortiz swings away, we expect him to increase Boston's chances of scoring by .036 runs on an expected value basis. (For the purposes of this chapter, to simplify things, we're going to assume that Ortiz is always batting with no one on and no one out. Of course, that's not the case, but adjusting for runners and outs doesn't change the basic conclusions.)

Now, let's imagine a world where David Ortiz looks down the third-base line, sees plenty of space, and decides to bunt. If he gets the bunt down, we will assume that either the pitcher will field the ball and throw him out or that he will push it past the pitcher for a single. Again, an out reduces Boston's run expectancy by 0.216 runs and a single increases it by 0.363 runs. Ortiz didn't normally bunt, so we don't know if he was any good at it, but let's assume that he would have been average at it, checking in with a 58.2 percent success rate.

Table 23. Ortiz's Expected Value Bunting Against the Shift

Event	Chance of happening	Run expectancy change	Expected value
Out	41.8%	(.216)	(.090)
Single	58.2%	.363	.211
Total	**100.0%**	**N/A**	**.121**

Ortiz bunting against the shift, even if he gets thrown out a good chunk of the time, would still have been worth three times more to his team than if he were to swing away.

During the real second inning of that Memorial Day game in 2014, David Ortiz swung away and flied out to center field.

WHY DIDN'T HE BUNT? IF TEAMS WERE ABLE TO CONVINCE their fielders to accept the math behind shifting, why can't those same teams convince those same fielders to bunt against the shift when they come to bat? The answer is that it's never quite as simple as it sounds. Ortiz is playing a game within a game. There are other things that he needs to consider in making his decision on whether or not to bunt. Here we enter the land of a branch of math known as game theory.

Let's return to David Ortiz in the batter's box in the second inning. Ortiz knew a few things that we haven't yet considered. He knew that he would get a second and a third plate appearance in this game, and perhaps a fourth and a fifth. He would face the Braves again the next day at Turner Field, followed by two games against the Braves at Fenway Park. The Rays were coming to Boston for a weekend series, and they probably had an advance scout in the audience. Ortiz knew that there were four more months left in the season. Presumably, he knew that he had a few more years to play. In other words, his choice in this at-bat was going to affect how other teams defensed him for the next couple innings and perhaps the next couple days and years.

Suppose that David Ortiz had taken advantage of the shift in the second inning by bunting and even gotten a base hit as a reward. When he came to the plate two innings later, what would the Braves have done in response? Would they have put the shift on again? Maybe (now former) Braves manager Fredi Gonzalez would have thought, "Well, he got us once, but I doubt he'll do *that* again" and stuck with the shift. Perhaps Gonzalez would have decided that Ortiz was a threat to bunt again. Gonzalez would need to make a countermove, and the numbers say his first priority should be to stop David Ortiz from bunting. (Ponder that sentence for a moment.) Gonzalez could keep three infielders on the right side, but move the left-side infielder toward the third-base line. It would stop Ortiz from bunting, but it would open a hole in the shortstop area. Still, that "free" bunt hit is so valuable that if Ortiz shows that he's going to take it over and over, the Braves would be fools not to remove that option. So would the Rays, once their advance scout relays the information back to Tampa that Ortiz is now bunting to beat the shift.

If he's too eager to grab those freebies, Ortiz runs the risk of drawing attention to himself and having the Braves (and the rest of the league) take away his best opportunity to provide value for his team.

*   *   *

WHEN DAVID ORTIZ DID HIT THE OCCASIONAL BALL TO the left side of the infield, it was almost exclusively to the area where the shortstop plays in a traditional two-right-two-left defense. He nearly never hit the ball down the third-base line. Because teams employing a three-on-the-right shift usually station their remaining infielder near that shortstop area, many (though not all) of those Ortiz grounders became outs in real life. Had the defense been guarding the line to take away the bunt, it means that those grounders to "short" that were gobbled up and turned into groundouts would likely have become singles.

At some point, Fredi Gonzalez might have thought to himself, "Why am I stationing a fielder on the third-base line when Ortiz never hits it there? Why don't I move him to the place where Ortiz at least hits a few balls?" At that point, with the third-base line wide open, Ortiz steps up to the plate, smiles, and bunts.

Now, Gonzalez has to make a decision. If he's committed to three infielders on the right side, there are two holes in the defense (the shortstop spot and the third-base line) and he can only plug one of them. Which one is more important? Between 2012 and 2016, David Ortiz hit a ground ball that went to the shortstop area of the infield and was thrown out in 1.5 percent of his plate appearances. If the defense had been guarding the line, it's likely those would have all gone for singles, rather than outs.

We're back to playing a game of probability. If Gonzalez knows for a fact that Ortiz will never bunt, there is minimal danger of a ball down the third-base line. He might as well tell his fourth infielder to stand near the shortstop spot and take care of the few grounders that Ortiz does send that way. Now suppose that Gonzalez knows for a fact that if Ortiz sees a clear third-base line, he *will* bunt 100 percent of the time. Since Ortiz is a much more dangerous hitter bunting down an open third-base line than he is swinging away, Gonzalez should logically station his fielder on the third-base line. The key piece of information for Gonzalez is how likely he thinks it is that Ortiz would bunt against an open third-base line. He has to guess, because Ortiz isn't going to tell him.

We estimated above that if Ortiz bunts against a fielder playing off the line, his run expectancy added would be .121 runs. We've also estimated, given Ortiz's seasonal line, which was mostly generated by swinging away against a shifted defense, that he would add an average of .036 expected runs. If he bunts against a fielder who's guarding the line, it's likely to be an automatic out, which would mean a run expectancy "added" of -.216. If he swings away but the fielder is on the line, we estimate that he would have had singles (rather than outs) in an extra 1.5 percent of his plate appearances and we can adjust his run expectancy for that set of circumstances upward to .045.

Table 24. Run Expectancy, Possible Scenarios for David Ortiz vs. the Shift

	Ortiz bunts	Ortiz swings away
Fielder on the line	(.216)	.045
Fielder at SS	.121	.036

In Ortiz's perfect world, he would come to the plate every time with no one covering the line and he would bunt. He would then somehow convince the opposing team that he wasn't going to bunt the next time, and yet do it again and again and again and again. He could basically live in that bottom left square and have the greatest offensive season of all time, even if it was mostly bunt singles.

Of course that's not going to happen, someone would catch on and guard the line, although that's not a horrible outcome for Ortiz either. He won't be able to use the bunt to his advantage, but with the fielder guarding the line, he's a slightly more dangerous hitter (.045 runs vs. .036 runs) swinging away. By luring the other team in to guarding the line, the occasional balls that he shoots through the shortstop hole will now go for hits and that's extra value for the Red Sox.

Since the defense has to show their hand first, it means that Fredi Gonzalez needs to tell his infielder whether or not to guard the line and lock Ortiz in to an expected value of .045 runs for the at-bat. How low would Ortiz's bunting tendencies have to fall before it made sense for Gonzalez to move that fielder back to the shortstop area? We can again use the equation for a break-even point that we discussed in Chapter 2. In this case, p represents the likelihood of Ortiz's bunting. The equation here is:

$$.121 * p + .036 * (1-p) = .045$$

In this case, p is equal to 10.6 percent (or .106). Leaving the fielder in the shortstop area means that Ortiz could grab a free base hit, but as long as he does it less than 10.6 percent of the time, teams are better off not bothering to defend against it. In theory, had Ortiz behaved rationally, he would have used the bunt option a tiny bit less than 10.6 percent of the time that defenses were shifted on him (which was most of the time). If the other team was behaving rationally as well, they would never have bothered to guard the line, and just lived with the fact that once every two or three games, Ortiz could have had a "free" base hit (or at least a 58 percent chance at one).

LET'S AGAIN RETURN TO THE TOP OF THE SECOND INNING on Memorial Day. If Ortiz had laid down a bunt, it would have been his first time doing so since August of the previous year. At his next plate appearance, all of the following statements would have been true.

1. David Ortiz bunted in one of the last one times that he came to the plate against the shift.
2. David Ortiz bunted in one of the last 10 times that he came to the plate against the shift.
3. David Ortiz bunted in one of the last 100 times that he came to the plate against the shift.

Based on "previous data" we can make a case that Ortiz will bunt 100 percent of the time, 10 percent of the time, or 1 percent of the time when shown an open third-base line. In that next plate appearance, should the Braves guard the line? The Braves don't actually have a lot of information to go on, because they aren't privy to Ortiz's innermost thoughts. It's possible that he had made a decision the night before to bunt against the shift every time he saw it from here on out and his bunt in the second inning was the first of what he hoped would be many. If that's the case, then the proper thing to do is to put a fielder on the third-base line.

It's possible that Ortiz went to the library, took out a book on game theory the night before, and ran some calculations in his hotel room. He realized that he could bunt about 10 percent of the time and the other team wouldn't take it away from him. He couldn't do it all the time, but he could get away with it once in a while. In that case, the Braves should not guard the line, but should politely request that all Atlanta area libraries burn their books on game theory.

It's possible that Ortiz realized that he could get away with using the bunt once in a while (though he doesn't realize how often he could), and this just happened to be one of those days when he figured he'd drop one, "just to keep them honest." The Braves should curse Ortiz's mischievous ways, but not bother guarding the line until they see more evidence of extended mischief.

David Ortiz probably knows something else about humans. They tend to overvalue recent information. It's called recency bias. The fact that Ortiz bunted in 100 percent of his plate appearances today will be more salient in the minds of Fredi Gonzalez and his coaches than the fact that Ortiz bunted in only 1 percent of his previous 100 plate appearances. In the case of the shift, there's even more irrationality to consider. The shift, despite the fact that it has grown in popularity, is still seen as something "different." If the Braves shifted and got burned, it's obvious. As we learned in Chapter 3, people react differently to someone who *did something* (in that case, pulling the trolley lever). Braves manager Fredi Gonzalez would likely have felt pressure to guard against this sort of embarrassment again, even if it wasn't actually a danger to happen.

So Ortiz, being a good student of human behavior, knows that if he drops a bunt in the second inning, the next time that he comes up, and probably for awhile afterward, his opponents will take the bunt option away from him by guarding the line. Is it really worth using his very valuable bunt card on a random second inning at-bat in May? In Chapter 3, we briefly discussed the concept of "leverage." There are some points in a game that are more important than others. One at-bat in the eighth inning of a 15–1 game is mostly meaningless. What happens in the eighth inning of a tie game might determine whether the fans go home happy or sad at the end of the day. Add in the fact that not all games are equally important (Game 162 of a season is meaningless for a 70–91 team, but means everything for a team tied for a Wild Card spot), and Ortiz has to ask himself, "If I can only grab a free base hit once in a great while, is this really the best time to do it?"

What if, later on, there's a ninth-inning, down-by-one scenario? That might not happen in today's game, but tomorrow there will be another game. And the next day. That card is really valuable. When David Ortiz comes to bat and sees no one guarding the line, he can choose to swing away, which we estimate would add about .036 runs, or he can supercharge his expectancy to .121 by bunting. For that one plate appearance, he is .085 runs better than he would have been, and if he picks his spot right *those expected runs mean more* to the outcome of a game or even a season than they do during a second-inning plate appearance in May.

So, the answer to my father's question of why David Ortiz ignored the wide swath of space down the third-base line is that it was in his best interest to develop a reputation as a guy who didn't really care about bunting. It was just something that he did once in a very great while on a whim. That way, when he did grab the occasional freebie base hit, opposing teams would interpret it as the exception to the rule, rather than something that they needed to worry about and (over) correct for. More importantly, he could preserve the option to play his ace in the hole at the time when it would count the most. To have that option though, he essentially had to live below the radar. While logically, it would actually make sense to "allow" Ortiz to get away with the bunting strategy every couple of days, Ortiz knew that his opponents wouldn't act that way, so he had to operate not below the logical threshold, but below the *illogical* threshold of the other team.

In other words, David Ortiz didn't bunt because he was a psychological mastermind and a game theory genius.

*   *   *

BEFORE WE CONGRATULATE DAVID ORTIZ FOR BEING SO clever, there's a rather unflattering piece of math that we can do that shows maybe he wasn't a genius. Ortiz may very well have been saving his bunt card for "the right moment." Rather than bunting in the top of the second, maybe he envisioned a particularly key situation down the road where he *would* use the card and he wanted that third-base line clear then. Maybe it would be one which was 10 times more important than this situation.

What if Ortiz, instead of waiting around for a situation that might never come, exercised absolutely no restraint and bunted every single time that he saw the shift? Teams would fairly quickly realize that they needed to guard the line and they would pull their extra defender from the shortstop area to the third-base line. Pretty soon, Ortiz would never have the bunt option presented to him.

That's not the end of the world. We saw earlier that Ortiz, having lured the fielder over to the line, is now .009 runs better swinging away than if the defense was *not* concerned about his bunting. because he occasionally hit a few ground balls toward that shortstop area that would now be unguarded. This is the important piece: he gets that .009 bump in *all* of his plate appearances. Here, we remember our second rule of probabilistic thinking, the one about a small effect repeated over and over being more valuable than a one-time large effect.

A full-time player like Ortiz normally records 600–700 plate appearances during a year. Over 600 plate appearances, if Ortiz was getting a .009 expected runs boost each time, he would generate an extra 5.4 runs just by making the fourth infielder *afraid* that he might bunt. If he holds on to the card, which is worth .097 runs in isolation, even if he plays the card in a situation where those runs were effectively 10 times more important, he's still well behind the value he would generate with the "bunt until they take it away!" strategy.

The optimal strategy for David Ortiz would have been to bunt *every* time that he saw no one was guarding the line. He wouldn't get a base hit 100 percent of the time, but even at a 58 percent success rate, he would have done more good for his team than he would have swinging away during those plate appearances. He could grab whatever freebies were given to him as the teams learned that he wasn't just fooling around. The kicker is that the real prize wouldn't be the bunt hits, but the additional base hits through the shortstop hole that Ortiz would have gotten *after the other teams realigned their defenses.*

So, we're back to the question of why David Ortiz didn't bunt. If he really was holding back on bunting because he figured he'd only get one or two chances to *really* use it and wanted to save the tactic for a very specific moment, then he miscalculated the way in which he could best benefit his team. The miscalculation is based on another human failing. The fact that Ortiz probably could have envisioned *the* situation where he would have liked to use the bunt tactic made it much more real. The ability to see yourself doing something in your mind's eye is powerful. Who envisions themselves accidentally poking a ball through the shortstop hole once in a while past an infielder who wasn't there?

I THINK IT'S WORTH ASKING THE QUESTION OF WHETHER the shift itself continues to make sense. It seems a strange question given that the league has been overrun with shifts. Clearly, *someone* thinks they work. If it really is working, we should be able to find evidence that the shift turns more balls into outs. There's a stat known as BABIP, or Batting Average on Balls in Play, which is perfect for looking at this. It looks at all plate appearances in which the defense could have made a play, by excluding all strikeouts, walks, HBP, and home runs.

This chart shows BABIP on ground balls hit against the shift compared to ground balls against a non-shifted defense. If you just look at this chart, the shift looks like a smashing success.

Table 25. League-Wide BABIP on Ground Balls, by Year, Against the Shift vs. No Shift

Year	GB BABIP vs. the shift	GB BABIP, no shift
2012	.208	.234
2013	.196	.234
2014	.210	.241
2015	.206	.238
2016	.224	.240
2017	.224	.243

Before we celebrate the success of the shift, we need to remember our third rule of probabilistic thinking: When evaluating a strategy, we need to think both about what happens because of a strategy and what *doesn't* happen. To start, let's look at another chart, this time looking at BABIP for *all* balls put into play.

Table 26. League-Wide BABIP on All Balls in Play, by Year, Against the Shift vs. No Shift

Year	BABIP vs. the shift	BABIP, no shift
2012	.293	.296
2013	.281	.298
2014	.290	.299
2015	.291	.299
2016	.298	.298
2017	.293	.299

The shift makes it more likely that teams will stop a *grounder* from becoming a hit, but the effect on the *overall* number of hits is much smaller. How did that happen?

The numbers above are league-wide numbers. We have data on individual players as well, and we can use them to take a closer look at what's going on. One thing that might drive the differences between shift and no shift is that different *types* of hitters are shifted against. This is a problem known as selective sampling. For example, if the hitters who were shifted against were simply better hitters, we'd expect better outcomes league-wide against the shift, not because of the shift itself, but because of whom the shift was used against.

If the shift is actually helping to stop batters from getting hits, then we should see that the same set of players will record fewer hits (per opportunity) against the shift than they do when not shifted. For example, let's say that a hitter had a BABIP of .300 when he wasn't being shifted and he had 100 PA with the shift on. If the shift didn't actually make a difference, we would expect to see 30 hits from him. If the shift was a better defense, then we would see fewer than 30. There might be some variability in an individual case, but we can then sum across the entire league to see whether the shift is making the difference that we think it is.

The following table shows how many hits we might expect if the shift was exactly as good as the standard two-left-two-right defense (expected hits) and then how many hits those same players actually recorded against the shift. I also looked at the number of total bases from those hits, both expected and actual.

Table 27. Expected vs. Actual Hits and Total Bases, Batters Facing the Shift

Year	Hits (expected)	Hits (actual)	Total bases (expected)	Total bases (actual)
2012	1,018	1,055	1,334	1,362
2013	1,653	1,556	2,159	1,984
2014	2,632	2,767	3,423	3,490
2015	3,874	3,844	5,024	4,895
2016	5,246	5,472	6,788	7,009
2017	4,737	4,849	6,123	6,246
Total	**19,160**	**19,543**	**24,851**	**24,986**

(Minimum: 100 PA non-shifted)

The number of expected hits increases in each year because the number of plate appearances in which a batter is facing the shift has kept going up. Overall, the number of hits that happened against the shift is slightly *higher* than we would have otherwise expected *once we control for the hitters who get shifted against*. By these data, the shift is making defenses slightly worse.

Why that happens is important. Similar to my analyses above, I looked at how often batters pulled the ball in non-shift situations and used that as a basis for an estimate of how many pulled balls we would expect if everyone made no adjustments at all when faced with the shift. Again, totals are summed across the league.

Table 28. Expected vs. Actual Pulled Balls, Batters Facing the Shift

Year	Pulled balls (expected)	Pulled balls (actual)
2012	1,495	1,385
2013	2,309	2,123
2014	4,023	3,914
2015	5,382	5,120
2016	7,403	6,882
2017	6,600	5,863
Total	**27,212**	**25,287**

(Minimum: 100 PA non-shifted)

We see that batters, when confronted with a shift which punishes them for their pull-hitting tendencies, tend to do the obvious and *not pull the ball as much*. They aren't becoming opposite field hitters, but they are adjusting a bit.

There's something else happening though, that we need to account for. While everyone's busy looking at what happens on the ground balls that are hit in front of the shift, what about the ground balls that never happen? Here are the number of line drives that we expect batters to hit in front of the shift compared to what actually happened.

Table 29. Expected vs. Actual Line Drives, Batters Facing the Shift

Year	Line drives (expected)	Line drives (actual)
2012	773	786
2013	1,213	1,258
2014	1,922	2,031
2015	2,823	2,818
2016	3,862	3,906
2017	3,313	3,477
Total	**13,906**	**14,276**

(Minimum: 100 PA non-shifted)

We see that batters are hitting a few more line drives than we might expect when the shift is on. It's possible that pitchers are changing the way that they pitch in front of the shift, and that this is in some way making it easier for batters to square up a pitch every now and then. The effect isn't very large, but it doesn't have to be. Below, we have the BABIP from 2017 for different types of batted balls.

Table 30. BABIP, by Type of Batted Ball, 2017

Batted ball type	BABIP
Fly ball	.130
Ground ball (shift)	.224
Ground ball (non-shift)	.243
Line drive	.682

The shift makes the ground balls that are hit somewhat easier to turn into outs. However, a few of those ground balls seem to be turning into line drives instead. In 2017, a ground ball hit into the shift had a BABIP that was 19 points lower than a ground ball hit into a two-left-two-right defense. However, a line drive had a BABIP that was 439 points higher than a ground ball. For each additional line drive that's introduced into the system, it undoes the beneficial effect that the shift has on 23 ground balls.

There's more to it. The only shift data that are publicly available are for balls that go into the field of play. We don't know how many walks, strikeouts, hit batsmen, and home runs happened when the shift was on and how that compares when the shift was off. At first, it seems like it wouldn't matter, because the shift is about defense and those are outcomes where the defense isn't involved. However, if pitchers are changing the way in which they pitch with the shift on, and this indirectly makes it easier for a batter to walk or hit a home run, that's a very big problem. What we do have are the numbers of balls and strikes that happened during plate appearances against the shift, although only the ones in which the ball was eventually hit into play. Again, we can adjust for how many balls and strikes we would have expected this time based on a pitcher's performance in plate appearances with no shift behind him, and to compare apples to apples, we'll limit ourselves only to plate appearances in which the ball was hit into play.

Table 31. Expected vs. Actual Called Balls and Strikes, Pitchers with the Shift Behind Them

Year	Pitcher strikes (expected)	Pitcher strikes (actual)	Pitcher called balls (expected)	Pitcher called balls (actual)
2012	9,408	9,473	4,543	5,060
2013	14,200	14,381	6,816	7,680
2014	26,726	27,118	12,657	14,076
2015	33,838	33,582	16,024	17,426
2016	50,274	49,286	23,822	25,387
2017	47,857	46,801	22,935	24,345
Total	**182,303**	**180,641**	**86,797**	**93,974**

(Minimum: 100 PA non-shifted)

We can see that pitchers, when backed up by the shift, are throwing (a lot!) more balls than they usually do and fewer strikes. That's not a good combination. Since these data specifically only cover plate appearances in which hitters did *not* walk (or strike out or hit a home run), we can't conclusively prove that the shift leads to more walks or fewer strikeouts, but we can come right to the doorstep of that conclusion. If the shift *is* leading to more walks, it's going to wipe out more of whatever benefits the shift actually has in making ground balls easier to field, and perhaps it will take us into negative territory. You can't throw a guy out who gets to walk to first.

When we take in to account *all* of the effects of the shift, there's a very real danger that it is doing more harm than good. The shift was sold as a wonder drug, but like all drugs, there are side effects to worry about, and sometimes, the cure is worse than the disease. In this case, I worry that teams have been so caught up in the shift fad that they forgot to look at the effects of the shift on the entire baseball ecosystem.

THE QUESTION OF WHY DAVID ORTIZ DIDN'T BUNT IS A tribute to how a seemingly simple question can sometimes have a very complicated answer. We need to consider both how humans should rationally behave and how humans are particularly averse to behaving rationally. Logically, David Ortiz should have bunted in the second inning of that Memorial Day game, both for the hit that he might have gotten in that moment, but also for the extra hits that he might have gotten later in the year. But he didn't.

It's possible that it really was just a matter of masculine pride. If Ortiz were able to bunt against an empty third-base line all the time, he would have been a nearly .600 hitter, although almost all of his hits would have been singles. That would have been immensely more valuable to the Red Sox than the guy who hit "only" .263 but with 35 home runs. At some point, you realize that pride points don't go on the scoreboard, and you have to go beyond your initial emotional reaction—beyond the icky feeling—and figure out whether what you're doing is the best thing you can do to help your team win.

The shift itself is a lesson in unintended consequences. What started out as a simple ploy to put three defenders on one side of the infield for a couple of specific hitters grew into a movement. The data show that, on the whole, it changed the ways in which pitchers pitched and the effects of that canceled out most or all of the benefit that teams thought they were getting.

When you change one part of a system, you change the whole system. There are always side effects.

The most important lesson though, is that simple answers can sometimes mislead us. In baseball (and in life), there's no shortage of simple theories about how the world works. Some of them are true, but you have to really dig in to find out which ones are which, and you have to be ready and willing to look at the entire system to figure it out. When you embrace the complexity of it all, you sometimes find out that the answer is not what you think.

– *6* –

This Isn't a Babysitter's Club

IT'S RARE, BUT EVERY ONCE IN A WHILE, I GET TO PLAY THE doctor card. One of the privileges of having a Ph.D. is that I can call myself "Doctor" and even have some expectation that others will do the same. Except for my grandmother. When I floated the idea to her that she would have to call me "Doctor Carleton" after I graduated, she said in no uncertain terms, "I changed your diaper. I don't have to call you anything."

I became "Doctor Carleton" in August of 2009, after completing my clinical internship, which is the last requirement of most clinical psychology programs. I spent a full year seeing therapy patients under the supervision of a mentor, supposedly in preparation for the days ahead when I would have my own practice and see my own patients. Apparently, it didn't work. That August marks the last time I ever saw a patient. If there is something that I learned in graduate school, it's that mental health is a very noble profession. It is also the wrong profession for me.

When I did see patients though, they were mostly kids. Fate had handed me a specialty of working with elementary school-aged boys who mostly were diagnosed as having Attention Deficit/Hyperactivity Disorder (ADHD) or Oppositional Defiant Disorder (ODD). ADHD and ODD are two of the most common problems diagnosed among young males, and oftentimes I would be assigned a case because the family had requested a male therapist for their son. Since I was a male working in a field that was more than two-thirds female, that was usually me. I spent a lot of time working with parents around strategies for parenting a child with behavior problems.

The irony is that while I was counseling parents on their parenting techniques, I had no children of my own. It wasn't until I was (almost) finished with my doctorate, and was supposedly an expert on parenting, that I finally became a parent myself. In some ways, it's a shame that I don't see patients anymore, not because I was an amazing therapist (I wasn't), but because now I have experience as a parent, and being a Da.D. would be a lot more useful than having a Ph.D.

What I've discovered about parenting is that the mechanics of it aren't all that hard. After all, as a culture, we are fine with 14-year-olds babysitting, though tellingly, we spend hundreds of millions of dollars a year on prevention programs to keep those same 14-year-olds from becoming parents. When babies are born, they need to be fed and changed and bathed and held and stared at, and those are all things that can be taught in an hour or two. As they grow, their needs become more complex, but you learn as they grow. The tough part about being a parent isn't the actual act of parenting; it's that you rarely get to leave "parent mode." Changing a diaper isn't all that hard. Changing one at three in the morning and then soothing the baby back to sleep when you aren't sure how you are currently vertical is the tough part. You find yourself searching for a song that will put the kid to sleep and marvel at the fact that you just used "Psycho Killer" by the Talking Heads as a lullaby. Hey, it worked.

Even beyond the sleep deprivation, the hardest thing for me to adjust to was the fact that I no longer had autonomy over my own schedule. A fellow adult will understand if you say, "I need five minutes by myself, then I'll come and help you." Kids don't. Becoming a parent means living for someone else on someone else's schedule, every day for a couple of decades. One of the (many) reasons that we, as a society, don't want 14-year-olds to become parents is that while they can be capable of the mechanics of parenting, they don't usually have the maturity to sustain the commitment needed.

Had I been a parent back during my days of clinical work, I would have better understood when I saw parents being "too lenient" with their kids. I might have instead interpreted it as a parent who needed a break from that constant demand. Parenthood is a draining business. There's no one event that gets you. Like a car that runs out of gas, there wasn't a specific mile that was to blame. It's the fact that you weren't able to stop to refuel.

* * *

THE JOB OF BASEBALL MANAGER MUST BE ONE OF THE most maddening on the planet. You have to do your job with thousands of people looking on. There are radio talk shows which are dedicated to people babbling about your decision-making skills. People whose only experience is playing video games are convinced that they could do your job. It's just figuring out when to pinch-hit in the seventh inning, right? On top of all that, if you point out how hard the job really is, they'll point out that you get a front-row seat to a baseball game every night. And get to wear a uniform. And get to hang out with baseball players. On top of that, you totally made the wrong call in the eighth inning when you didn't call for a bunt. At least that's what Ed from Lakewood said on the radio. Ed should be the manager. Ed is convinced of this.

There's a great imbalance between the way that people who are living through a baseball season experience the game and how fans experience it. For one, even the most dedicated fan need only invest a few hours each night, usually at home in the comfort of a nice chair. The guys in funny pajamas run around the screen and the announcer tells amusing anecdotes about their madcap adventures. Between innings, there are commercials for car dealerships and beer and various pills for various maladies. And frankly, if a fan wants to turn the game off and go bowling, it's a free country.

The manager isn't so lucky. After he makes that eighth inning non-call on the bunt, he talks to a bunch of guys who just gave maximum physical effort for three hours and lost. He answers the same five postgame questions from the same five sportswriters. He has a few meetings with the trainers and the coaches and the staff. He thinks about tomorrow's game, because there is going to be a game tomorrow and he can't go bowling. He goes back to the team hotel and calls someone back home to hear a friendly voice, but he falls asleep thinking about one of his relievers who has a nagging injury that no one knows about publicly. Maybe he did screw up not calling for that bunt, but even if he did, for some reason he's the one person in the world who isn't allowed to make an occasional mistake.

The next morning, he will wake up and have breakfast and then go to the ballpark to have meetings with the coaches again. He'll get some bad news about one of his guys on the disabled list who's had a setback. It means sticking with that kid from AAA at third base for another week, even though he shouldn't be up in the bigs right now. He'll see players straggle in. Some of them are rested and ready to go. Some may have gotten to bed at 5:00 AM. There are meetings and batting practice and bullpen sessions and there's lunch in there somewhere. Then there are the same five pregame questions from the same five sportswriters. Then he'll talk to the team before the game. Not the rousing speech from the movie that calls everyone to action. The quiet conversations where he checks in with everyone, including that kid from AAA, to see how he's doing. He tells the kid that he's doing fine, despite the .205 batting average. It's a lie, but he doesn't say, "You don't belong up here," because he *needs* the kid to have at least some confidence in himself. Maybe that'll buy an extra base hit.

It's an all-day job for the manager. While most people watch the game from 7:00 to 10:00 PM, the manager has to take care of his team from 10:00 PM to 7:00 PM. However, if you're still convinced that your video game skills qualify you to be the manager, I'm going to give you the chance to prove how awesome you would be at managing a major league team. You can't actually manage one right now, but I've drawn up a list of things that you'd have to do as a manager that don't involve calling for a bunt. Try a few of them out.

* * *

WELCOME TO SPRING TRAINING. SEE THAT GUY OVER THERE? He's 28 and has never made it to the majors. He doesn't have amazing talent but loves the game of baseball more than anything, and he's hung around in the minors for seven years now. He shows up on time every day and actually listens to the coaches. He puts in extra BP and fielding practice and taught himself to play a passable third base because he figured it might help him get to the majors. He's a legitimately nice guy. He signs autographs for the kids outside the AAA park and does appearances at the local elementary schools. He knows that he'll never be a Hall of Famer, but he's hoping for that cup of coffee so he can say he played in the majors. If ever there was a guy you were cheering for because he just wanted it so much, it would be this guy.

Your job is to tell him that he's being released. The dream is over.

While you're at it, do the same for the 35-year-old veteran guy who's been around for a while and stood up for you in the clubhouse when some of the younger players were getting out of hand last year. He's being cut for a 23-year-old who thinks that he's God's gift to baseball.

When I taught classes in graduate school, one thing surprised me. After my first quarter of teaching, I had a couple of students who had "earned" Fs. They had all regularly skipped classes and been surly toward me when they did bother to show up. They didn't take assignments seriously and what they turned in showed a lack of effort. At the end of the quarter, I went to enter grades into the university website. The process was as simple as typing "B" or "C+" or "A-" into the field next to the student's name. Then I got to the first of *those* students. I'd never given an F before. I found myself hesitating to type the letter. With one keystroke, I was going to electronically declare someone a failure. I didn't even have to look them in the eye to do it, and yet I found myself hesitating over someone who actually deserved that F.

Few people ever have the experience of telling someone that they have failed. It's a hard thing to do. Now imagine doing that and as a result breaking the heart of a good kid who's worked hard and wanted this one thing all his life.

*   *   *

YOUR SECOND BASEMAN IS HOMESICK FOR THE DOMINICAN *Republic and doesn't have a lot of friends on the team. Your left fielder has a drinking problem. Your LOOGY is having problems with his wife. You can see that it's affecting their play. Congratulations! You just became a Spanish-speaking social worker, a substance-abuse specialist, and a couples counselor.*

As fans, we see the three hours of actual game time. If we're lucky, we get a five-minute interview with a player when he's mostly throwing out clichés about "teamwork" and "wanting to win." So, what does he do during the other 20 hours and 55 minutes of the day? For some reason, there's this odd disconnect between the little blobs running around the TV screen and the fact that they are human beings. When you get down to it, a baseball team is a collection of twenty-and-thirty-something-year-old men, and there are a lot of life events that happen during that time. Guys get married and guys get divorced. They have kids and miss them and wish they were back home. They try to figure out what they want to be when they grow up and worry about how they'll get there. And yeah, some of them have problems.

A manager has to deal with 25 males on his roster, and men are less likely to seek out mental health services if they need them. So if our manager sees that one of his players is in need of help and that he isn't going to seek out help on his own, the manager either has to do something or deal with a player who isn't at his best.

*   *   *

TONIGHT WHEN YOU PLAY YOUR VIDEO GAME, PLEASE PUT the difficulty on expert (there aren't any novices in MLB). No spending five minutes getting a sandwich so you can think over a pinch-hitting decision in your head. Play with the "warmup pitchers" mode enabled, because you have to think ahead like that in a real game. Try to play your video game as realistically as the settings will allow. Real pitchers throw once every 20 seconds or so, not at the frenetic five-second pace that the video game pitchers do. It means that the game and your concentration must last for three hours.

If you lose, you can't play another game to knock the taste of losing out of your mouth. Remember, in real baseball, you have to go to bed knowing that you don't get a chance to redeem yourself for another 21 hours. Don't do that thing where you're losing by five in the eighth inning, but the system freezes for a moment, and so you hit the reset button because the system was obviously going to need it anyway. When you're winning, you wait it out. Cheater.

A real manager doesn't get to hit the reset button. He has to be thinking 10 minutes ahead and about multiple things that could happen in those 10 minutes. Then he has to make split-second decisions when the moment comes. He also doesn't get to hit the pause button. There are times he has to manage despite the fact that his stomach or his bladder needs some attention. There are lots of little emotional luxuries that your video game allows you that you don't get in the real chair.

IT'S THE NINTH INNING, AND YOU'RE UP BY ONE. YOUR TOP two relievers are Smith and Jones, and both are fresh and available, which is great, because you're in the thick of a tight pennant race and need this game. Smith is generally better than Jones and usually gets the call here, but there's a complication today. Smith has a daughter who has a chronic medical issue. He's a private man and doesn't discuss this with the press, because he wants to keep his family out of the limelight. He got some bad news about his daughter earlier and has been walking around with his head down all day. You've seen him like this before. He'll say he's okay, but he

can't concentrate, and his performance suffers to the point where Jones would actually be the better pitcher tonight to nail down that lead.

It's easy to say that you'd go with Jones in this situation, but if you do, there will be those same five reporters in your office after the game. All of them will ask why you didn't go with Smith. Is there a closer controversy? Is Smith injured? When you mumble something about "better matchups," they'll go to Smith to ask him how he feels about losing his job as closer to Jones, and Smith definitely does not want to answer those questions tonight. If you tell the truth, but kindly ask the reporters to leave that out of the game story, some idiot might put it on Twitter anyway, because he...gets...to...break...a story!

You could go with Smith, and hurt your team's chance of winning in the middle of a pennant race. Maybe he blows the lead, you lose, and the team misses the playoffs by a single game. Great. You just sacrificed an opportunity for the other 24 guys to protect one player from having to answer a couple of questions about his daughter. Maybe he gets the save anyway and you cheat death one more time. So for whom do you ask on the bullpen phone? There is no right answer. There's not even a good answer. You must live with this. After the game, Ed from Lakewood is probably going to be mad at you, no matter what.

When we talk about managers, we usually talk about the strategic decisions that they made. They call for a stolen base. They call for the closer in the ninth inning. While that's a part of managing, I'd argue that it's not even the most important part of being a manager. What we usually think of as "managing a baseball team" is the equivalent of babysitting a baseball team. It's spending three hours with a team at night and then getting out. Real managers have to be parents. It's more than just clicking the button to insert the lefty reliever. It's an around-the-clock commitment to 25 people, any of whom could end up being the one that gets you fired from your job. This isn't a babysitter's club.

✱　　✱　　✱

LET'S BUILD THE PERFECT STRATEGIC MANAGER WHO DOES everything the way that the numbers say he should and is up on all the latest research at Baseball Prospectus. We're going to play within the bounds of reality. We're not going to give our manager any superpowers, like the power to predict the future. We're just going to compare him to what we might expect from a standard issue manager who follows the same strategic "book" that everyone else seems to follow. What does a manager actually do during a game?

1) He decides who's starting today.

He at least decides which position players are starting today, because the starting pitcher is whoever is next in the rotation. In Chapter 4, we talked about some more exotic rotation options than the 5-6-7 method, but we saw that many of those options just aren't realistic. The one that could be implemented with a minimum of fuss would be skipping over the fifth starter when a team doesn't have games five days in a row. Everyone else would still be pitching on a "normal" schedule with four days of rest, and the strategy redistributes a few starts that would have otherwise gone to the weakest link. It might net a team half of a win.

As far as position players, most teams have a regular lineup. It's usually pretty obvious who should be starting, assuming no one is hurt or needs a rest. The manager is in charge of resting his players once in a while, and research has shown that rest does have a very small positive effect on hitters for about week after their off-day. The problem is that when a player takes a day off, he is replaced by a bench player, who by definition isn't as good. If he was, he would be starting. The value gained from the rest and the value lost from having the utility infielder in there for a day about cancel each other out. It's important for a manager to balance the need for rest with the need for keeping his best players on the field, but in terms of tactical management, there's not a lot of advantage to be gained.

2) He makes the lineup.

In previous generations, the fast guy hit first, the guy who was good at bunting hit second, the best hitter was third, the guy who hit a bunch of home runs hit cleanup, and the rest tailed off in spots five through nine. It turns out that's not quite the best way to construct a lineup.

As an example, we don't want a hitter in the leadoff spot just because he's fast. Instead, we want someone there who is good at *not making outs* for the simple reason that the leadoff hitter comes up the most often and *outs are bad*. If a player is good at both not making outs and stealing bases, that's wonderful. When you can't have both, you have to pick the skill that provides the greatest amount of value. Here again is a snippet from our run expectancy chart for 2017.

Table 32. Runs per Base-Out State, 2017 MLB

	No outs	**One out**	**Two outs**
Bases empty	0.523	0.286	0.109
Runner on first	0.895	0.541	0.235
Runner on second	1.110	0.690	0.330
Ratio of home to first value to first to second value	1.73	1.71	1.32

If we have to choose between a guy who is good at getting to first, the base that famously cannot be stolen, or the guy who is good at stealing second, we can see that simply getting on the bases is more important than getting from first to second.

The nice thing about a stolen base is that it essentially turns a single into a double, and that's one reason why managers have liked putting speedsters atop the lineup. If a hitter is gifted in getting to second base by swiping a bag, that's wonderful, but what if the batter just hits a double instead? Then he doesn't need to steal the base. He's already done the work with his bat and he's just as much on second base as the guy who singled and stole second. Why must we have a leadoff hitter who can swipe 45 bases, but a leadoff hitter who can hit 45 doubles is weird?

Still, the numbers tell us that lineup order matters far less than we generally give it credit for. Researcher Tom Ruane published a study in which he used a computer simulation to create an "average" team. The team had one player who had the aggregate stats of all leadoff hitters in baseball (using data from 1993 to 2004), one who had the aggregate stats of all second hitters, and so on. He then simulated a large number of games for every mathematically possible lineup combination of those nine "league average" players. He found that the difference between the perfectly optimized lineup in his simulation and the "he's clearly trying to sabotage the team" lineup was about a tenth of a run scored per game. The difference between the traditional lineup and what the computer considered the perfectly optimized lineup was roughly one hundredth of a run per game. Even over 162 games, a team would score an extra run and a half per year by optimizing their lineup. That's about it. There are gains to be had from a manager who knows how to write down those nine names in the perfect order. What's surprising is that those gains end up being fairly tiny.

3) He calls for the sac bunt.

In Chapter 2, we saw that the "successful" sacrifice bunt is actually a failure. The situation "runner on first, no outs" produces more runs on average than does "runner on second, one out." While that's true, it doesn't tell the whole story. It's instructive to look at one situation where no one bats an eye if the manager calls for a bunt: the pitcher is at bat with a runner on first. Pitchers tend to be awful hitters. So, while a runner on first base and no one out, with a league average hitter at the plate (what the run expectancy matrix assumes), might be worth 0.895 runs, the outlook is not that rosy with a pitcher up. The bunt is a way to get the pitcher out of the batter's box while doing something marginally useful. Research has shown that managers usually bunt with weaker hitters hitting in front of stronger hitters.

Not all sacrifice bunts end with the batter retired and the runner having moved up one base (though about 70 percent do). Some end up as surprise bunt singles or fielding errors. Some end up as double plays! When we incorporate all of the possible outcomes into our analysis, bunting isn't as bad as it initially appears. When we look at how managers use the bunt in practice, the net effect is still negative, but only by a few hundredths of a run each time. In 2017, the average team bunted 20 times with its position players in sacrifice situations, so the net effect of bunting is less than a run per year. A perfect tactical manager might claw that run back, but that's all that he would get compared to a garden-variety manager.

4) He calls for the stolen base.

We've seen that to break even on stolen base attempts, teams need to be successful a little more than 70 percent of the time. In 2017, the success rate for steals was 73 percent, meaning that overall, managers are more-or-less breaking even with the stolen base attempts that they do call for. We'll never know what would have happened to all of the runners who were unsent. Maybe there were individual cases where a runner could have made it, or at least had a better-than-break-even chance.

Even still, let's say that we had a manager who could somehow intuit the best time to send a runner *and* turn his runners into Olympic sprinters. In 2012, writer Sam Miller ran a thought experiment in which he used noted Cincinnati Reds speedster Billy

Hamilton as a proxy for a near-automatic stolen base. Miller's idea was that Hamilton might be used as a pinch runner at the point of highest leverage in the game and that the manager would somehow know that no greater leverage point was coming later. He used real games that the Reds played in September 2012 and assumed that Hamilton could successfully steal a base 83 percent of the time (Hamilton's career minor league SB success rate at the time). How much win probability would Hamilton have added to the Reds? About a tenth of a win over the course of a month, which would be about six-tenths of a win over a full season. That's what would happen if our manager could magically turn his baserunners into Billy Hamilton *and* predict the future. If Billy Hamilton plus psychic powers is worth around half a win a year, again we see that mere mortals wouldn't be able to squeeze much out of this either.

5) He decides when the starting pitcher has had enough.

The complete game has become a relic. In 2017, Corey Kluber and Ervin Santana led all of baseball with five of them. In 1997, that would have been good for a tie for 10th place. In 1977, Kluber and Santana would have tied for 69th place. The complete game has gone away largely because of an intensified focus on pitch counts for starters, particularly over the last two decades. In 2017, there were only 23 games in which a pitcher threw more than 120 pitches. In 1997, there were 383!

In Chapter 4, we saw that it would be hard for teams to completely break away from the idea of having a small stable of pitchers who are tasked with delivering bulk innings (i.e., starters), but the data show that the percentage of innings thrown by starters has receded further and further over the years. Baseball has become a game where it's not a question of whether the bullpen will be involved in the game, but rather how much of the game that bullpen will have to cover.

Table 33. Percentage of Innings Thrown by Starters

Year	Percentage
2017	61.9%
2007	64.8%
1997	67.2%
1987	68.1%
1977	70.3%

While there are those who pine for the old days of hurlers who routinely went the distance, the reality is that teams need to be worried about injuries to their pitchers, particularly catastrophic injuries like the ones that require the dreaded Tommy John surgery, which can rob a pitcher of an entire season on the mound. Research into the effects of single-game pitch counts has shown that each time a pitcher exceeds 110 pitches in a game, his risk of sustaining a catastrophic injury increases by a small, but significant, amount. This is why most managers start getting antsy around the time the starter throws his 100th pitch. Pitch limits might not be aesthetically pleasing to some fans, but the evidence to back them is fairly strong.

Sometimes managers also face a decision of when to *tactically* remove the starter from the game. That is, the starter could throw a few more pitches, but there's someone better out in the bullpen. It's hard to really assess a manager here, because the decision of whether to give the starter the hook will depend on how rested (and how good) the bullpen is. Even more than that, the manager has other things to think about. He could pull the starter in the fifth inning, rather than rolling the dice for one more batter, but if he does, someone else will have to pitch. The manager could give the extra work to one of his better relievers, but he has to guard against that reliever burning out over the course of a season from overuse. He could give the extra work to one of his lesser relievers, but at that point, is that really a better idea than sticking with his starter?

There are moments in every season where a manager leaves the starter out there for one batter too many and has to walk out to get him *after* he gives up the three-run home run. Those are awful to watch and they stick in the memory bank, but just citing those obvious system failures is not a fair way to evaluate a manager. We don't know what would have happened had the reliever come in. He might have given up that same home run. We also don't really know about the moments where the manager had an inkling to take out his starter, decided against it, and the batter grounded meekly to second.

What we do know is that managers really do consider more than just the short-term when deciding whether or not to go to the pen. The evidence for that comes from an interesting place: how managers use their bullpen in a game before a day off, when the manager knows that he literally doesn't have to worry about tomorrow. We see very little effect on how he uses his pitchers.

Table 34. Pitcher Usage, Before a Day Off vs. No Day Off, 2013–2017

	Before a day off	**No day off**
Batters faced by starter	24.29	24.38
Outs recorded by starter	17.08	17.06
Pitches thrown by starter	91.15	91.42
Number of relievers used	3.18	3.10
Number of relievers facing two or fewer batters	0.53	0.48

It's tempting to analyze all pitching moves that a manager makes as if they all took place in Game 7 of the World Series. Game 70 of the regular season is a different situation. The reality is that a decision that might look bad in the context of a single game is justifiable in the context of a season, and we don't have a good method for figuring out what the best strategy actually is for balancing those.

6) He decides who pitches in relief, and when.

We learned in Chapter 3 that the most important relief pitching decisions that a manager makes are the ones made when the game is *close*. There will be relievers brought into the eighth inning of a game where the score is already 9–2, but those don't much matter. At that point, the manager is just trying to keep guys sharp.

Most "by the book" relief strategy still revolves around the save rule, even though we've seen that the save rule leads to some irrational behavior on the part of managers. There have been proposals on how managers might structure their bullpens differently to protect those small leads. For example, what if the closer—if he really is the best reliever of the bunch—were asked to pitch both the eighth and ninth inning with a one-run lead? What if the closer pitched either the eighth or ninth, depending on which hitters were likely to be coming up in those innings?

The evidence suggests that it wouldn't actually make that much of a difference. Here's a look at how often teams enter one of the late innings with a save-worthy lead and how often they exit that inning with the lead still intact.

Table 35. *"Save" Situation Conversion Rates, by Inning, 2013–2017*

	One-run lead	Two-run lead	Three-run lead
Top of the seventh	75.7%	89.5%	95.1%
Bottom of the seventh	70.8%	88.5%	95.2%
Top of the eighth	76.6%	90.6%	96.4%
Bottom of the eighth	77.0%	90.7%	96.3%
Top of the ninth	78.3%	90.9%	96.1%
Bottom of the ninth	78.4%	90.3%	95.7%

We can see that while eighth-inning relievers aren't *quite* as good as their ninth-inning brethren (and the seventh-inning crew is not quite as good as the eighth-inning guys), they all usually get the job done. Even if we assume that ninth-inning pitchers would pitch equally well in a two-inning stint or that eighth-inning relievers could handle the pressure of a ninth-inning save situation (and those are *very* large assumptions), moving a few of those percentages around would mean an expected return of some small fraction of a win over what teams are getting now.

There is a place where teams could do a lot better than they are now with their bullpen. In Chapter 3, we talked about managers and their reluctance to use their closer in the bottom of the ninth in a tied game. (For some reason, this seems to be a good time to bring out the team's fifth best reliever.) Between 2013 and 2017, with a lead of one run in the bottom of the ninth, teams avoided giving up a run 78.4 percent of the time, probably with the closer on the mound. When *tied* in the bottom of the ninth, they avoided giving up a run (which would mean that they lose the game) only 70.4 percent of the time. By simply making the decision to treat a tie game as a priority situation and using his closer, a manager could increase his chances of holding on to the tie by 8 percent, or about a 4 percent chance of eventually winning the game.

In 2017, the average team was involved in seven games where they were the visiting team and the game was tied going into the bottom of the ninth. By ceding a 3.75 percent of a chance to win each time by sticking to a strategy of bringing in an inferior reliever, they give away a quarter of a win each year.

This is not an exhaustive list of tactical decisions that the manager makes, but it's a pretty good one. We can see that even if our manager was fully statistically optimized, the value added to his team—compared to the standard "book" used right now—wouldn't be all that much. Still, if we squeezed all of these together, it would produce something around an extra win for his team, and that's if he does all of them perfectly. Most of that value would come from two decisions: being more willing to skip over the fifth starter and treating a tie game as a priority, decisions that, curiously, few managers seem to be willing to make.

It seems that tactical brilliance can have an effect, but I don't think that tactical brilliance is the most important characteristic of a manager. What is?

*   *   *

IF YOU TALK TO A PROFESSIONAL BASEBALL PLAYER ABOUT his lived experience, you're guaranteed to hear a particular phrase within the first five minutes. It's even more guaranteed than hearing phrases like "throw a fastball," "swing the bat," or "comport with the platypus." You'll hear about "the Grind." By the time the calendar turns to August, it's hot, he's tired, and he's been living out of a suitcase for four months. Every night he has to play a game that requires intense concentration and lasts for three hours. Yes, it's hard to feel pity for a guy making $10 million per year, but he is human and those are tough working conditions.

We know that over the course of a season, plate discipline, which is the ability to make good decisions within the strike zone, erodes. No, players do not become free-swingers or completely lose track of the strike zone by mid-September, but the data show some falloff. I created a simple measure of plate discipline that starts with the assumption that "strikes are bad." I looked at whether each pitch produced a strike (bad decision) or not (good decision). From 2013 to 2017, hitters made "good" decisions on

61.7 percent of all pitches thrown to them. Using a technique known as logistic regression, I estimated the chances that a batter would make a "good" decision, based on the number of days it had been since Opening Day.

Table 36. Estimated League-Wide "Good Decision" Percentage, by Days from Opening Day

Days since Opening Day	Projected "good decision" percentage
0	61.96%
30	61.92%
60	61.87%
90	61.82%
120	61.78%
150	61.74%
180	61.70%

It's not the sort of effect that you can see with the naked eye. It's a pattern that only becomes apparent after analyzing a big data set, but there's a very obvious slowly descending line. Still, with such small differences between those numbers, you may think "so what?" In Chapter 2, we talked about how a small effect can be very important over a large number of repetitions, and this effect impacts every pitch that a team faces, and the average team saw 23,444 pitches in 2017.

We see that between Opening Day and 90 days in, our projected "good decision" rate falls by 0.14 percent. Over 23,444 pitches, that 0.14 percent difference would mean 33 extra pitches that did *not* result in strikes, although that's just a league average. Each of those is worth about a tenth of a run. What if some managers are better than others at preventing this sort of falloff, and thus creating value for their team? It turns out that some are.

The math here gets a little more complex, but essentially what I did next was to ask the computer to adjust the line showing how quickly plate discipline eroded over the course of a season for each individual manager. We want to be careful not to credit (or debit) a manager for the talent of the guys in his lineup, nor for the quality of pitchers that his team was facing, but we can statistically control for that. In theory, on Opening Day, a league-average batter and pitcher would have the same projected "good decision" outcome, no matter what manager they were playing for. As the season wears on, that same matchup might produce a slightly better or somewhat worse outcome, based on the identity of the manager. A statistical program is able to see those patterns where the naked eye is not.

Using data from 2013 through 2017, I looked at what the computer projected each manager's effect would be on a matchup between a league-average hitter and pitcher (61.7 percent "good decision" rate) on the 90th day (the mid-point) of the season. It turns out that part way through the season, some managers are estimated to have players who are still pretty sharp, perhaps even sharper than they were on Opening Day. Others have players who have fallen off. Here are the top and bottom five managers, from that time period (among managers active in at least three of those five seasons).

Table 37. Estimated Manager-Specific "Good Decision" Percentage for Hitters on the 90th Day of the Season, 2013–2017

Top five managers	Estimated "good decision" rate	Bottom five managers	Estimated "good decision" rate
Bruce Bochy	61.83%	Craig Counsell	61.52%
Ryne Sandberg	61.82%	Walt Weiss	61.53%
Robin Ventura	61.80%	Pete Mackanin	61.59%
Bryan Price	61.79%	Terry Francona	61.60%
Terry Collins	61.79%	Brad Ausmus	61.61%

The difference between the top manager (Bruce Bochy) and the bottom manager (Craig Counsell) is about 0.2 percent at the 90-day mark. If a team managed by Bochy played the same way that they played at 90 days into the season all year long, they would make more than 30 extra "good" decisions over the course of a year than a team with an average manager.

Over the course of a season, the best manager in the league is likely worth about seven runs or most of one win more than the worst manager *based only on his ability to keep his hitters from experiencing the negative effects of the Grind on their plate discipline.* That's just the batters. We haven't even yet accounted for running these same analyses on whether managers can keep their pitchers slightly fresher over a long season, but we can.

When we add those effects (hitters making slightly better decisions, pitchers inducing slightly worse decisions in their opponents) together, the best managers come out 10 to 15 runs (a win to a win and a half) ahead of the worst ones. We don't know if this is all the manager's doing, but insofar as the manager is ultimately responsible for the well-being of his roster, it seems proper to assume that the credit is his.

Here are the five best (and worst) managers in fighting the Grind, based on their performance from 2013 to 2017 (minimum three seasons managed).

Table 38. Estimated "Grind Runs" Saved for Pitchers and Hitters, 2013–2017

Top five managers	Estimated "Grind runs" per season	Bottom five managers	Estimated "Grind runs" per season
Buck Showalter	7.38	Walt Weiss	-7.57
Terry Francona	5.98	Mike Matheny	-4.78
Ryne Sandberg	5.88	Joe Girardi	-3.25
Terry Collins	5.52	Jeff Banister	-3.17
Bryan Price	3.78	John Farrell	-2.84

(Note: numbers are relative to an "average" manager)

Earlier in this chapter, we suggested that the perfect tactical manager might squeeze out an extra win for his team with his tactical maneuverings if he did absolutely everything right. These analyses suggest that certain managers are already having just as great an impact on their team in how well they help their players to fight against the Grind. A lot of that work is done behind the curtain in the clubhouse. It's the conflict between two players that never gets out of hand because the manager, or his *consigliere*, stepped in and mediated it. It's the little note in the lunchbox that encourages the second baseman to keep trying, even if he's had a couple of tough nights. It's realizing when a guy needs a day off to clear his head. It's the stuff that you know when you're the parent and not the babysitter.

If there is something that I think baseball analysis has gotten wrong over the years, it's evaluating managers based only on their tactical decision-making. Sure, tactics are part of the job and the easiest to get data on, but it's only part of the story. The behind-the-scenes piece, as much as we can measure it, can be just as valuable. Perhaps more valuable. When players talk about a manager who can keep the team on an even keel throughout the season, that might not be just another player spouting clichés. That might be the sound of real value being added to a team that no one ever sees.

The nice thing is that this isn't an either/or choice. A manager can be both up to date on all the latest strategic research *and* good at helping his players get through a long season. We ignore either of them at our own peril. So, Ed from Lakewood, if you're out there reading this, maybe you really could be a decent babysitter for the team for a night or two. But please, don't confuse that with the hard work of actually managing one.

- 7 -

Nitrogen and the Forgotten Fourth Starter

THE FIRST JOB THAT I EVER HAD WAS SELLING BASEBALL cards. My father's assistant manager at the parking garage had a side business selling cardboard on weekends. He needed someone who could do enough math to make change and who didn't mind sitting around thinking and talking about baseball all day. I was 10 and to this day, it was the greatest job I ever had.

This was during the early 1990s, a period of time now known among card collectors as the "junk wax" era, but we didn't think of it that way back then. Baseball cards had been produced even in the 1800s, but it wasn't until the 1950s and 1960s that baseball cards came into their own. Before the 1950s, most sets were one-off, small-batch collections that featured well-known, All-Star-level players, and were meant to be prizes that would help to sell cigarettes or chewing gum. In 1952, Topps—a chewing gum company—tried something different. They issued a set of 407 cards, including the now-iconic Mickey Mantle and Willie Mays rookie cards. It was the largest set of baseball cards ever made by a country mile. It also flipped the sales model upside down. Topps sold the cards in packs of five and the chewing gum was the nice little prize. A few decades later, they stopped bothering to include the gum.

By the 1980s, the kids of the 1950s had grown into adults who had developed the most universal disease of adulthood, nostalgia. Those who had been card collectors in their youth began reaching back for pieces of their childhood, only to find that few of those baseball cards had survived, mostly by hiding in attics for 30 years. As tends to happen, the number of nostalgic adults exceeded the number of attics and the forces of economics took over. Prices for old cards began to climb, as the first generation that had grown up with card collecting as a hobby grew into adults who had incomes capable of supporting the chase to hold a few extra moments of youth in their hands.

The high prices that baseball cards were fetching drew plenty of newcomers to the business. In 1981, Topps, after functionally having a monopoly on baseball cards for a few decades, was joined by upstarts Fleer and Donruss. Score and Upper Deck cards would appear a few years later, all of the companies producing sets of several hundred cards and all hoping that not only could they sell cards to baseball-loving kids, but that serious adults would see the cards as an investment. What resulted was a spectacular crash, and like every other crash in history, it seems obvious in hindsight, though we missed it (or chose to ignore it) when it was happening in front of us. The market massively overproduced inventory to the point that cards from that era can now be had for the cost of shipping them. Thankfully, I wasn't an investor back then. I was a kid who was just happy to open a couple of packs.

The 1952 Topps set is normally discussed in terms of the Mantle and Mays rookie cards, which continue to fetch six-digit prices on the open market, but I'd propose that the most important card in the bunch actually belonged to Willie Ramsdell. (He was listed on the card by his given middle name of Willard.) In 1951, "Willie the Knuck"—Ramsdell was a knuckleballer—had gone 9–17 pitching 196 entirely forgettable innings for the Cincinnati Reds. For his efforts, he was traded to the Chicago Cubs before the 1952 season. After 67 innings as a Cub, he fell out of Major League Baseball, never to return again. Because of the rarity of the 1952 set, Ramsdell's card still fetches a few dollars, but it's likely that most of the people reading this book have no idea who Willie Ramsdell is. That's the point.

Ramsdell was the fourth starter on a team that had finished the 1951 season with a 66–86 record in the 18th largest city in the United States, and yet he was deemed worthy of enshrinement in cardboard and specks of bubble gum–scented sugar dust. Whether the Topps Company specifically planned it or not, their decision reflected—or maybe spurred—a major breakthrough in how fans thought about baseball. With a set of 407 cards, and only 16 teams in Major League Baseball at the time, it meant that Topps was producing cards for more than 20 players on each team. No longer were cards reserved for famous names like Yogi Berra and Warren Spahn, who would have been well-known even outside their hometown fan base. There was room for just about everyone. This was a strategic risk for Topps. There were plenty of serious baseball fans who wouldn't have recognized Willie Ramsdell on the street, even if he was in uniform. It meant the distinct possibility that fans might plunk down their hard-earned nickels for a pack of baseball cards, only to discover that all five were obscure role-players on teams that they'd never seen play.

A somewhat less charitable interpretation of the Ramsdell gambit might have been that Topps was hoping to use the principles of gambling in their sales strategy. If every pack had a Stan Musial or a Ralph Kiner in it, then someone buying a pack would have the thrill of nabbing an All-Star every time they opened one. Topps may have been trying to space out the "good" cards with cards that they knew that few would care about. It would reduce the number of times that the card buyer had the thrill of encountering an All-Star, but it would make them chase that high by spacing out that reward at random intervals, rather than satisfying that itch every time. Topps essentially turned the experience of buying otherwise worthless pieces of cardboard into something resembling a slot machine.

Whether Topps was priming nine-year-olds with their first taste of casino action or whether they simply thought that the public had a right to know Ramsdell's 1951 stats and his place of birth (and before the internet, where else could one find this information?) the cards slowly became collector's items. Sure, Mantle and Mays would fetch higher prices than Ramsdell, but soon, people were collecting *sets* of baseball cards. It was as important to have Ramsdell as Mantle. The set was not complete without both.

A set of baseball cards is a tangible collection of baseball *in its entirety* at some moment in time. All (well, most) of the players who played regularly in 1951 are in that set, from the superstars to the backup catchers, each with his own eight-and-three-quarters square inches of cardboard real estate. Collecting cards of individual players is a cult of personality. Collecting the set is to savor the game itself. It's a philosophical statement. There are no unimportant parts of baseball, there are just parts that get more attention than others. If you take any of those parts away, even the little parts that don't seem to do much, it stops being a set. It stops being baseball.

For baseball junkies, Willie Ramsdell is like nitrogen gas, which comprises nearly 80 percent of the air we breathe in, even though the body doesn't actually use it. We simply breathe it back out. Yet that gas fills the entirety of every space that we occupy in life. It's easy to dismiss nitrogen (or Ramsdell) as unimportant, but chemically, nitrogen gas is a stable compound and without it the atmosphere would be far less stable. That atmosphere keeps us alive even if we're only interested in the 20 percent that's oxygen—or Willie Mays. Mays wouldn't be there without the Willie Ramsdells of the world to pitch to him.

I caught the baseball-card bug early in life, thanks to my parents. For Christmas when I was seven, they got me a full 1986 Topps set. I still have it. When I got it, it was already in an album, arranged uncreatively in order from card number 1 in the set to number 792. Players from different teams were strewn about the pages with no rhyme or reason other than whatever logic (if any) Topps put in to numbering their cards. I had to hunt to find pictures of my beloved Cleveland Indians. While baseball cards are social objects that facilitate friendships among children (I traded cards with the best of them), they also have an awesome one-player mode. I felt the need to bring order to the chaos that was the seemingly random assignment of one through 792. So, much to my mother's horror, all 792 cards came out of their sleeves and onto my bedroom floor. I decided to organize them.

At first, I organized the players by team, but that seemed so banal once I was done with it. Out they came again onto my floor.

This time, I decided to alphabetize the players. Orioles pitcher Don Aase was happy for a while; Braves shortstop Paul Zuvella was not, but eventually I grew tired of alphabetical order and decided to sort the players by position. (Sorry, Mom.) The 1986 Topps set had a little circle on the front of the card with the player's preferred position printed in it. Most players had just one position listed, but I was struck by the fact that some players had two. At the time, it didn't occur to me that these were largely interchangeable utility infielders. I figured that they must be some sort of special super-athlete to play both second base *and* shortstop. They got their own section of the album, and I still have a strange affinity for utility infielders.

That's the beauty of baseball minutiae. It's a game full of nooks and crannies and the occasional rabbit hole. There are thousands of little pieces of information about the game. Some of them are more important than others, or perhaps it's better to say that some are more appreciated than others. Sometimes, even if something isn't all that important, it's still fun to understand how it works.

That 1986 Topps set taught seven-year-old me classification and sorting skills in a way that no schoolbook could ever teach.

Reorganizing my baseball cards was the first time that I ever played around (literally!) in a data set, and something fun happens when you start playing around in any data set. You start noticing patterns and asking questions that begin with "Why...?"

I remember being struck by the fact that there were so many "SS-2Bs" and not a lot of "OF-3Bs" and wondering why that was. The answer to that question might not be important to understanding the game, but it planted the seeds of exploration in my head. The fact that this book exists can be traced back to that same sense of wonder.

I probably would have kept going with my reorganization of those 1986 cards, finding different ways to group the players together, but eventually the 1987 set ended up under the Christmas tree. My 1986 set is still in a closet at my house, sorted by position, and once in a while it still feels good to pull out that album and breathe in that air from when I was seven. There's the nitrogen, the oxygen, the nostalgia, the curiosity about utility infielders, and Andy McGaffigan, the Cincinnati Reds' fourth starter that year.

I'VE NEVER CAUGHT A FOUL BALL. I'VE BEEN TO A COUPLE OF games where I was in the right section, but I never got a chance to make a play on a batted ball off the bat of a major leaguer, even if it was one that went the wrong way. Once, when I was 10 or 11, I was sitting at the end of a row in the lower deck of Cleveland Municipal Stadium when a member of the Minnesota Twins lined a ball foul off to the side, directly up the aisle-way.

(Thankfully, no one was in the way!) The ball ricocheted off the facing of one of the concrete stairs that led to the concourse and it bounded back down the aisle where it landed on the step one row behind me. I jumped to snare the pearl but was beaten to it by about half a second by a guy in his thirties. Had I been a few years younger, I might have been more spry, or perhaps I could have pulled the "cute kid" trick and the guy might have given me the ball. Alas, the ultimate baseball raffle prize has never fallen from the sky into my outstretched hand.

Most baseball fans see foul balls as a source of souvenirs. To catch one is to take home a tangible piece of the game that you went to see. From a gameplay perspective though, foul balls are annoying. They don't really *do* anything. With two strikes, they don't even move the count along. They are just a null space in which a pitch was thrown, but nothing technically happened. What could possibly be worth looking in to about foul balls?

Foul balls may not move the game along, but they do contain information. We know that the batter swung and we know that he didn't miss. Below we have numbers from 2017 showing what happens when a plate appearance starts out with a 0-1 count.

Table 39. Outcomes on 0-1 Counts, Non-Pitchers Batting, 2017

	AVG	OBP	SLG
All plate appearances (0-0)	.255	.324	.426
All 0-1 plate appearances	.223	.268	.359
First pitch was swinging strike	.205	.255	.338
First pitch was called strike	.226	.273	.362
First pitch was foul ball	.235	.281	.390

We can see that a first-pitch strike is not a great outcome for a batter, but we also see that it matters how that strike got there. A foul ball gets better results than a called strike, and both get much better results than a swinging strike. The fact that the batter *didn't miss* tells us something, even if he didn't hit the ball in the right direction. These findings even hold when we statistically control for the overall quality of the batter and pitcher. This means that even if we had the same batter and pitcher, but three different plate appearances, one starting with a called strike, one with a swinging strike, and one with a foul ball, we would still expect the same basic pattern of outcomes.

Let's look at two-strike foul balls.

Table 40. Outcomes on Two-Strike Counts, Non-Pitchers Batting, 2017

	AVG	OBP	SLG
All plate appearances (0-0)	.255	.324	.426
All two-strike counts	.176	.250	.281
Fouled off at least one two-strike pitch	.193	.291	.321
Fouled off no two-strike pitches	.172	.237	.271
Fouled off just one two-strike pitch	.187	.279	.310
Fouled off more than one two-strike pitch	.204	.314	.343

Again, we see that a two-strike count is a bad idea for a hitter, but they do happen. In fact, in 2017, more than half of all plate appearances got to two strikes. A batter who fouled off a ball when he got to a two-strike count actually gets somewhat better results than we might otherwise expect. (Again, these findings hold even when we control for batter and pitcher quality.)

Intuitively, this makes sense. The more two-strike pitches that a batter spoils, the more he forces the pitcher to labor and the more chances he gives the pitcher to make a mistake.

This isn't the kind of value that people tend to look for in a baseball player, but it's value. Even batters who foul a two-strike pitch off are hitting well below the league average, because they are, by definition, dealing with a two-strike count. We might look at the slash line of .193/.291/.321 and wonder who would *want* that? Someone who was stuck in a situation where the expected slash line is .172/.237/.271, that's who. If a hitter is good at generating foul balls, he'll be better able to cut his losses in a bad situation. Added value, even if it's just taking things from "very bad" to merely "bad," is still added value.

And you thought that they were just souvenirs!

A RUNNER STANDS AT FIRST OR, TO BE MORE PRECISE, A few feet away from first. A pitcher turns and throws over to the first baseman and the runner takes a couple steps back to the bag. The first baseman throws the ball back, and the runner takes a few steps back off. Everyone knows what's going on. In 2017, there were 16,721 throws made to first base to "check in" on a runner. A measly 1.5 percent of them resulted in a pick-off. There were another 0.7 percent of those throws where the pitcher threw the ball away allowing the runner to advance. That means that 98 percent of the time, a throw to first doesn't "do anything" other than make the fans a little more antsy in their seats. Everyone knows that it doesn't make much difference, but it happens anyway. It's baseball's way for the pitcher to say to the runner, "I haven't forgotten about you." Maybe it's his way of saying, "I know what you're thinking about…" Maybe there's more going on there than meets the eye.

In 2017, the runners who most often got a "check in" were Delino DeShields Jr. (64 percent of the time he was on first), A.J. Pollock (61 percent), Trea Turner (60 percent), Byron Buxton (59 percent), and Jonathan Villar (59 percent). On the other side of that list, no one bothered at all to check in on Kendrys Morales or Victor Martinez in 2017. Salvador Perez, Nelson Cruz, and Joe Mauer all got throws over less than 3 percent of the times that they stood at first. I'll let the reader figure out the pattern there.

Surprisingly, throws to first don't act as a deterrent to runners trying to steal. Using data from 2013 to 2017, we can isolate all situations in which a runner was standing on first with second base open. We know that some runners like to try to steal more than others, so we'll need to statistically control for that, as well as for some other factors that we know affect whether runners try to swipe a bag (the number of outs, the inning, whether the score is close). But even once we do that, we see that when a pitcher makes a throw over to first, the runner is actually *more* likely to try for second later in that at-bat than we might otherwise expect.

There are a couple of reasonable explanations for why this happens, none of which we can directly prove. One would be the "challenge theory," which says that a runner might see the throw from the pitcher as a challenge. ("Oh…you think I'm going to run? I'll show you.") In Chapter 3, we talked about how managers are more likely to try to send a runner after having one caught stealing. Perhaps the same dynamic is playing out here. The other possibility is that pitchers can recognize situations when runners are more likely to make a break for it, and while they can't stop a runner from trying, they can at least throw over and make him stay a tiny bit closer to the bag.

While a throw to first doesn't deter runners from trying for second, it does have an effect on whether a runner makes it to second safely. Again, when we control for all of the same factors above, including how successful a runner usually is in his steal attempts, we find that when a pitcher has thrown to first, a would-be thief is *less* likely to be successful, by about 6 percentage points, controlling for everything else. That's a pretty big effect. Reducing a runner's chances of stealing by 6 percent is worth .04 runs of expected value to the defense. That might not seem like much, but it just takes a nice soft toss over to first to reach out and grab those runs.

Runners commonly take a lead of a few feet off first. Eventually, a stolen base comes down to a race between how quickly the runner can traverse the 90 feet between first base and second and how quickly the pitcher and catcher can get the ball to the second baseman. By getting a lead, the runner is trying to move the odds in his favor by shaving a few feet off his journey. A fast—but not blazing fast—runner might be able to average 20 feet per second on the bases. So, for every two feet—less than the average length of a step—closer to first base that the pitcher can make him stand, the runner will need roughly an extra tenth of a second to make it to second base. Those tenths of a second matter. The pitch-catch-throw-tag sequence usually takes around 3.4 or 3.5 seconds from the moment the pitcher releases the ball, so an extra tenth of a second is 3 percent of the time that the runner has available to make his mad dash.

A runner on first can't stray too far off first base, lest he get picked off. Logically, he should choose the distance that is the furthest he can get away from the base while still feeling comfortable that he can get back if he needs to. Pitchers know that runners will be picking a distance that they are fairly sure is safe, and that actually recording a pickoff is rare, yet they throw over anyway. Why bother? It's because the pitcher knows that the runner is human and humans have a tendency to overcorrect.

If a runner was able to make it back to first with a lead of 10 feet, then he should be able to do it again. After all, he *just did it*. That's not what the human mind does though. By throwing over to first, the pitcher has put the thought into the runner's head that he can (and will) throw over. Of course, the runner already knew that, but now that thought is front and center in his mind. It might mean that he takes a slightly shorter lead or hesitates just the tiniest fraction of a second more when trying to decide if the pitcher really is going to throw home this time. In a cat-and-mouse game where there are less than four seconds to get away from the cat, those fractions can be the difference between a stolen base and a caught stealing. The data suggest that this is exactly what happens.

The real reason that a pitcher throws over isn't that he thinks he'll pick the runner off. If that happens, it's a nice bonus, but he's really playing a mind game with the runner. The prize he's going for is that extra half-step that no one notices.

*   *   *

IN 2017, MAJOR LEAGUE BASEBALL COMMISSIONER ROB Manfred made what looked to be a minor change to the rules of the game. The intentional walk, long a staple of strategy in the game, would be no more—at least the part where the pitcher throws four purposefully wide pitches so that everyone can pretend that this is an actual at-bat. Instead, the manager was allowed to signal to the umpire for an intentional walk, and the batter could just trot down to first.

Strangely, my defense of the "classic" intentional walk—the one where you have to actually throw four balls—begins with the center fielder, but first, we need to meditate on the absurdity of the center fielder, a man standing 300 feet from the spot where the action is. In most other sports, it isn't even physically possible to have a defender that far away. Three hundred feet can fit the length of three basketball courts and one-and-a-half hockey rinks. Three hundred feet marks off the distance from end zone to end zone in football. In baseball, a 300-foot fly ball is rather pedestrian. There's even more real estate out there beyond the center fielder. A baseball field is a very large place.

That has some consequences. It means that a good number of the seats in the ballpark are also several hundred feet away from the place where the ball is launched. Unlike soccer or basketball where the location of the action moves around the playing surface—which means that at different times, seats will be closer to or further away from the game action—the batter's box doesn't move. It means that the two most important people in any at-bat—the pitcher and the batter—are confined to only a few square feet worth of space, 60 feet, six inches apart, and 500 feet away from the guy who paid $12 to sit in the center-field bleachers.

Baseball looks very different when watched at close range. I remember clearly the first time that, when I was in high school, my friends and I snuck down into the lower reserve section at Jacobs Field and watched half an inning from the first row behind the backstop. (Even my teenage rebellions involved baseball.) Eventually, an usher politely asked us to remove ourselves from that area, lest we be removed from the park, but I remember it well. The pitches *moved*. It wasn't video game movement. They still obeyed the laws of physics, but they moved. And the batter muttered. And the pitcher danced. There was emotion coming from all of the participants after each of those pitches. It was its own little soap opera.

For most of my life, when I had gone to a baseball game, I sat in those $12 seats. I knew that the outcome of a pitch, whether ball or strike, was important, but I mostly considered it important because I knew that a strike brought the batter closer to a strikeout and a ball brought the batter closer to a walk. All you can really see from center field is the ball being thrown down the chute and the umpire making a call.

There's a lot of action that goes on between the pitcher and hitter on all of the pitches. It shows up a lot better on television than in the bleachers. The center-field camera gives a decent perspective on the ball's movement and the body language of the pitcher and batter after each pitch, so I knew some of what was going on. The thing is that there once was a time when baseball games were not shown on television. That might not seem like a big deal, but it means that baseball spent a great deal of its early existence where there were only two ways to experience the game. One was on the radio (once it was invented) and the other was in person, probably sitting a few hundred feet from the batter's box.

BASEBALL IS A GAME PLAYED IN TWO PARTS. THERE'S THE dance of the batter and pitcher and then there's what happens at the end of that dance when (and if) the batter hits the ball. Much of the first part of that dance is played out in the realm of inches. Plenty of pitchers live either just on the corner of home plate or just off of it. The difference between a "good" slider and a bad one might be a couple inches of break. It's the sort of resolution that even the best human eye can't get from a few hundred feet away. From that distance, they all look the same. But a fly ball hit in the air 300 feet from the batter's box? That was easy enough to see.

That too had consequences. In baseball's formative years, a language grew up around the end of the dance. Hitters "singled" or "grounded to third" or "flied out to center field." From this language, there came forth numbers that became culturally important, almost all of them based on summarizing what had happened at the end of a player's turn in the box. Batting average summarizes the outcome of a hitter's at-bats. On-base percentage summarizes the outcome of a hitter's plate appearances. Home runs are a specific outcome that can end a turn at the dish. So are strikeouts.

Baseball's culture grew to speak of its heroes in terms of how their plate appearances ended. There's nothing wrong with that. That is eventually the object of the game, but what would have happened if baseball had built all of its ballparks with all of its seats behind home plate, close enough to watch the dance of the slider? What if Abraham Lincoln himself could have turned on the television to watch a game? What if a language had developed where we talked about both Babe Ruth's career home run total, and also the number of pitches just off the corner that he was able to lay off?

But alas, that never happened. The physics of the game called for a center fielder and seats that were too far away to fully appreciate that batter-pitcher tango. By the time radio and television were widespread, baseball already had an entire language, poetic and numerical, that it used to talk about itself. The fundamental assumption of that language was that what happened at the end of the at-bat was what mattered, with special preference given to things that the fans could see from the stands. Television might be able to show the movement of the pitches, but by the time television came around, there were few words to describe how pitch movement affected the game and the fans watching at home didn't grow up speaking them.

Table 41. "Not in Play" Events per Game per Team, 1976–2016

Year	K per game	BB per game	HBP per game	PA per game	"Not in play" percentage	Minutes per game
2016	8.03	3.11	0.34	38.01	30.2%	184.77
2006	6.52	3.26	0.37	38.71	26.2%	171.91
1996	6.46	3.55	0.31	39.10	26.3%	175.77
1986	5.87	3.38	0.19	38.24	24.7%	168.99
1976	4.83	3.20	0.18	38.06	21.6%	149.17

Major League Baseball took a look at these data before the 2017 season and decided that it had a problem. Games had grown noticeably longer, by more than half an hour over the course of 40 years, despite the fact that patrons still got to see almost the exact same number of hitters come to the plate. There's another trend that has walked alongside that increase. Driven almost entirely by an increase in strikeouts, hitters were putting the ball in play a lot less than they used to. Over 40 years, the number of plate appearances ending with a "not in play" event jumped by almost 10 percent.

The issue of game *length* and game *pace* are separate, though related problems, and baseball has never been clear on which one it's trying to solve. Maybe the answer is "both." The game has grown up with a clear cultural preference for the ball being hit into play, but it has also evolved past seeing strikeouts as a moral failing as it once did. (Karma did not punish Casey for his hubris by having him ground to third.) Instead, strikeouts are now seen as an unfortunate, though bearable side effect of behaviors that teams do like. Power hitters strike out a lot, but they also hit a lot of home runs. Whatever their moral valence, strikeouts are hard to appreciate from 500 feet away, and even though television can show the anguished face of the batter after he flails at the forbidden candy that he shouldn't have chased, we are still programmed to associate "action" with "hitting the ball."

This left MLB in a strange position. They couldn't command teams to strike out less. They did what they could, instituting suggestions, like requiring the batter to keep one foot in the batter's box, even when he was adjusting his batting gloves. If they couldn't induce more balls in play, they could at least say, "C'mon guys, let's get this over with."

The psychologist in me sympathizes with the gentlemen who are on the field taking an extra moment before stepping into place. Baseball is a game of sustained attention in a low-stimulation environment under conditions of sleep deprivation. Baseball is a game where most of the time nothing happens, but you have to pay close attention anyway because when something does happen, you have to react quickly. That's hard to do when the team plane landed at 3:00 AM last night.

Table 42. Length of Time Between Pitches, by Inning, 2017

Inning	Time (seconds)
1	19.61
2	19.78
3	19.71
4	20.32
5	20.41
6	21.17
7	21.81
8	22.42
9	22.57

(Note: bases empty only)

As the game wears on, things start taking just a bit longer. That makes sense. When people in laboratory settings are asked to perform a sustained attention task without rest, their reaction time slows as the task gets longer and they have more lapses in attention. It's not surprising if hitters take an extra moment to reset their focus before climbing into the batter's box to face a 98 mph fastball that could literally kill them. MLB could legislate that they not take those extra moments, but they'd be legislating against the realities of neuropsychology. Their reward would be players who aren't *quite* on their game.

Here we need to ask again whether the cure is worse than the disease. Yes, games could be shorter, but there wouldn't be quite as much thrill from seeing some of the hemisphere's best athletes playing a game at the highest possible level that it can be played. There are going to be days when the score is 8–3 and the eventual outcome of the game isn't much of a mystery, but in any one plate appearance a player can make a highlight reel–worthy catch or hit a home run that breaks the tape measure. Even if the game is a dud, the fans can at least go home talking about *that* play. Take away those little extra pauses and you take away some of the player's abilities to generate those moments. It's like cutting a few minutes off *Swan Lake* by sending in the junior varsity ballet dancers, because they pirouette a little faster.

*   *   *

WHEN I WORKED AS A THERAPIST, IT WAS IMPORTANT TO understand not only the problem that a person was bringing to the therapy room but why they believed that it was a problem. In baseball's case, they have identified the clock as the problem. For a business which makes its money by selling an entertainment product, it's a perfectly reasonable fear to have, but MLB has a fear of being boring. Like anything else, boring is in the eye of the beholder, though MLB has a business interest in making sure that as many eyes as possible are beholding the game.

I rather like spending three-and-a-half hours at the ballpark, but even I recognize that an 8–3 snoozer is no one's idea of a good time. And yet, while baseball complains about long games and extended pauses, they sure do sell those moments when it suits them. Watch the television feed of a close game and you are guaranteed to see close-ups of a reliever as sweat drips down his face and he takes a deep breath before shaking off his catcher. The batter takes an extra moment before stepping in and has a determinedly placid look on his face as he wiggles his bat a little bit. Back to the pitcher, who comes set as the crowd noise swells behind them both, and then...the batter calls time. Baseball can be such a tease.

Suddenly, in a close game, the very issue that baseball had declared as the reason for boredom is now a *dramatic moment*, despite the fact that "nothing" is happening. Now the pause is a reason to love the game. It's a reason to luxuriate in the fact that the game is in the balance and might be won by the heroes or the villains, and we have no idea who. It's an invitation to become emotionally invested. It's the setup for what is often called a "Hollywood ending."

I'd argue that baseball doesn't have a time-of-game problem. It has a narrative-pacing problem. It wants to tell a good story. To solve it, maybe baseball can take a few lessons from another art form: film. Filmmakers don't tell a story in the most efficient way possible, because humans don't perceive stories in terms of efficiency. Instead, film uses a complicated visual language all its own that we often don't even recognize, but one that conforms to the way that people absorb narratives. When a scene opens, the filmmaker rarely jumps right to the action, but instead leaves an "establishing shot" on the screen for a few seconds. If the characters will be interacting at a diner, the screen will show that diner from the outside. The establishing shot doesn't actually move the plot along, but the brain needs a moment to transition from the last scene where they were in a laundromat. Or a spaceship. Or Mount Rushmore.

Filmmakers also play around with time in their composition. It's a standard film technique to use slow-motion footage during a particularly important moment in the film. Efficiency would be showing the event at full speed, which is how things actually proceed, but it's not how humans experience big events. When people experience crisis moments in real life, they will often recall the event by saying, "It's as if time slowed down." It didn't, but there's a very real cognitive reason why it seems that way. During normal operations, the human brain has millions of pieces of information that it could pay attention to. The problem is bandwidth and capacity. To pay attention to every single detail all the time would be maddening.

Instead, the brain is predisposed to pay attention to certain bits of information, process others on auto-pilot, and ignore others. In a crisis situation, as the brain realizes that this is an important moment, it begins collecting as much data as it can for this short burst. We are used to a certain amount of information representing a certain amount of time, but the brain's short-term information-gathering binge messes with that ratio. Filmmakers have learned to use that to their advantage, mirroring the brain's natural tendency to slow things down as a signal to the viewer. *Pay attention. This scene is really important.*

The intentional walk is a counterintuitive strategy. The pitcher is not supposed to want the batter to reach base, and yet there he is doing something that will guarantee the batter does. This must be an extraordinary moment if they are resorting to doing something that they aren't supposed to. The intentional walk is most often placed at an important juncture in the game, and like a filmmaker who is trying to set a good narrative pace, the IBB slows the game down and allows a bit of time for baseball's version of an establishing shot as we watch two grown men play catch exactly four times. The whole process used to take a minute or so in the good old days when you actually had to throw the pitches, and now we can shave most of that minute off the game. But at what cost? Yes, we could get rid of that establishing shot and it would cut a little bit of time off of the movie, but would the movie actually be better for it?

I think there's value in the "classic" intentional walk. We need those four pitches because they are part of the unspoken, visual language of the game. As the narrative of the game unfolds, the seconds that those four sham pitches consume actually serve a purpose in making the game fit with how humans process information, and therefore making the game more engaging. It's not realistic to expect that a non-obsessed fan will watch every pitch of a game, especially one that doesn't have much drama in it. It might even be a little much to ask the obsessed ones to do it. The rules of basketball and football provide for "action," with the rules scheduling it on a regular and predictable basis. Baseball suffers from an unpredictability problem in that sense. To be a baseball fan is to have no idea when the next bit of "action" might be.

So I say bring back ball four. Make the pitcher actually issue an intentional walk, rather than just point the batter to first. Leave alone the language which baseball has evolved to work around some of its own limitations. Yes, they might seem like four useless lobs, but they do a job that's much more important than just allowing the batter a free pass to first. And they're worth the 45 seconds that it takes to make them happen.

*   *   *

THE HIGH SCHOOL YOU WENT TO TURNS OVER ITS ENTIRE student population every four years. The teachers who were there when you were 16 eventually move on to other jobs or retire. Yet, even though most of the people are gone, there is a connecting thread that somehow still makes the school feel familiar. At my high school, the cafeteria still smells like tater tots and 300 adolescent boys crammed into a small space. Somehow that part never changes. When I went to school there, I never really stopped to notice that smell. It took me time being an outsider before I realized how much that smell comprised the atmosphere that I breathed on a daily basis. It took even longer before I realized how much breathing that air shaped me as a person.

When Rob Manfred proposed the rule change concerning the intentional walk, there were plenty of strong reactions. That seems to happen any time baseball proposes a rule change, even something tiny and seemingly irrelevant. In the case of the intentional-walk rule, even the people who were against the change expressed frustration with their difficulty in explaining why they were even upset over something that meant so little. One day, when I was back visiting my high school, I had the same sort of reaction when I saw that they had replaced all of the old hallway lockers, including *my locker*. Sure, it had trouble closing half the time and probably should have been replaced 10 years before I got to the school. It wasn't even really mine, given that plenty of other students had used it before and since I graduated, but it represented an object that linked me back to another time in my life. Yes, the school and its walls were still there and there was still a (new, impostor!) locker in that space, and yet I felt a profound sense of sadness about the loss of a malfunctioning piece of metal. When something is important to your life, there aren't any unimportant parts. Maybe intellectually, there's a case to be made that the new lockers or the new intentional-walk rule is measurably better, but emotionally, it stung.

When you grow up to be an obsessive baseball junkie like I did, you start to notice the little things and they become a part of you. I find baseball captivating because it provides so many opportunities to look at these seemingly small pieces of life and to recognize what a big impact they can end up having. Change one and the entire game—or your entire self—can change. What might seem irrelevant, like the nitrogen gas that we breathe in and breathe right back out, turns out to have a profound effect that few bothered to notice. There aren't any unimportant pieces. There are just pieces that we haven't yet given their proper attention.

- *8* -

Putting Down the Calculator

RANSOM HALL IS A SMALL, GRAY BUILDING IN THE MIDDLE of Kenyon College, which is in the middle of Knox County, which is in the middle of Ohio, which likes to think of itself as the Midwest. It's perhaps telling that Knox County doesn't have a single mile of interstate highway running through it. It's hard to accidentally end up there.

Ransom Hall housed the admissions department for Kenyon, as well as the registrar's office, where students went to declare their majors. When I eventually declared mine, the clerk on the other side politely nodded as I handed her the form. Her response seemed wildly disconnected from what that paper represented in the story of my life, but for someone who processed major declaration forms all day, I suppose I was just another number.

This was the fall of 1997. My beloved Cleveland Indians were clawing their way toward what would eventually be a heartbreaking Game 7 loss in the World Series, and I was a high school senior looking for a college. My father and I had already established a

ritual of touring some candidate college every Saturday. Distance
didn't matter to my dad. He would have driven to the moon, loved
every minute of it, and bought a t-shirt from their bookstore.
When I expressed interest in seeing some colleges in Philadelphia,
he packed up the car and we started driving east. That day, somewhere in rural Pennsylvania, I learned how to change a flat tire,
by the side of the interstate in the middle of a snowstorm.

This particular weekend, we took the somewhat tamer two-
hour trek down I–71 and State Route 13 and ended up in Ransom
Hall. My father had thought to call ahead, so the admissions department was expecting us. The admissions worker on duty that
day was a fresh-faced 23-year-old recent college graduate named
Jed. Though only six years separated us in age, he appeared to me
a fully formed adult, while I was a mere fledgling. Mr. Jed gave us
the standard tour of campus and he even did a small interview
with me, which I later realized was an admissions interview. I
remember thinking that Mr. Jed was the nicest man named Jed
whom I'd ever met. After the formal interview, we engaged in
some light banter and the topic of baseball came up. Since the
Indians were deep in a playoff run and I was from Cleveland, it
was an obvious go-to topic. Mr. Jed was also a baseball fan and
confided, in a moment of self-disclosure, that his dream job was
to one day work for a team in Major League Baseball. I told him I
had the same dream.

In 2011, 14 years after my first time walking around the campus of what would eventually become my alma mater, I saw the
news that the Chicago Cubs, having recently hired Theo Epstein
to be the President of the team, had also tapped then–San Diego

Padres general manager Jed Hoyer to take a similar position on the North Side. Reading through a profile of Hoyer in one of the Chicago papers, I read that, prior to working in baseball, Hoyer's first job out of college had been as an admissions worker at a small, liberal arts college in the middle of Ohio. Seems that Mr. Jed got his wish.

In the meantime, I was accepted at Kenyon, and at age 18, I moved into the halfway house to adulthood known as the college dorm. A few weeks before the school year started, my parents and I drove down to see my new dorm room, open an account at the local bank, and to get the lay of the land. My mother was most concerned about the fact that this would mark the first time that I had been fully responsible for my own laundry. One of the problems of growing up is that clothes don't magically clean themselves anymore, and so my mother gave me a crash course in that particular aspect of adult life. There were coin-operated washing machines and dryers in the basement, and my mother helpfully pointed out that everyone in college did their laundry on Sunday, so it was best to avoid Sunday.

The time came to do my very first load of laundry on a sunny Saturday afternoon. Three of the tiny basement washers were available and that was enough room to hold all of the clothing in my worldly possession. I remembered my mother's instructions on the intricacies of permanent press. After 45 minutes, the washing part was apparently a success. On to Phase 2! I loaded the now-wet clothes into a dryer, popped in a quarter, and remembered my mother's advice about pushing the "medium heat" button and...nothing happened. I knew that dryers worked their magic by spinning around, but my clothes were apparently not feeling cooperative that day. Here I was, valedictorian of my high school class, trying desperately to figure out how to turn on a dryer.

After five minutes or so, the heavens sent a helpful messenger in the form of a young woman who apparently was also doing her laundry on a Saturday afternoon. While the most straightforward approach would have been to simply admit that I had a small problem and ask for her guidance, I was not nearly mature enough to walk that route. I needed to play this one carefully, so as not to appear silly to the young lady, and more importantly to myself.

"Hi," I began, trying not to startle her. It didn't work. "Hey, have you...ever had any trouble with these machines?" I pointed to the dryer that I had previously spent five minutes quietly lecturing with some four-letter words of Germanic origin. She looked at me puzzled, probably more for the fact that someone had talked to her in the laundry room. I interpreted it as the universal sign for "You idiot." Perhaps both interpretations were correct.

Before she said anything, I continued, "So, I put in the clothes, obviously, and put in the quarter here," pointing, as if there was another place to put the quarter, "and I hit the button, but for some reason, it won't start for me." Perhaps she too had experienced moments of terror in the face of nascent adulthood and decided to take pity on the poor soul who was experiencing his own time of need. Maybe she just wanted me to shut up.

She walked over to the dryer, cocked her head to the side, let out a sigh that most certainly was the universal sign for

"You idiot" and pushed the button clearly marked "START." The dryer obediently began spinning. There are times in life when the fact that you were valedictorian of your high school class won't save you.

I tried unsuccessfully not to blush, but I did thank her for her help. She nodded and walked back up the stairs, never having spoken a word. Adulthood was going great.

LET'S PLAY FAMILY FEUD! NAME SOMETHING THAT YOU need to be able to do on your own in order to be considered a "real" adult. Most people start with things like "cook your own food" or "create a budget" or, for some reason, "do your own taxes." Your list may vary. Now ask yourself at what age (assuming it's in the past) you started doing those things independently. It's likely that you accomplished different items at different ages. That's common. Nothing magical happens on your 18th birthday. Eighteen-year-olds are replacement-level adults.

Scientists who study human development have begun to regognize the concept of *emerging adulthood* as a distinct and important phase of life. This covers the years roughly between ages 18 and 25, but the bigger point is that adulthood is a process, rather than an accomplishment. In my case, I moved into a dorm and was doing my own laundry (once I figured out the dryer) when I was 18, but didn't have my own apartment and wasn't paying my own bills or doing my own taxes until age 22. I knew how to cook a little when I moved to campus, but it wasn't until the summer when I was 21 and I stayed on campus without the meal plan that I was going to the grocery store and cooking for myself every day. I had a bank account at 18, but my parents were at least partially supporting me financially up until I turned 25. At what point did I become a real adult?

Major League teams routinely draft players at the end of their senior year of high school, usually when they are 18. They can sign players from outside the United States at the age of 16. However, even if our teenage prospect is going to eventually make his way to the majors, it's going to take him a few years. In 2017, 262 players made their Major League debut, and the median age of those debutants was 24. In other words, minor league players are likely to be right in the middle of those emerging adulthood years.

The Major League salary structure is set up so that players in their first six years in the big leagues are systematically underpaid. In their first three seasons, players get a minimum salary and have little bargaining power to increase it, even if they put up an MVP level season. In years four through six of their careers, salaries are set by an arbitration system that is widely known to underpay young players, compared to what they might receive if they were free agents. Teams have millions of incentives to make sure that when their young players reach the majors, they are able to contribute as much value as possible.

Plenty of the development that goes on in the minor leagues is related to baseball skills. Coaches are trying to teach pitching prospects how to throw a good slider, but does anyone teach them how to drink alcohol responsibly? If not, will our pitcher show up hungover for his bullpen session the next day? Maybe he just doesn't know how to do laundry and feels self-conscious all the time because his clothes stink. Maybe he's distracted while his coach is trying to show him this one weird trick to get the ball to break a little more. Maybe our prospect is putting on too much weight. Maybe he's feeling lonely and depressed and has a hard time concentrating on learning to hit line drives.

We most often encounter baseball players as little blobs of pixels that run around our TV screens or as characters in video games who obediently swing when we hit the "A" button. The reality is that players do not go into hibernation between the hours of 10:00 PM and 7:00 PM. These are men who go home to significant others, shave, eat breakfast, and walk the dog. They have thoughts and insecurities and hobbies and (gasp!) political beliefs. Some of them are cooking their own food for the first time. Some of them are away from home for the first time. Some of them are living in a foreign country. Some of them are probably wondering how they ended up in Iowa.

Teams need to think about both player development and *human* development. While there will never be a database on how well minor leaguers are mastering adulthood the same way there are databases on how well they are mastering striking hitters out, we are not totally adrift in trying to understand this issue better. The Centers for Disease Control and Prevention (CDC) regularly conduct surveys of high school students as part of their Youth Risk Behavior Surveillance System (YRBSS). This survey asks a nationally representative sample of youth about their experiences with certain health habits and risky behaviors. Using data from 2015, we find that among 12th grade males:

- 20 percent had been in a car with a driver who had been drinking alcohol and 12 percent had driven after drinking alcohol in the past 30 days.

- 9 percent had an episode in the last 30 days where they drank 10 or more drinks in one sitting. (Five drinks is generally considered a "binge" drinking episode, and 26 percent of respondents reported doing this within the past 30 days.)

- 12 percent had made a suicide plan in the last 12 months and 1.4 percent had made an attempt that resulted in them receiving medical attention. Nearly a quarter (24 percent) reported that they felt sad and lonely almost every day for at least two weeks.

- 43 percent did not use a condom during their last sexual intercourse. Another study (also conducted by the CDC, though not using the same data source) found that among adolescent females, more than 80 percent of those who were sexually active had not received any formal sex education prior to their first time having sex and 9 percent reported no formal sex education at all by the age of 17. It's likely that the number of males who can say the same is similar.

- 7 percent had eaten *no vegetables at all* in the past seven days.

- 77 percent averaged fewer than eight hours of sleep in the past seven days.

Not everyone has one of these risk factors present in their lives. However, some high school seniors do and some are going to be reporting to Rookie Ball after the June Draft. Most of them will be navigating the world of adult decision-making for the first time. What happens if they are already engaging in risky behaviors or have undiagnosed mental health needs? What if they have developed eating and sleep habits which aren't really compatible with peak athletic performance? What if one of them never had "The Talk" growing up?

Fortunately, there's plenty of research on topics like how to encourage people to have safer sex or engage in responsible drinking that are proven to work in the "real world." Many of them would likely work in the context of a baseball team as well, but as any good public health worker will tell you, understanding the culture of the people whom you are trying to reach is vital to tailoring a program so that it will both reach people's ears and change their behavior.

IN THE SUMMER OF 2014, I SET OUT TO RESEARCH THE question of how MLB teams approach these human development issues. I put in some phone calls and emails to some very gracious (and anonymous) "friends" who worked in player development and baseball operations departments for Major League teams. Later that year, I presented my work at an annual gathering of baseball researchers known as SaberSeminar. I also used a very different research method. There were no numbers to draw on, so I used a *qualitative* rather than *quantitative* approach. I started with a list of questions to ask, but let the conversation wander where it may. My goal wasn't to solve the issue or to calculate the answer to the third decimal place, but to understand the problem better. I was doing research...without a calculator.

A few things came up over and over again. For one, players come into an organization with a wide range of "adult-ing" skills. Some draftees are college seniors who are 22 and have already been living a thousand miles from home. On the flip side, there may also be a player who is 17, and is not only living apart from his parents for the first time, but also living in the United States for the first time. He might have been so focused on baseball since the time he was 12 that he effectively missed out on a lot of adolescence too. How does a team craft its instructional programs so that it doesn't waste the time of the 22-year-old, but meets the needs of the 17-year-old?

There's also a language and culture issue to be considered. Baseball is a game already played in two primary languages (English and Spanish), and with the further global expansion of the game, more are being added. On top of that, there are cultural differences in how people define being an adult, to say nothing about cultural differences in approaching difficult, sometimes taboo, subjects. Remember that we're talking about topics like alcohol, sex, and mental health. How does a team start a conversation about responsible alcohol use when one player has grown up with parents who completely abstained from drinking and another who grew up having a glass of wine every night with dinner?

Teams tended to take a very pragmatic approach to the subject. They were of course concerned about issues like substance abuse, cultural assimilation, and healthy eating, but one front office member talked extensively about how his department saw teaching anger management as its most important mission. His logic was simple. There are 25 young men who have to live in close physical proximity to each other every day. In the minor leagues, long bus rides are a way of life. There will be conflict between people and it's best that they know how to diffuse it before it gets out of hand. Other teams stressed that they had invested in language learning software for their minor leaguers, with the hope of both teaching Spanish-speaking players to speak English and teaching their English-speaking players to speak Spanish. Those skills help on the field *and* in building relationships among teammates.

Then, I came to the question of how to convey this information. In public health prevention work, the message is usually pretty obvious ("Don't drink and drive"). The hard part is how to frame the message in a way that the audience will listen to it. When I spoke to my informants, they began talking like public health workers.

Most teams held informational seminars for minor leaguers and rookies during Spring Training, for the twin reasons that it was one of the few times that everyone in the organization was in the same place and that it was at the beginning of the work year. Teams differed in how they got the message out. Some had "a couple of meetings" while others had dedicated weekly seminar time. Some teams used the "everyone in a room" approach, while others tried to identify good candidates for one-to-one meetings.

Then there was the question of who the messenger should be. For example, when discussing good nutrition, was it better to have someone with a degree in sports nutrition science or was it better to have a former player who knew a little bit about healthy eating? The nutritionist is a subject matter expert and would be able to answer more questions. The ex-player might be more relatable to the people in the room who needed to hear the message.

In 2015, the Washington Nationals hired former Major League pitcher-turned-outfielder Rick Ankiel to fill a newly created role of "life skills coordinator." Ankiel had developed a reputation as a good teammate and "clubhouse guy" during his playing days and his new job was to travel the Nationals' minor league system and talk to players about how life was going. Where he was able, he could offer advice from the perspective of someone who had "been there." When needed, he was a conduit between the players and management. If a team can benefit from having strong connective tissue between the players and the help that they might need, Ankiel was hired to be that connective tissue. Clearly, the Nationals believed that Ankiel's credibility as someone who can say "I've been through the same things that you are going through" was more important than having a degree. It's better to give someone with that kind of credibility a crash course in being a good social worker rather than the other way around. The credibility of the messenger matters more than their credentials.

Beyond the Spring Training seminar sessions lay another question. Once March is over, there are another six months until the end of the season. What to do when the warm glow of being in a real Spring Training camp has worn off and now it's just another day on the road? What to do with the player who isn't hitting well and hasn't really become friends with any of the other guys on the team? He feels isolated and lonely and maybe it's starting to creep in to his play. How can a team best reach out to him?

Again, the teams that I spoke to were prepared for these issues. Many spoke of having point people embedded in the organization. Some had one person who was chosen because the team believed that she or he was "approachable." Some referred their players to the person who would most likely be able to handle such an issue (e.g., questions about diet were referred to the team trainer).

As someone who has worked in mental health, I was struck by how much a Major League organization resembled a public health agency. There were outreach workers and case managers and interventionists (though none of them called themselves that) who were all trying to identify and fix problems. Teams had well-reasoned prevention and intervention strategies. We often think of Major League teams as doing nothing more than seeking out baseball talent to acquire. What I found was that teams are hiding an entire social services structure inside their walls!

It's tempting to begin the next paragraph with a discussion of "Which team is doing the best job?" I think that's the wrong question. There is, of course, a wrong way to do things, but there isn't one correct answer. When trying to set up a system that connects players who need help with the help that's available, the biggest barrier is often just getting the player himself to say the words "I need help." It doesn't help that United States culture, particularly United States *male* culture, sends plenty of messages equating asking for help with weakness and failure. In a baseball context, the people a player might feel comfortable approaching might also be the ones controlling his playing time. Once a player admits that he needs help, connecting him to the right resources is a matter of a couple of phone calls. What I came to realize was that it mattered little how those connections were set up. It's going to look different from team to team, and that's okay. What really seemed to matter was the strength of that connective tissue.

At the end of my phone calls, I didn't walk away with an answer. I walked away with something much more valuable than that. I learned how to conceptualize the problem. Sometimes, it's better to put down the calculator and to ask a few questions. As St. Yogi of the Bronx reminded us, "You can observe a lot by watching." A baseball team might not look like a social services agency, but there are plenty of parallels. Thankfully, there's already plenty of research in the real world about how to run a good social services agency. It doesn't take much imagination to see how improving those services could eventually lead to real value on the field. While teams don't often talk about these issues, they do invest in them.

WRITING IN HIS 2010 BOOK *THE BULLPEN GOSPELS*, FORMER major (and minor) league pitcher Dirk Hayhurst recounted his time in the minors, particularly his life off the field. While a few minor league players—generally those taken in the high rounds of drafts—are given multi-million dollar bonuses and can draw from those to support themselves, most minor leaguers sign for a few thousand dollars and live on small minor league salaries. For meals, Hayhurst reported that he and his teammates were given a small per diem allowance and told to fend for themselves. Not surprisingly, with little money and a job that required the expenditure of a lot of energy, players often settled for cheap, calorie dense, but nutritionally questionable fast food, especially when they were on the road. At that point, they had few options for getting food other than where the team bus happened to drop them off. When I read that, it surprised me.

The effects of poor nutrition run deep. Weight gain puts extra stress on the body, particularly the joints, which can lead to a greater likelihood of injuries. There have been several prospects who have lost their blue-chip status to the potato chip. Poor nutrition also has other not-so-obvious consequences, which take the form of things that *fail* to happen. There's a rather apt comparison here: In many places, school districts offer breakfast to low-income students who might be coming to school hungry. A hungry child will have trouble learning, and school boards have realized it's cheaper to offer breakfast than it is to bear the costs of kids repeating grades or eventually dropping out of school. If kids in school need proper nutrition to learn, shouldn't minor leaguers?

Minor leaguers are trying to develop pattern recognition and muscle-memory skills that will make them better baseball players. Learning requires the construction of new synaptic pathways in the brain and the brain needs raw materials to build these neural links. More nutritious food means more raw materials with which the body can work. A well-cared-for body sleeps better, and sleep is the time when the body and brain consolidate what they learned all day. Every day where a player doesn't have a proper meal or a good night of sleep means a lost opportunity for laying down a few synaptic pathways. Those are the hidden cognitive effects of poor nutrition and rest. It's the slow creep of what might have been, but wasn't. Over a day, it won't be apparent. Over a few years, it's not that a player will fail to develop, but that perhaps *he could have been more*. Teams were shooting themselves in the foot. Slowly.

A few years after Hayhurst wrote his book, news stories started popping up about teams making investments in providing better food for their minor leaguers. I don't know that Hayhurst prompted the change as much as simple math did. After all, the math wasn't all that hard. Most teams have seven minor league affiliates. If we assume that each team has 30 players and coaches, and that they are playing for the team for 180 days out of the year, and that it would cost $50 per person per day to have a healthy catered lunch and dinner brought to the players, that comes to $1.9 million in costs per year. Add in the cost of someone whose job is to coordinate all that and the full cost would be around $2 million. It might be a little more or less, but that's the correct order of magnitude.

Two million dollars is not an inconsequential amount of money, but we need to think of it in baseball terms. Teams routinely spend $2 million on a utility infielder or a back-of-the-bullpen reliever from the free agent pool that they don't actually want. If being more food secure is the push that *one* of a team's 200 minor leaguers who might not have been quite major league material needs to make him good enough to sit on the end of a bench, then they can forego paying that $2 million in free agency. Any other benefit that they get is frosting on the cake.

Then there's the issue of rest. Baseball has the unique challenge of being a daily sport. Football games come but once a week. Basketball and hockey players might play three or four games within a week, and even when they do play on back-to-back nights, it's rare that they would play a game 15 hours after finishing the previous one. In baseball, this is known as "Sunday." Baseball is a game that is set up to reward the well-rested.

All sports involve physical effort, which will be affected by fatigue, but baseball demands something else. Players spend large amounts of time waiting for something to happen, not being entirely sure when it will. When it does, a player needs to react quickly to run and track down that fly ball. That sort of vigilant concentration is hard to maintain even when a player is *well*-rested. When the body is malnourished or tired, the brain begins playing a game of triage with cognitive functions. The first ones to go are the more complicated neurological functions, like attention, pattern recognition, and planning/decision-making, followed by fine motor control. Those are skills that really need to be functioning at top efficiency when playing baseball.

Teams have begun tackling this one too. In 2013, the Boston Red Sox built a "sleep room" in Fenway Park, so that tired Red Sox players could take a nap on the job. Baseball will always have a demanding travel schedule, and a quick nap isn't going to make all of the fatigue go away, but even if it sharpens players' abilities a little bit, the effect is probably worth more to the team than the cost of hiring a contractor to redo a room.

In 2015, newly hired Los Angeles Dodgers director of player development (and former outfielder) Gabe Kapler made news when he announced that all Dodgers minor league affiliates would have a Spanish-speaking coach on staff. For a league in which 34.5 percent of the players on Opening Day rosters in 2017 were born outside the United States, most of them in countries where Spanish was the primary language, it seemed strange to think that teams *wouldn't* routinely have a Spanish-speaking coach on staff, but that's what he found. Perhaps the Dodgers had previously balked at the cost of an "extra" coach on each minor league affiliate's staff. Kapler's calculation was that whatever that cost was, the ability to communicate directly with the team's Spanish-speaking prospects was more valuable.

The 2010s may end up being remembered for other things, but I think the most enduring legacy of the decade might be one that no one sees: the shift in the way that teams view the proper care and feeding of their players, especially their young players. Programs that might have once been seen as unnecessary costs were instead reframed as chances to realize on-field value at a cost that was much lower than that of the free agent market. Baseball is a hard game to play even in the best of circumstances, but especially when you're hungry, tired, and have no idea what the manager is saying. Why not make it easier?

BASEBALL IS A PHYSICAL GAME, BUT AS ST. YOGI OF THE Bronx again reminds us, "Ninety percent of the game is half mental." Baseball requires the ability to recognize patterns and to anticipate what the pitcher is going to do next. It takes the ability to formulate and execute a plan to get the hitter out. It takes restraint and impulse control to learn to lay off a pitch. It takes good judgment and emotional regulation skills to navigate the inevitable highs and lows of a baseball season. All of those things are known in neuropsychology as "executive" functions and are governed by a part of the brain known as the prefrontal cortex (PFC).

If you smack your forehead (gently, please) with the palm of your hand, the PFC is on the other side. It's the part that does all the complex stuff that we humans are so proud of as a species. This particular area of the brain goes through a great deal of development when a person is in their twenties—or for the purposes of the current conversation, the time when teams are desperately trying to sculpt their lumps of athletic clay into fully formed masterpieces capable of winning a Cy Young Award.

On average, men stop growing physically around the age of 17, which means that when Major League teams are out scouting high school seniors, they can get a decent idea of what a player's body type is before drafting him. He might add muscle later on, but the basic "frame" is there. On the other hand, the human brain continues to develop into a person's early thirties, meaning that a young baseball player is far from a finished human being. In fact, he's in the middle of a neurological growth spurt. Teams looking at an 18-year-old high schooler might have a pretty good idea what he will *look* like at age 27, but will have a harder time projecting what he will be *thinking* like.

Neurological and cognitive development is not a gradual, linear, standardized process. It can defy prediction. It happens in fits and spurts. It happens at different times for everyone, just like it did in junior high. We normally think of baseball player development as a physical, rather than as a neurological, process, but both end up being important. There are players whose PFCs develop more quickly, and they are better able to use those high-end mental skills that turn a raw athlete into a ball player. Some 19-year-olds are ahead of the curve; some 35-year-olds *still* haven't gotten there.

Baseball is aware of this effect, even if they don't frame it as a neuroanatomy lesson. Scouts often tout a kid with good "makeup," despite having difficulty describing what "makeup" is. It's often a player who "doesn't get too high or too low" (i.e., he has good emotional regulation skills) or a player who has great work ethic (i.e., he's able to focus on and plan for long-term, rather than short-term, goals), things that sound to my psychologist ears like the effects of a well-developed PFC. On the other end of the player life cycle, one wonders whether "clubhouse guys," often veterans on the wrong side of 35, are prized specifically because from the perspective of PFC development, they are on the good side of 35!

In fact, baseball is rather pointedly aware of the role that the PFC plays in the game. The Joint Drug Agreement (JDA) between Major League Baseball and the MLB Players Union specifically bans the use of certain stimulants, including Adderall and Ritalin, which are commonly prescribed to treat Attention Deficit/Hyperactivity Disorder (ADHD, also commonly called by its older name ADD). Players can be suspended for the illicit use of these drugs in the same way that they are suspended for the use of steroids. Adderall and Ritalin are medications which are specifically meant to affect the PFC.

There are legitimate reasons that an adult might have a prescription for Adderall. There is a great misperception that ADHD is only a disorder of childhood. Indeed, clinicians used to believe that people "outgrew" ADHD. It turns out that ADHD never really goes away. Some people need Adderall to control their ADHD symptoms in adulthood, and yes, some of them are professional baseball players. There's a therapeutic exemption rule in the JDA for players who are using the drug under the guidance of a doctor, because it would be cruel to deprive people of medicine that they really need. Reports have suggested that 9 percent of MLB players have such an exemption, even though prevalence estimates from the National Institutes for Mental Health suggest that slightly more than 4 percent of adults in the United States currently have the disorder.

People are often surprised to learn that ADHD is not a disorder of "having too much energy." Children and adolescents who have the disorder do often run around as if they are driven by a little motor, but the problem isn't that the gas pedal has been pushed to the floor. The problem is with *the brakes*. Neurological research on ADHD has shown that the area of the brain tasked with *inhibiting* behavior—the one that stops you from following any impulsive thought you might have or paying attention to whatever shiny object appears in the room—is compromised in some way. That area is in the prefrontal cortex.

People are also often surprised to hear that a disorder of "too much energy" is treated with a stimulant. While ADHD medications are stimulants in the chemical sense, they work by targeting the prefrontal cortex and stimulating the brakes. For children and adults who have ADHD, the medication brings the activity level in that part of the brain up to where it needs to be. Under proper physician care, stimulant medication can help people to live up to their full potential. Once the brakes are working, it's a lot easier to focus.

Like all drugs, Adderall and Ritalin can also be abused. Some people crush the pills and snort them, with effects (and side effects) much like those that stem from snorting other stimulants. Others take the drug in pill form, and sure enough, it goes to the prefrontal cortex, where it stimulates the parts of the brain that regulate focus, just like it was designed to do. College students have been known to use the drug when pulling all-nighters specifically for these focus-improving effects. Those effects probably have a certain allure for baseball players as well. In a game where sustained attention is required and rest is often at a premium, it's not surprising that some players turn to Adderall when caffeine and "energy drinks" just won't do. The problem is that if someone does not actually need these medications, taking them will *over*stimulate that part of the brain, and that can have serious neurological side effects.

The question of whether performance-enhancing drugs *should* be allowed in baseball is one that's beyond the scope of this book, but it's telling that while drugs that helped players to build their bodies got most of the headlines in the 1990s and 2000s, players were also using drugs that worked on their brains. It's a quiet admission that baseball is a game of thought and focus, in addition to being a game of running and throwing. If there are ways that teams can (safely, legally) help their players improve as physical athletes, they would be silly not to do so. At the same time, if there are ways that teams can (safely, legally) help their players improve their mental functioning, they should do that as well. One of the next frontiers in understanding baseball will be understanding that mental development process, and perhaps figuring out additional ways to support and nurture that development and brain functioning. The science of baseball is beginning to acknowledge that St. Yogi of the Bronx was right all along. Ninety percent of the game really is half mental, and all of this squishy-mental-brainy-feelings stuff has real value.

IN 2015, MAJOR LEAGUE BASEBALL ADVANCED MEDIA INTRO-duced the StatCast system to the baseball-watching world. The slightly Orwellian information-gathering apparatus collected real-time positioning data for the ball, the batter, the runners, and all nine fielders as each play of a game unfolded. It was now possible to track how hard the batter hit that line drive and how fast and how far the center fielder had to run to snare it. As cool as that level of detail is and as many questions as it may help us answer, it can't tell us everything.

For example, how does a player handle things when he has a bad at-bat? Does he sulk or does he get over it? How does he get over it? Baseball is, after all, a game of failure. There's the oft-repeated line that Hall of Famers fail seven out of 10 times

and if you can get down to six in 10, you're a legend. But failure doesn't feel nice, especially when you hit a ball to the wall,
only to have someone make an amazing catch to steal away your
home run. It's perfectly natural to feel a little disappointed in
that situation. Often, it results in someone yelling out *that* word.
The F-word. "Fiddlesticks!"

Now, "Fiddlesticks!" is a very salty word and perhaps not
fit for polite company, but sometimes doo-doo happens and
you just have to yell it. And so, I would humbly request that
StatCast should begin recording instances of when players say
"Fiddlesticks!" That might revolutionize our understanding of
baseball more than knowing a player's top running speed.

Consider for a moment what screaming "Fiddlesticks!" does
for a person. After a disappointment, whether a lost game or a
lost at-bat, a player might naturally feel anger. These guys got
where they are by being extremely competitive and they just lost
a competition. Anger needs an escape valve. In the therapy room,
the best way to handle anger isn't to tell a person not to get angry.
You work with them to find a way to let the anger out construc-
tively, or at least non-destructively. More than once, I actually
suggested to someone that (when no one was around) they yell
out "Fiddlesticks!" as a way to release anger.

Humans are creatures of ritual, especially when confronted
with strong emotions. When someone dies, we have funeral rituals. When someone leaves for the day, we have separation rituals.
When we are anxious, we have all sorts of superstitious rituals.
That's how humans manage emotion. Rituals might seem silly,
but they serve a very important function. Rituals take all of that

negative emotion and allow a person to *do something with it*, even if that *something* is just yelling out a word. That negative emotion becomes part of the ritual act.

Screaming "Fiddlesticks!" allows a person to take all of that pent-up angry energy and divert it into...screaming. It's a forbidden and rather violent word to yell, so the screamer gets the satisfaction of doing something naughty, but the word disappears into the air. No one gets hurt and everyone can move on with life. That's important in a game that doesn't really stop. A pitcher who gives up a home run has about 45 seconds before he has to throw another pitch. He can't be sitting out there beating himself up or stewing over the fact that he gave up a gopher ball. He has to get over it. Soon. Sometimes that means screaming "Fiddlesticks!" into the air in front of 40,000 people.

What I'm really talking about here is one of those executive functions I mentioned earlier. In this case, the ability to regulate emotion. Over the course of a three-hour game (and a six-month season), there will be highs and there will be lows. It's hard enough trying to get enough sleep while playing baseball without lying awake at night thinking about the ball that got away. Baseball requires intense focus. There's little room for being distracted, because it really is a game of inches played at insane speeds. It might seem strange that we're in the middle of a sports book talking about feelings, but the ability to manage emotion is important. It may only have a small effect here and a small effect there, but over time, as our second rule of probabilistic thinking reminds us, a little plus a little plus a little eventually adds up to a lot.

The problem is that we have absolutely no data to study whether shouting "Fiddlesticks!" might make a difference. There's a reasonable case to be made that emotional-regulation skills can have an impact on a player's performance, the same way that his running speed can. We're good at measuring the things that a player does with his body, but not his mind. Just because something is hard to measure, it doesn't mean that it's not important. What if all that mental and emotional stuff is the key to identifying value that no one knows is there? In a perfect world, we perhaps have a "Fiddlesticks!" Index (FI), or perhaps a "Fiddlesticks!" Utterance in the Context of a Strikeout Percentage to work with. It might provide a way for a team to get some low-cost wins, just by identifying guys who are good at yelling "Fiddlesticks!"

*   *   *

EVEN FOR RESEARCHERS LIKE ME WHO LOVE A GOOD MATH problem, sometimes it's best to put down the calculator and pay attention to the human element of the game. Not everything in life can be solved with 10 million lines of data and yet another semipronounceable acronym. Not everything in the game is about physical motion. Sometimes you're dealing with things that don't fit neatly into numbers...and that's okay. There have been very few numbers in this chapter (by design) and we've still learned some things about baseball. The point of baseball research should never be to somehow reduce baseball players to number-generating algorithms. They're people too, even though a lot of times, fans forget that. We should embrace that humanity and all the messy complexity that goes with it.

We also want to do that in a way that doesn't fall for sappy narratives that sometimes pass for "analysis" in sports. That scrappy minor leaguer isn't now raking in the majors because he wished for it harder than anyone else. It was not preordained by something that his Little League coach said when he was eight. There are lots of Little League coaches who make lots of prophecies about lots of kids and lots of them turn out to be wrong. There's a middle ground somewhere between viewing baseball players as random number generators and viewing them as fairy tale characters. That's where we find the real "human element."

It's possible to appreciate the humanity in a baseball player *and* be scientific about it. We know that baseball players are going through a period of growth and development. We know that their mental makeup can have an effect on their play. We know that managing emotion is important, even if we can't gather data on it in a baseball context. We know all of this because baseball players are human and we have information about humans who *don't* play baseball to draw from. If you take nothing else away from this book, let it be this: To do proper science about the game of baseball, you eventually have to account for the humanity of the players who play the game and that is not a contradiction at all. It's an opportunity.

– *9* –

Did You Say "Guessing"?

IN 2009, I HAD AN OPPORTUNITY THAT MOST PEOPLE don't get. I became a major leaguer.

Sort of.

By that point, I was *almost* "Dr. Carleton," although 2009 wasn't the best time to be graduating into the labor market. I had swung and missed a few times looking around for psychology post-docs and was staring to get frustrated. One day at the dinner table, my wife—who was in the middle of her own post-doc—suggested that since I'd always loved "the baseball thing" I should see if any MLB teams were hiring. By that point, I had done some of my own independent research on baseball, and so in a fit of naiveté, I put together 30 packets containing my resume and a few of the "greatest hits" from my research and cold sent them to 30 general managers.

Back then, there was still a separation between teams who had embraced the power of data in their decision-making process and those who hadn't. There were a few teams who had an "analytics department," but not everyone was there yet. I got a few formal "Thanks, but no thanks" letters back and a particularly emphatic response from one (now former) general manager who said in no uncertain terms that if his team ever decided to go away from using time-honored methods for player evaluation, he might consider giving me a call. He never called back.

A few weeks after I sent out that volley of resume packets, I literally got a call from up the street. I was finishing my clinical internship at an agency in downtown Cleveland where I could see the light towers of Jacobs Field from the parking lot. It was the Cleveland Indians calling. They wanted to talk. Six-year-old me was over the moon. So was 29-year-old me. Maybe they'd even let me play third base.

The next week, I was sitting in the front office—or at least I was sitting in the conference room in the front office. The Indians had read my work and were impressed. They already had an analytics department with a couple of dedicated employees, but they wanted to know if I was interested in doing some freelance projects for them. They would send me questions and I would use my magical spreadsheet powers to answer them. Since they asked nicely, I agreed.

I have to be upfront about how truly tangential my involvement was in the Indians' front office. I did work on projects and communicated my findings back to them, but I wasn't in the middle of the "fun stuff." A simple story will perhaps illustrate my very limited role.

In July 2011, the Indians sent pitchers Alex White and Drew Pomeranz, along with two other prospects, to the Colorado Rockies in a trade deadline deal for starter Ubaldo Jimenez. At that point, White and Pomeranz represented the two most recent first round picks that the Indians had made. A deal of that magnitude doesn't just happen in five minutes via a few text messages, fantasy-baseball style. It's likely that Indians then–general manager (and eventually club president) Chris Antonetti said to the front office staff, "We're thinking about Ubaldo."

There were probably a few others names on that list as well. He probably asked for some research from "the stats people" before they went ahead with the deal. I keep saying "probably" because I don't know for sure. I found out that the Indians were interested in Jimenez by reading the website MLB Trade Rumors and found out that the trade had happened when I got back from a family gathering and saw a news story. So yes, I was (sorta) a major leaguer and I have the tax documents to prove it, but I was also on the very edges of it all.

When people find out that I worked "on the inside," I often get *that* question. "How can I get hired by a Major League team?" There's always a bit of mystery surrounding "the front office" of a baseball team. It's kind of like being an astronaut. Sure, someone's in those spacesuits, but how did they even get there? I understand where the urge comes from. You love baseball. You hate your job. Two birds. One spacesuit. On top of that, we live in a culture where there is a multi-billion-dollar industry based around people pretending that they are general managers of teams that don't actually exist. There are discussion boards where people argue about what they would have done were they the general manager. If you'd be willing to spend your free time doing it, why not do it for real and get paid for it? It's not quite that easy.

The GM holds an odd space culturally. There is at once a reverence for the GM of the local nine that's mixed with a strong conviction by just about everyone else in town that they could do a better job. At least Ed from Lakewood thinks he could do better. The reality of working in baseball isn't as glamorous as the fantasy. Yes, these are people who get paid to think about baseball all day. Yes, they get to go to the games for free, but there are days where even the most fanatical baseball lover wants to think about something else. When you're a fan, if you don't want to think about baseball, you have the option to turn the game off. You can pay attention to just the fun parts of the game (exciting trade discussions!) and leave aside the more mundane stuff (scouting reports on a bunch of mediocre high schoolers!).

The actual office, aside from the baseball-themed décor, is... an office. There are cubicles and computers and a water cooler and people in business casual attire. They are, after all, running a business. They just have team logos printed on their polo shirts. There truly are some brilliant people wearing those shirts, but like Oz behind the curtain, they are mostly just guys from Nebraska talking about baseball and hot air balloons. A lot of times it's just people doing work. It can be boring. Sorry to ruin the fantasy.

When all you do is think about the fun parts (and the parts that are visible to the average fan), it's easy to believe that being a GM must be such a hoot. In reality, a GM and most of the rest of the staff spend most of their days thinking about and doing things that the average fan probably doesn't even realize are part of running a team.

Which area scout should we send to cover New Mexico? How's our catcher in AA progressing? Has he learned to stop swinging at every slider out of the zone? We might need him to be our backup backstop in three years. If things aren't going well, we might need to have "potential backup catcher" as something we pursue in trade talks this year. If we don't do something about the situation, it might mean that in three years, we'll need to divert $1 million to signing a backup, and that affects how big of an extension we can give to our budding superstar that we want to keep around. That's the kind of thing that you're signing up for. Can you think about baseball at *that* detailed of a level?

Almost everyone in the front office enters through the internship door, and the competition, even for those internship spots, is intense. Taking an internship—some of which are unpaid, others which pay near minimum wage—likely means moving to another city and spending a year or more living with a minimal or non-existent income. It probably means either drawing on previous savings, if you have them, to cover living expenses, or asking someone else to help support you, if you have someone in your life who can do that. At the end of the internship, there's no guarantee of a job. The hours can be long in part because, like working in a restaurant, the times when your company is producing its main product are the times when everyone else is going out *after work* and wants to be entertained. There's also a lot to do and much of it isn't very interesting.

Because there are a lot of people who want to work in baseball and who would be willing to do so for peanuts (and Cracker Jack), teams take them up on that fact. People earn less working for a baseball team than they could earn working in the "real world." Working in baseball also means giving up geographic control of your life. There are only 30 Major League teams in 26 cities (sorry, Oakland and Anaheim, you aren't fooling anyone). You need to be ready to move, across the country (or to Canada!) wherever there's an opening. Job security is a 68–94 season away from vanishing. If the owner decides to fire the general manager and "clean house," that means real people—and in this fantasy world, you—are losing their jobs. Baseball is a tough business to be in.

However, if the last couple of paragraphs haven't deterred you, the best advice I can give you about how to land a job in baseball goes like this: it's not enough to "love baseball" and "be willing to do anything" for a team. That describes 99 percent of the applicants and maybe more. Instead, it's important to think about what sort of work you actually want to do for a team. This is a job, after all. Teams don't pay people to sit around and pinch themselves because "I'm working for a team!"

You might be interested in scouting or athletic training or "the big data thing," but it pays to first become familiar with what a front office actually does and to develop some idea of how your unique skills and perspective might add value to a team. It's not helpful if you are simply well-read on what's been posted on the internet. Everyone in the front office can read. It's not enough to say that you'd be "willing to learn." You most certainly will learn things, but you also need to make the case that you add value that the team can't get anywhere else.

It helps to network as much as you can, but even then, that's no guarantee. Whether it's cosmically fair or not, it's often whom, rather than what, you know that lets you break into the system. Some teams advertise their internship openings and some don't. The ones that do can get more than a thousand applicants for one spot, and it's hard to filter through that many resumes in any reasonable way. Sometimes it's just easier to skip that part and go to the step where you ask around the office if anyone knows of anyone who might be a good fit. That might strike people as unfair, but it's reality.

Ed from Lakewood, if you still really want to work in a front office, I have one piece of advice. This is really hard work. Yes, there are some fun parts, but to acquire the depth of knowledge needed to do it means years of immersion deep in "the weeds" of baseball, the kind that normally removes one from being considered "an idiot" as you so graciously referred to the current GM yesterday. There are no perfect people in front offices, and yes, sometimes what they do doesn't work out, but I assure you, there are no fools in the front office either.

WHAT IS A GENERAL MANAGER WORTH?

This might be the hardest question to answer in the game of baseball. Players are comparatively easy to evaluate. We know everything that they did on the field and we can assign value to it. What about a general manager who spends most days behind closed doors in that baseball-themed office at the ballpark? When there's a trade or a free agent signing, that becomes a matter of public record, but what about all of the trades that the GM says "no" to? We rarely hear about those. How do we account for a GM who is smart enough to *not do* something stupid?

To complement our lack of information, we also lack a baseline for comparing a GM's performance. With players, everyone faces the same group of pitchers (or batters). If the GM hits big on the first pick in the draft but every other GM would have drafted the same player, is that brilliance shining through or just the luck of having the first pick? Since a team only has one general manager at a time, we never get to know what even one other GM would have done, much less a sufficiently large comparison group. We'll also never know what one team's GM would have done given a different set of circumstances. It's easy to lionize a general manager who just won a World Series, but maybe Ed from Lakewood really could have done just as well. We have no way to prove any of it.

One thing is clear. We have to evaluate the front office in a completely different way than we evaluate players. That doesn't mean that we can't look into the front office, by the numbers, and learn something. We just need to shift the kinds of questions that we ask. Even if we can't evaluate individual general managers the same way we do players, maybe we can at least learn something about the game by studying them.

There are three ways for a general manager to find players for the MLB roster: the player-development system, trades, and free agents. Trades end up being difficult to evaluate, because the most commonly made trade in MLB is one in which a team exchanges present value (usually a veteran on an expiring contract) for future value (minor league prospects). That usually means that to see the full results of a trade, we have to wait most of a decade for the prospects to mature and then play out their cost-controlled years for their new team. Sometimes, the team acquiring the veteran doesn't win the World Series they were hoping for. Sometimes, the prospects don't pan out. Sometimes both. By the time the full effects of the trade are known, both GMs are likely to have been fired already.

In the last chapter, we talked about how the economics of the game favor teams who are able to extract value from their young players. In an ideal world, a general manger would always have a bunch of young, cost-controlled superstars on his roster, but that's not how it often happens. That leaves our GM needing to sign a few free agents, and it turns out that the behavior of GMs (and owners) in the free agent market is a surprising case study in the collision between economic theory and actual human behavior.

In theory, a market should develop a sensible price structure for the goods that it is selling. Since the turn of the millennium, there has been a shift toward teams valuing free agents based on metrics like wins above replacement (WAR), which consider all the ways in which a player can add value, rather than single-skill numbers like home run totals. WAR has the advantage of being denominated in the one thing that teams ultimately care about: wins. Teams can reasonably project how many wins they expect a free agent to be worth, and then make decisions about where their needs are, but the market will eventually settle on a price per win—for the most part.

Work by researcher Matt Swartz suggests that the price of a win on the 2017 free agent market was around $10 million. The price-per-win number has changed each year as more money pours into the game, but it's generally accepted that a free agent third baseman whom we might expect to be a "one win" player might expect an annual salary around $10 million. That "$10 million per win" shorthand has its limits. MVP level players, who should be the best paid players in the game, usually put up seasons of seven or eight wins. If the rest of the market is getting $10 million per win and if the market is fully rational, there should be players with annual salaries in excess of $70 million. Even if the players that get those salaries don't turn out to be the best in the game (teams have to commit to a salary *before* the merchandise is delivered), the top end of the salary chart should be in that neighborhood. Instead, in 2017, the highest paid player in MLB was Clayton Kershaw, with a salary of $35.6 million. That's a nice paycheck, but perhaps he should make twice that?

Table 43. Highest MLB Salaries, by Year

Year	Highest paid player	Salary	Second highest	Salary	Third highest	Salary
2006	Alex Rodriguez	$21.7M	Derek Jeter	$20.6M	Jason Giambi	$20.4M
2007	Jason Giambi	$23.4M	Alex Rodriguez	$22.7M	Derek Jeter	$21.6M
2008	Alex Rodriguez	$28.0M	Jason Giambi	$23.4M	Derek Jeter	$21.6M
2009	Alex Rodriguez	$33.0M	Manny Ramirez	$23.9M	Derek Jeter	$21.6M
2010	Alex Rodriguez	$33.0M	CC Sabathia	$24.3M	Derek Jeter	$22.6M
2011	Alex Rodriguez	$32.0M	Vernon Wells	$26.2M	CC Sabathia	$24.3M
2012	Alex Rodriguez	$29.0M	Johan Santana	$24.0M	Prince Fielder	$23.0M
2013	Alex Rodriguez	$28.0M	Cliff Lee	$25.0M	Prince Fielder	$23.0M
2014	Zack Greinke	$26.0M	Ryan Howard	$25.0M	Cliff Lee	$25.0M
2015	Clayton Kershaw	$32.6M	Zack Greinke	$25.0M	Ryan Howard	$25.0M
2016	Clayton Kershaw	$34.6M	Zack Greinke	$34.0M	David Price	$30.0M
2017	Clayton Kershaw	$35.6M	Zack Greinke	$34.0M	David Price	$30.0M

One answer is that the players who sign these sorts of mega-deals often get a five- or six-year term, meaning that a player will still be paid like a superstar six years into the future, even though history tells us he will likely have at least tumbled a little bit from All-Star level. This is a strategy known as cost-shifting. Teams accept that the back-ends of those contracts might not be a great deal, but they are willing to live with that problem (in five years!) for the short-term gain. Players get some cover too. They lock in guaranteed money, preferring the certainty of having $150 million, rather than chasing after a few million dollars extra. Once you have $150 million guaranteed to you, what's another $20 million?

During the 2011 through 2017 off-seasons, contracts which were among the top 10 in annual salary had an average term of 4.43 years, while those ranked in 11th through 20th place got 2.74 years and those ranked 21st through 30th got 2.64 years. Players at the top of the payroll scale really are getting a year or two more tacked on to the end of their contracts. Even if we assume that in those extra two years, our All-Star level free agent will be *completely worthless* to his team, it sometimes still doesn't bring his contract in line with what the market is offering to lesser players, and really how much chance is there that an All-Star will end up completely useless in five years?

I found all position players from 1999 to 2012 who had finished among the top five in WAR at their positions three years in a row. I then looked to see how this group of All-Star level performers did during the next year, the third year after, and the fifth year after. Were they still All-Stars (top five in the league at their position)? Were they merely "pretty good" (ranked sixth–15th at their position) or perhaps they'd fallen to "good enough to start" (ranked 16th–30th).

Table 44. Outcomes for Consistent All-Star Level Position Players, 1999–2012

Comparative ranking	One year later	Three years later	Five years later
All-Star (1st–5th)	59.3%	38.1%	16.9%
Still pretty good (6th–15th)	26.3%	33.1%	29.7%
Good enough to start (16th–30th)	10.2%	15.3%	14.4%
Backup (31st and higher)	2.5%	7.6%	8.5%
Fringe (fewer than 200 PA)	1.7%	1.7%	2.5%
Didn't play	0.0%	4.2%	28.0%

There's a pretty good chance that, even five years from now, a player who has a sustained track record of success (i.e., the kind of player who would get a contract at the top end of the market) will at least still be a "pretty good" player. Yes, there is some downside risk that he might no longer be playing or producing much value, but there's some of that risk for players getting lesser contracts as well. It doesn't seem like back-end risk is fully explaining why superstars get such comparatively low salaries, relative to how the rest of the market seems to be getting paid.

I think the answer lies in something I call the Guinness Effect. When I was in college, I was a disc jockey at the campus radio station. Because the school was so small and had no communications department, the requirements for having a radio show were being willing to show up on time and not being drunk on the air. Having listened to the station a fair bit, the second one was apparently optional. One day, my father sent me a newspaper clipping (hello, 2000!) from the *Cleveland Plain Dealer* about a student at some other college who had set the world record for the longest continuous radio DJ marathon, staying on the air for several days in a row. Dad figured that I might want to try to break that one.

To my 20-year-old mind, that sounded like fun. I went so far as to contact the Guinness organization to ask about the regulations around breaking this record. They sent back a document that laid out the rules, but also requested that if I was going to make an attempt, I only plan to beat the previous mark by a small amount. This way, others might also have a chance to break it later on. It was a baffling request, because the entire point of breaking a world record is to etch one's name into immortality by being *the best* at something, even if "the thing" was only not sleeping for a few days and staying *just* awake enough to mumble, "You're listening to the Pizza Cutter Show on WKCO, 91.9 FM" in between playing songs by Barenaked Ladies and Letters to Cleo.

There's a certain cultural courtesy to the request that Guinness World Records made of me. It's not nice for someone to smash a record, even if they can, because we want everyone to feel like they have a chance at getting there. There seems to be a similar unspoken taboo that has tamped down the top end of the salary distribution in Major League Baseball. To even be allowed to set a new record, one needs to have a certain cachet as "the best player in the game" and the salary that sets the mark should only be a little bit higher than what came before it. In baseball's rather rigid social hierarchy, everyone else needs to fit under that cap.

It creates an odd dynamic. If the salary market is "capped" at roughly $35 million per year (and growth in that cap is slow), but the market also seems to value a win around $10 million (and the number has trended upward at a faster rate), then suddenly, players who project to be worth four wins or more can't really receive a market rate. There aren't a lot of those players, but there are enough that some are going to get squeezed. Why should teams splurge for a four-win player when a six-win player might be available for only a tiny bit more? If the dollars-per-win number continues to increase at a rate greater than the unofficial top salary ceiling then this pressure is going to build up even more.

Free agency represents a rational market economy up to a point, when an irrational desire to maintain social etiquette takes over. In that sense, the free agent market represents an accidental test of two competing hypothesis. If front offices want to maximize the value they get from their free agent budget, on a dollars-per-win basis, they should look to the top end of the market. If the market was behaving fully rationally, then a player who projects to be worth seven wins but was getting offers of "only" $30 million per year represents a pretty good value. If a team believed in the player, they might bid the contract up to $32 million. If a few teams catch on, they would bid on top of each other, until the usual contract for a superstar fell more in line on a dollars-per-win basis with contracts for middle-tier players. Alternately, teams might simply stop paying what is now "full price" for some of those players in the uncomfortable middle, since the superstars who are a couple wins better aren't *that* much more expensive. That would effectively lower the price per win throughout the rest of the free agent market to bring it in line with the unofficial cap. Maybe a little of both would happen.

So far, the evidence suggests that front offices aren't interested in being rational—and really, why should they? Rational here probably means "spend more money." The idea of a rational market seems to work perfectly well for the players whose salaries we care little about. But once we reach a point where a salary becomes *culturally* significant, things change. No one knows—or cares—who the 61st, 84th, or 92nd highest paid players in baseball are, but the highest paid player is another story. It will be interesting to see whether the market or the cultural norms win this one.

AT THE OTHER END OF THE SPECTRUM FROM HIGH-PRICED free agents are the players who are just entering the league. The Rule 4 Draft (which is the fancy name for MLB's annual amateur draft) takes place every June. There's pageantry, which is a fancy word for people trying to make a boring administrative event into a less-boring administrative event. There are random appearances by Hall of Famers. The end result of a year of hard work by 30 scouting staffs will come to fruition in the form of 30 teams making some wild guesses.

Wait. Guesses?

Every general manager has to deal with at least one "you could have had this All-Star guy, but you drafted this other guy" complaint. There's plenty of cases where a player who never made it to the majors was taken a pick or two in front of an All-Star. It's a testimony to how inexact a science the MLB draft is. Unlike the NFL and NBA, where draftees are put directly into the starting lineup, it's going to be a while before a team sees the fruits, whether luscious or rotten, of their draft. They have to project what a guy who only recently attained the right to vote will look like at age 27.

All 30 teams have a scouting department filled with people who measure their experience evaluating amateur talent in decades. They get access to all sorts of information that is not public. They have cross-checkers and big secret meetings. They all have player development systems with equally grizzled and talented coaches and coordinators to shape that future. They have every incentive to get this right because, at the end of the day, someone will be cutting a check with a lot of zeroes in it. And yet, all of them mess up.

In a world where everyone had a crystal ball, the team that picked first in the draft would take the player who would eventually provide the most major league value. The team picking second would take the guy who would provide the second most value. The problem is that the draft doesn't always work that way.

Instead, the draft used to be half proper draft and half auction. In ye olde days (things changed after the 2012 Collective Bargaining Agreement), teams with high picks would sometimes pass on players whom they believed to be more talented, but whom they saw as wanting too much money to sign. For example, in 2001, the Minnesota Twins drafted Joe Mauer first overall and gave him a signing bonus of $5.15 million. The second overall pick was Mark Prior, who got million $4 million from the Cubs. The Tampa Bay (Devil) Rays actually paid a little more for third pick Dewon Brazelton at $4.2 million, and fourth pick Gavin Floyd got $4.2 million from the Phillies as well. With the fifth pick, the Rangers got Mark Teixeira for $4.5 million. In those days, if you wanted to know how much a team really valued a player, the key piece of information was not his draft position (i.e., he was drafted 10th overall), but instead his signing bonus. Like everything else in life, follow the money.

With the benefit of hindsight, we know what became of Mauer, Prior, Brazelton, Floyd, and Teixeira as players. But how good are "the experts" at predicting the future overall? To find out, I looked at draft picks made in the first 10 rounds of the Rule 4 Drafts held between 2003 and 2010, along with their signing bonuses. (For the initiated, I normalized each signing bonus based on how much money was spent on signing bonuses for that year, to account for bonus inflation.) To figure out whether a draft pick was "successful" I used three indicators. One was a player's career WAR total as of the end of the 2017 season. Another was whether the player appeared in a Major League game. The third was whether or not he surpassed 5 WAR in his career.

Surprisingly, not even all first round draft picks make it to the majors. In the 2003 draft, 10 out of the 37 picks in the first round (including supplemental picks) never put on a Major League uniform. In 2004, seven out of 41 didn't make it. In 2005, it was 11 out of 48.

If all 30 teams could somehow know exactly how much value each draft-eligible player would produce once he got to the big leagues, then in an efficient market, a price structure would develop around those wins. We would see a very close relationship between the signing bonus that a player received and his contributions. In some sense, that's the whole point of the scouting system: to try to predict what's going to happen. How good were they?

Since the first outcome (career WAR) that we're interested in is a continuous variable and so is signing bonus, I used a Pearson correlation to test the strength of the relationship. A correlation of zero means that there is no relationship between two variables. A correlation of one means that they are perfectly aligned. The other two outcomes that we're interested in (Did he make it to MLB? Did he contribute five WAR?) are both questions that can be answered with "yes" or "no," so we will use binary logistic regression to test our hypotheses.

Now for a piece that's going to get a little nerdy. You can't do a correlation when one outcome is binary, so we're going to use a statistic known as Nagelkerke's R-squared, which we will then take the square root of to mimic a correlation. (Stay with me here.)

It turns out that the size of a player's signing bonus has a correlation with his career WAR of .30 in this data set. The "correlation" between signing bonus and whether or not a player made it to the majors was .43, and whether the player achieved five WAR or more, the "correlation" was .36. The maddening thing about correlations in the 30s and 40s is that you can't dismiss them out of hand, but they aren't all that impressive either. It means that teams have some clue what they're doing, but there's a lot of room for error. A glance back at the logs of previous drafts can tell us that, but now we have a number to put on it.

To make sure that the numbers weren't being spoiled by one bad year, I looked at each draft individually, with the following correlations (or pseudo-correlations) for each indicator.

Table 45. Strength of Relationship Between Signing Bonus and Player Outcome, by Year

Year	Career WAR	Appeared in MLB	Reached 5 WAR
2003	.22	.39	.32
2004	.27	.52	.40
2005	.50	.49	.49
2006	.39	.43	.34
2007	.27	.44	.34
2008	.31	.44	.39
2009	.12	.38	.29
2010	.34	.42	.33

Again, we see moderate correlations across the board, with the exception of a Mike Trout induced dip in 2009. (Trout was drafted 25th overall that year!) Teams have steadily been decent, but not great, at matching their signing bonuses to future results. Next, let's see if the old adage that college players are safer bets than high school players is true.

Table 46. Strength of Relationship Between Signing Bonus and Player Outcome, by School Status

Drafted from	Career WAR	Appeared in MLB	Reached 5 WAR
High school	.22	.43	.29
College	.34	.47	.40

There's a stronger correlation between signing bonus and eventual performance for players drafted out of college, which is consistent with the fact that when they are drafted, teams know more about them, and can get a better idea of what they might look like as finished products.

We can also look at pitchers and position players to see which ones teams have a better grasp on predicting success for.

Table 47. Strength of Relationship Between Signing Bonus and Player Outcome, by Position

Position	Career WAR	Appeared in MLB	Reached 5 WAR
Pitcher	.33	.46	.33
Position players	.29	.42	.38
High school pitcher	.22	.45	.24
College pitcher	.40	.46	.38
High school position player	.22	.43	.33
College position player	.31	.48	.42

Here, we see that teams are equally mediocre at assessing future performance from pitchers and position players, and that the high school/college split makes a much bigger difference. Finally, we can look at one more split, this time by round.

Table 48. Strength of Relationship Between Signing Bonus and Player Outcome, by Round

Round	Career WAR	Appeared in MLB	Reached 5 WAR
First	.32	.35	.33
Second	-.19	.01	.10
Third	-.01	.09	.12
Fourth	-.05	.15	.06
Fifth–10th	.08	.13	.11

Whoa! In the first round, we see some reasonable correlations between signing bonus (our proxy for how much teams value each player) and what they end up becoming a few years later. By the *second round*, there is almost *no* relationship between signing bonus and eventual outcomes. That means that teams are statistically performing no better than if they were simply guessing. Put another way, a good amount of your team's most valuable talent pool is being selected by people who are effectively throwing darts. There are players who emerge from the later rounds and end up being diamonds in the rough. However, there is little evidence that teams—at least as expressed through their signing bonuses—are good at knowing who those diamonds will be.

The moral of this story isn't "Scouts are bad at their jobs." Instead, I'd interpret this as "Scouting 17-year-olds is hard." In fact, the more accurate statement is probably "Predicting the future is hard." There's only so much that one can predict about who and what a human being will be in eight years. It's like looking at a room full of fifth graders and trying to project who will be the 10 tallest on graduation day in high school. Sure, you can make a decent guess as to who the tallest will be, but how would you figure out who will be the sixth vs. the seventh tallest? That's the job that faces a front office and a general manager. Sometimes "success" can be the fifth round pick who turns into an All-Star, even though no one, including that same general manager in the previous four rounds, saw that coming.

✱   ✱   ✱

IF THE LOCAL GM IS MAKING A LOT OF GUESSES, THEN PER-haps Ed from Lakewood really could do the job just as well?

Don't be silly. There's a difference between "there's a lot of luck involved" and "all GMs are clueless." To get to the point where one can be *moderately* successful in predicting the future takes a great deal of talent. Sometimes you do everything right and it doesn't work, but the flip side of that maxim is also true. You have to know how to do everything right so that *sometimes it will work.*

In baseball, there is an upper limit to how much we can know about the future. The first job of a front office and its general manager is to push the boundaries on that limit. It always has been. The first scouting departments were formed to gather and sort information with the best tools that they had. The first analytics departments were there to do the same thing, just with different tools. The game has evolved to where a GM's job is to aggregate all of that information into an actionable plan. It's hard to keep an edge in baseball. When all 30 teams have scouting and analytics departments looking for those little in-efficiencies, any edge that you might find can get wiped away quickly. It takes being as good as the experts from the other 29 teams just to keep up, but when everyone is on roughly equal footing with respect to knowledge, something else will have to separate them. Sometimes that's a guy who discovers a wicked curveball out of nowhere in AA. You hope that he just happens to be in your system when he does.

Beyond the luck factor, we lack a vocabulary to discuss what a general manager does. In Chapter 4, we talked about ways in which teams can create *emergent* value, the kind of value that is generated not by individuals, but by the way the *system* works together. We found places where these effects could have real value, but struggled with how to give the credit for that value, and sometimes even what to call that value. We know that there are ways to structure a roster to promote those emergent effects, but it's not like the players needed to realize that value show up randomly on the roster. That takes planning, it takes someone to execute the plan. A good chunk of a general manager's job is to be that organizing emergent principle.

A GM also has to think about time. Fans don't. A move made (or *not* made) today might affect the team both now *and* in two years, and sometimes the benefit in two years is more valuable. In the field of child development, there is a classic experiment known as the "Marshmallow Test." In it, a four-year-old child is presented with a marshmallow on a plate, and is told that if they can wait a short amount of time and do *not* eat the marshmallow, they may have two. It's a test of self-control and of willingness to resist short-term impulsivity for an even greater long-term reward. How does one credit a GM for *not* signing the shiny new second baseman that Ed from Lakewood *really* wants to see on the team? The GM knows that second baseman might make the team better in the short-run, but moving from 75 wins to 81 just means missing the playoffs by a little bit less. The money is better saved for next off-season, even though that means a longer wait for Ed to have a taste of sweetness. How do we credit a GM for mastering the Marshmallow Tests of baseball?

General managers like talking about their "process," a purposefully vague catch-all term for the ways in which they make key decisions. A good "process" will center on figuring out what things a team can control (and what it can't) and then creating as much expected value for the team as possible. To do that, you have to know *a lot* about the game. Even then, sometimes the best plans don't work. Luck will eventually put its thumb on the scale. The lament of the general manager is that while a hitter can appeal to expected value ("I hit a screaming line drive that just happened to get caught by the shortstop! Seven times out of 10, that's a hit!") a GM can't come out publicly and say, "Here are our deepest held competitive secrets that we used in putting the team together. Seven times out of 10, they work!"

In a game where we are used to giving out credit immediately to an individual for things that they do and do in plain sight of everyone, the front office's job is to think beyond the present, in terms of an organization rather than an individual, and where sometimes, the best move is to refrain from doing something (and we never find out about it). It's tempting to try to evaluate general managers and front offices through the same lens we use for baseball players, when they're actually playing a very different game. If we want to understand the front office, we have to ask different questions, and at this point, I don't think we even have a basic framework to start doing that.

– *10* –

Except That It's
Not Actually True...

WEDDINGS ARE CULTURAL EVENTS, PERHAPS *THE* MOST culturally-infused event of the human life cycle. All cultures have birth rituals, though no one remembers their own, and death rituals, where people tend to play a passive role. That leaves weddings one of the few times in which humans actively participate in one of their own major life events. And is there ever a great deal of ritual and tradition—along with its plus-one: superstition—involved in a wedding! There's an entire wedding-industrial complex around planning and etiquette and cake baking, despite the fact that the only requirements for a wedding are a valid license, an officiant, and a couple of witnesses to countersign the document that makes it legal.

Before we got engaged, Tanya and I had been talking about getting married. On a six-hour drive from Cleveland to Chicago after a weekend visiting my parents, we had a long conversation—the sort that all adults considering marriage *should* have—about whether this was what we wanted. Both of us came to the end of that conversation with a "yes" in our hearts. Somewhere along the Indiana Turnpike, I looked at Tanya in the passenger seat and asked "Did we just get engaged?" She answered, "Yeah, I think we did."

So much for the grand romantic gesture of asking for someone's hand in marriage. We were awful at this tradition thing, and it was only getting worse. I promised her that I would propose "for real," because it would be fun. In response, since I was now somewhere between her boyfriend and fiancé, Tanya started calling me her boy-ancé. Somehow, there is no word for the space between having a sensible conversation about a major lifetime commitment and a silly ritual in which that commitment becomes formalized. We invented one.

I went ring shopping and found one that both looked nice and was affordable on a graduate student budget. The saleswoman at the jewelry store asked me whether I wanted to pick up the ring or have it shipped. This was puzzling because I lived only a few blocks from the jewelry store and I told her I could somehow walk the half-mile for something this important. She explained that if I shipped the ring out of state, I could save the sales tax. All I needed was a reliable person to receive the ring who was not in Illinois. If anyone in the Illinois Department of Revenue is reading this, I bought that ring for my father.

My dad received the ring from FedEx, but didn't feel comfortable shipping something that valuable back through the mail. He decided that he was going to drive the ring to Chicago himself. I was still trying to maintain some amount of secrecy around my plan to pop the question, but that meant I had to come up with a cover story for why my father had randomly decided to drive to Chicago for no apparent reason. I settled on "My father randomly decided to drive to Chicago for no apparent reason." Thankfully, my father is the sort of person where that story makes perfect sense. It was the only piece of the deception that I managed to pull off.

The timing of the actual proposal was hilariously not a secret. There was no grand surprise where I swept Tanya off her feet unaware, like the movies told me I was supposed to. I did use the fig leaf of not telling her *exactly* why I had asked her to come for a picnic in the Lincoln Park botanical garden, but when she got to my apartment, I told her that I had gotten some watermelon like she had wanted and that I had a big knife for cutting it. She laughed at me and said, "You're going to propose to me with a big knife in your backpack?"

I had decided to propose in the penguin enclosure of the Lincoln Park Zoo, which was demolished a few years later, because we had an inside joke in our relationship about penguins. There were plenty of people at the zoo that day and I figured that maybe I could make a socially appropriate scene out of this major life event. Once we were in place, I knelt down, produced a Beanie Baby penguin with a note affixed to his flippers that said "Marry Me" and just to be sure there was no confusion, I asked Tanya the question verbally. I already knew that the answer was going to be "yes."

No one noticed. I had figured that one person kneeling down in front of another with a ring would draw a crowd of cooing people, but I guess the penguins were cuter. No matter. We walked out of the zoo an "officially" engaged couple.

I booked our wedding date over a hazy Labor Day weekend. Tanya had gone to Atlanta to visit her parents and do some wedding dress shopping, which left me the job of booking a church. Despite the tradition that a wedding should take place in the bride's village, we had decided to get married in Cleveland, for the fact that I had a much bigger family. When I went to meet with the priest who would eventually officiate our wedding, I brought my mother along. For someone who's read a bit of Freud, the implications were not lost on me.

I called Tanya that night and confirmed the date with her. Now that we had "a ring and a date," we could start talking about real wedding planning. Our first promise to each other was that we were going to have a superstition-free wedding. Crazy young idealists that we were, we figured that the health of our marriage would be based more on our willingness to love and be patient with each other than on whether we had the correct font size for our reply cards. Later that night, Tanya sent me a picture of the dress she had found. She was wearing the dress. Take that, superstition!

On the day of the wedding, my parents had arranged for a limo bus to drive the bridal party from the hotel where most of them were staying to the church. That included me and Tanya, who of course, weren't supposed to see each other before the ceremony, or else our marriage would be doomed. As people walked into the church atrium, they were surprised to see the two of us standing in plain sight of each other, greeting family members.

The actual marriage ceremony was beautiful. In the Russian tradition, the best man (my brother) and the maid of honor (Tanya's friend from high school) hold crowns above the heads of the bride and groom. It's a ceremony that takes about 20 minutes. The problem is that the human arm is not made to be held aloft for 20 minutes, especially holding something heavy. It's a wonder my brother didn't need Tommy John surgery afterward. Allegedly, it's bad luck if the crown touches the head of the bride or groom before the ceremony is complete, although for some reason, someone thought to put padding on the bottom of the crown, just in case. Let's just say that the padding came in handy.

Near the end of the ceremony, Tanya and I were standing up near the front of the church as the priest was talking to our assembled witnesses, leading up to the point where he would say the legally binding words "By the power vested in me..." I noticed something by the altar area that I hadn't before that moment. There was a large floral arrangement, which was lovely, although we hadn't ordered any large, lovely floral arrangements. As I focused on it, I noticed that it was decorated with a ribbon that contained the words "Beloved Grandmother." Beloved Grandmother? I think Tanya saw it at the same time, because while Father was still talking about...something...we caught each other's eye and simultaneously looked over at the arrangement and then looked back at each other. In that moment, I knew this marriage was going to work, and it was because someone forgot to remove the bouquet from the funeral that was held in the church earlier that afternoon.

The rest of the day was a flurry of activity. There was dinner. People danced to songs about local workout and social service organizations. Cake entered my nostrils. My brother made a very touching toast to our happiness. My newly-minted father-in-law gave a toast "about the reproductive system." I swear that I am not making that up.

We're going to fast forward a bit to the next day. Tanya and I were scheduled to leave for our honeymoon that afternoon, but before we left, our parents wanted to meet us for brunch. We met at a restaurant near my parents' house and after some light banter recapping the previous day's events, my mother pulled me and Tanya aside and said, "I have something to tell you." Unfortunately, she said it in the tone of voice that's usually followed by dire medical news.

"You know your cake from last night?"

Okay, not cancer. Good.

"Yeah, Mom, what about it?"

"Well, were you guys planning on saving the top layer of it?"

"What do you mean?"

"Well, last night after you guys left the reception hall, Dad and I put all of the stuff from the gift table into the back of the van, and they gave us the top layer of your cake. After we got back to the house, Dad opened up the hatch and... the cake fell right out and went ker-splat on the driveway. We actually thought about not telling you and just getting a new one made. I know a lot of couples keep that top layer and then eat it on their first anniversary."

My mother looked genuinely worried that she had doomed us to divorce within six months.

Tanya and I laughed. "Who eats year-old cake?" was all I could manage.

*   *   *

YOU PROBABLY DIDN'T PICK UP THIS BOOK FOR THE WED-ding planning advice, although if you're planning a wedding (*mazel tov!*), you're welcome to it. Instead, I offer you this story as a tutorial in sound research methodology. My wife and I broke several "rules" of weddings, and despite the implied, and ever-so-vague threat of "bad luck," we have managed to stick together through three cities and five kids. How have we managed such an astounding feat given how many "rules" we broke? I assume, reader, that you are muttering that of course, none of those superstitions are actually true. You wouldn't fall for such completely baseless and emotionally loaded garbage, would you? You're a rational person, much smarter than that. It's just a bit of fun on a big day, right?

By the way, the playoffs are coming up and this year's match-ups are looking good. There's the series with the team of grizzled postseason veterans who has been to the playoffs the last three years against the team of upstart youngsters who are on a mission to shock the world. There's the team that won their division by 12 games and coasted into the playoffs after clinching in mid-September against the team that fought all the way down the stretch and only punched their playoff ticket on the last day of the season. Who do you think is gonna win it this year?

There's nothing like a good bit of uncertainty around something important, like committing to spend the next seven games and/or the rest of your life with someone, to create a bit of anxiety. And are the playoffs ever an uncertain and important time of the year! Your entire season is boiled down to a short series against a team that is, by definition, playoff-caliber, where one random bounce could mean that six months of work has gone down the drain. If you win, your prize is another short series against another playoff-caliber team, where you are again at the mercy of some random bounces. If you win that, you get another one!

The reality of playoff baseball is that you have two mostly evenly matched teams facing off against one another in games that are essentially coin flips. To even say that a single game has reached the point where one team is a 60/40 favorite to win, you'd have to assume that if the two teams played each other (and only each other) over the course of a 162-game season, the favored team would win 97 of those games. It's rare that a team wins 97 games in a season when they also get to play the bad teams for part of it. Even if we did assume that two playoff teams could somehow be mismatched to the tune of a 60/40 split, the laws of statistics tell us that the lesser team would win three out of five games 31 percent of the time and four out of seven games 28 percent of the time. That's for two teams that don't belong on the same field. What happens when one team might only be *slightly* better than the other?

It's hard to predict anything in baseball. Sometimes the best team doesn't win and there's no good reason why. That leaves us in a very uncomfortable position culturally, because it means that while both playoff teams in a series are immensely talented and hardworking, they are likely equal to each other to the point where talent mostly cancels out of the equation. *Something* has to separate them over the next week and a half, and it might be which team gets more fortunate bounces of the ball.

There's a taboo in United States culture, as well as sporting culture, about crediting luck for anything. Everything must have an explanation, preferably one that involves someone *working harder*. After all, if luck was the deciding factor, then do I really deserve to be holding this trophy? Even when it's patently obvious that a team got a lucky bounce, players and fans and talk-show hosts will talk about *anything* but that. Victory will be credited to dedication and perseverance and experience and leadership and drive and grit and heart and the fact that Smith wore his lucky necklace that was given to him by his fairy godmother. As if Jones on the other team didn't also have a fairy godmother. Humans are amazing in their ability to hold two contradictory beliefs and to not even acknowledge the conflict. A team filled with veterans has an advantage because they know how to handle pressure. A team filled with young players has an advantage because they are hungry and don't know they should be scared! These things can't both be true, but we allow both to be true anyway. It means that no matter the outcome, we have something that can *explain* what just happened, rather than having to live with randomness as the answer.

It's easy to miss the point when we talk about the role of luck in baseball (and life). The team jumping up and down after winning the World Series is not "just lucky" in the same way that anyone might have their name drawn out of a hat. Here, "luck" is more like a team who has put in a lot of work to unfurl their giant sails, but still need an eastward wind to blow in them. Without that work, even if a strong breeze came by, the boat isn't going any-where. With the work, that wind will power them to the World Series. It's just that there are a lot of other hardworking sailors out there. Sometimes you do everything right and someone else wins.

*   *   *

LET'S TALK ABOUT BIG MO. MOMENTUM. DOES IT HELP A team in the playoffs if they had to fight their way through September in a heated pennant chase, keeping their skills sharp? The fact that they made the playoffs means that they probably won some emotional (but exhausting) victories. Perhaps it's bet-ter to be the team that wraps up a playoff berth early, rests its stars, but risks losing its edge? Usually, the answer that people give depends on what route their favorite team took into the playoffs. We will instead ask the data to decide for us.

I looked for how often teams played "meaningful" games in September from 1995 to 2017. To be a "meaningful" game, the following three things had to be true.

The team entered its game(s) that day having *not* clinched a playoff spot, either division or wild card.

The team had to be within three games, in either direction, of a playoff spot. So, if a team was more than three games back, both in the division race *and* the wild card race, the game that day isn't "meaningful." Same goes for having a lead of more than three games.

There had to be an available playoff spot that the team could still obtain (i.e., there hasn't been a clinch on their division *and* the available wild cards). It's useless to be three games back with two to play.

That's not a perfect definition, but it's a pretty good one, and so I counted up how many games, out of the team's final 15, were "meaningful." Now we know whether a team was involved in a dogfight down the stretch and has some "momentum" built up or whether they cruised in on auto-pilot. How big of an effect does Big Mo have? None really.

Here's a breakdown of playoff series wins from 1995 to 2017, which is the "Wild Card era," separated out by how many "meaningful" games, out of their final 15 regular season contests, a team played down the stretch.

Table 49. Percentage of Playoff Series Won, 1995–2017

Number of "meaningful" games in final 15	Playoff series won
None	47.0%
1–5	48.6%
6–10	53.1%
11–15	50.0%

There's very little evidence that the way that a team enters the playoffs makes much of a difference. A more sophisticated analysis (for the initiated, a chi-square) showed that the slight differences between these groups is almost certainly random chance, in the same way that you can flip a fair coin 100 times and sometimes get 52 heads. If there is any effect of momentum, it is tiny and far out of line with how much emphasis people place on it coming into the postseason.

If teams can't build momentum into the playoffs with a big stretch run, then perhaps they can claim it in the middle of a series. There is nothing more momentous than a late-inning, come-from-behind victory, ideally one with a big walk-off hit as the exclamation point. When one of these moments happens, there's a quick narrative that is guaranteed to spring up. The victorious team has "seized the momentum" and in their next game will have a decided advantage from the emotional lift that went with the glory of *that* moment. The defeated team might as well just pack up and go home. The problem is that it's not true.

I found all playoff games from 1995 to 2017 in which a team entered their batting half of the ninth inning either tied or behind, but eventually managed to win the game. This means that at some point, they had a dramatic hit that made some announcer swoon that the victors had "it." Then I looked at what happened in the next game of the series. (Momentous hits that closed out a series were not counted.) There were 102 of these games in the playoffs during this time period, and the momentum-having team won the next game 59 times (58 percent!). Score one for momentum? Not so fast! If we instead asked "What percentage of teams who won a game—in any fashion—also won their next game?" we'd find that in the same time period, the answer is 54 percent. If momentum provides any advantage in the next day's game, it is again a relatively small bump.

The common narrative of momentum is that after the game, the losing team feels so devastated by their loss that they can't possibly go on. Once again, we forget that baseball players do other things than play baseball. After the game, members of the losing team can scream "Fiddlesticks!" into their lockers, have a group hug, take some time to remind each other that the next game starts with a score of 0–0, and get a good night of sleep. Baseball teams are small societies, and all societies have ways of both celebrating happy events and mourning losses. A baseball season gives them plenty of chances to practice both. Teams do not sit there sulking after a loss. They grieve and they cope, and in doing so, they get ready for tomorrow. That's part of the game, and if a team doesn't know how to do that as a collective, they probably aren't in the playoffs to begin with.

THERE ARE TWO HARBINGERS OF THE RETURN OF SPRING in the United States, and Punxsutawney Phil is one of them. In a ritual so bizarre that only the United States could think of it, onlookers gather on February 2nd of each year in a small Pennsylvania town that is famous entirely for *this*. A man in a top hat pulls a rodent out of a hole in the ground and then makes a prediction about the extended weather forecast, allegedly based on whether the rodent saw his shadow or not. How this is communicated from the annoyed groundhog to the man in the top hat is not entirely clear. Perhaps the hat gives him the ability to speak to animals.

The other sign happens about a week and a half later, when baseball-starved fans hear the five words that they have been longing to hear since the last out of the World Series. "Pitchers and catchers report today." It's an odd landmark, because the pitchers and catchers don't do anything on that day other than check in to the team hotel and let management know that yes, they have arrived. The next day, they play catch with each other, but they do it with hats on, and hats make it official.

The next day, the worry begins. No one ever said, "You can never have enough catchers." But the pitchers, oh the pitchers! There are never enough good ones and they tend to break down a lot. Nearly two-thirds of all trips to the 60-day disabled list are made by pitchers. Teams justifiably lose sleep over the thought of one of their "arms" feeling a little twinge in his elbow, for fear that it will lead to the two most dreaded words in the sport: Tommy John.

Tommy John surgery, named for the former All-Star pitcher who, in the 1970s, became the first player to reestablish himself as an effective pitcher after undergoing it, is an operation that from a historical perspective would seem a minor miracle. A pitcher who otherwise might have vanished can now be repaired by replacing his ulnar collateral ligament. The miracle comes at a high cost, though. The recovery time from the surgery is about a year, meaning that the pitcher usually misses an entire season.

There are plenty of theories around what might put a pitcher at higher risk for needing a major surgery such as Tommy John. The list of suspects has included throwing really hard, throwing breaking balls too often or too early in life, throwing too many pitches in a game, throwing too many innings in a season, and the one that is the most well-validated: throwing.

Because these major injuries happen to pitchers at seemingly random times, most of the theories to explain why they happen seem to be based more on the need for an explanation than actual data.

Most famous among these explanations is the "Verducci Effect," named after sportswriter Tom Verducci (Verducci himself named it the "year-after effect"). His hypothesis was that serious pitcher injuries and sudden drops in performance stem from teams overworking their tender young arms. A pitcher who was young (25 or under) and who had seen an increase in his workload of 30 innings or more in the previous season, including work in the playoffs, was at significant risk, according to Verducci's hypothesis.

This makes sense intuitively. If you are training to run a marathon, you don't go from maxing out at one mile to maxing out at 10 in the space of a week. You have to build up your endurance along the way. Rick Peterson, who has been a pitching coach for several teams, has given the Verducci Effect his imprimatur. There *have* been several cases where a young pitcher saw an increase in his workload and suffered a major injury or a major decline in performance. So far, our evidence file contains an imperfect analogy, expert testimony, and case examples. As someone who's a stickler for proper research methodology, I see a few problems. None of those forms of evidence (analogy, testimony, or example) are legal tender as proof of anything. That's not how science works. Analogies can gloss over important differences between things, experts can be wrong, and as one of my favorite quotes goes (by Frank Kotsonis) "the plural of anecdote is not data."

Still, Verducci's hypothesis is at least *reasonable*. Better than that, it's also *testable* with data that we have available. Using data from 2006 to 2012, I found a group of pitchers who fit Verducci's criteria—they were 25 or under and in the previous year had experienced an increase in their combined (minors, majors, and postseason) workload of 30 or more innings. I also found a control group, who were also starting pitchers aged 25 or under, but had *not* seen an increase of 30 innings. Then, armed with a database of injuries, including both "day-to-day" and ones that required a trip to the disabled list, I looked to see which group was more likely to have problems.

In the Verducci group, 68 percent of pitchers reported some sort of injury during their "at-risk" year, compared to 54 percent of the control group. A Verducci victory? Before we consider the case solved, there are more numbers worth looking at.

Table 50. Time Lost to Injury and Performance Change

	Control group	Verducci group
Days lost to injury (all pitchers)	21.09	15.08
Days lost to injury (among those suffering an injury)	39.04	22.17
Went on disabled list	29.2%	24.0%
ERA increase of 1 run or more	19.4%	15.9%

When we look a little deeper, we find that the Verducci Effect group was slightly healthier and they were not actually more likely to suffer a drop in performance than the control group. The Verducci group *was* more likely to have an injury reported about them, but those injuries tended to be less severe. That's the power of a control group. By comparing young pitchers who have been extended in the previous year to a control group, we find that the biggest risk factor for injury isn't their youth or their workload, but the fact that they are pitchers.

Using the same data set, I looked in to whether we could find factors that really did predict pitcher injuries. It turned out that the biggest risk factor for a pitcher was whether he had sustained an injury *the year before*. More than that, the effect was body part specific. A pitcher who had a shoulder injury last year is more likely to have a shoulder injury this year, and the size of the effect was compelling. For example, if a pitcher had an elbow injury in the previous year, his chances of having an elbow injury in the current year were 27 percent. Among those who had healthy elbows the year before, the elbow injury rate was only 2 percent.

I also looked at whether single-game pitch counts were a predictor of injuries and using a slightly different statistical technique (for the initiated, a Cox Regression), I found that when pitchers had games in which they exceeded a pitch count of 110, their risk of suffering a catastrophic injury, including injuries that require Tommy John surgery, increases. Extending beyond 130 pitches in a game pushed the risk even higher. Increased risk is not the same thing as certainty that our pitcher will develop an ouchie, in the same way that not everyone who plays with matches will set fire to the house, but it's still not a good idea to play with matches.

The take-home message isn't all that surprising. A pitcher who throws a lot of pitches in a short period of time is more likely to get hurt. A previously injured body part is more likely to get hurt again. Despite cultural messages around "manliness" and commentators who crow at the idea of a pitcher being held to a 100 pitch limit, the data show that pitch counts help to prevent injuries.

The appeal of the Verducci Effect was that it was more interesting than "pitching is hard on the arm." It "explained" emotionally charged events (catastrophic injures to young pitchers) in a way that promised an easy solution. According to the Verducci Effect, teams needed only to plan ahead and ration out a pitcher's innings. My research doesn't offer such comfort. Once a pitcher is damaged, he's not guaranteed to get hurt again, but the risk increases. So, we can either tell him not to throw another pitch or we can live with the uncomfortable fact that sometimes pitchers get hurt.

AUTHOR BERNARD MALAMUD, WHO WROTE THE BOOK *THE Natural* (which was turned into the Robert Redford movie of the same name with one *tiny* difference), is quoted as saying "The whole history of baseball has the quality of mythology." That's true in the sense that there's a great deal of poetic majesty in baseball, but there's a sly double-meaning in there. Another quality that baseball shares with mythology is that there are a lot of old stories about it that aren't factually true.

There's the one about how you shouldn't put two lefty starters back-to-back in the rotation, because a team would get used to seeing the ball coming from the left side on the first night and use that advantage to tee off on the second night. We can look in to that using the data. We can check to see whether teams facing off against a lefty on two nights in a row perform any differently than what we might otherwise expect based on their seasonal stats. It turns out that there was no discernible effect for facing two lefties in a row or two power/high-strikeout pitchers in a row or two fly-ball pitchers in a row or even two left-handed-high-strikeout-high-fly-ball pitchers in a row. It's almost as if hitters, even if they haven't faced a lefty in a couple of days, can still remember back to last week.

There's the one that says that you shouldn't hit three left-handed hitters in a row, because a team could use a left-handed reliever against that part of the lineup later in the game. It's true that left-handed batters don't hit as well against left-handed pitchers. In 2017, left-handed batters hit .260/.336/.440 against right-handed pitching and .241/.310/.372 against southpaws, which is not reducing lefties to impotence, but that's a pretty significant effect. Later in the game, the three-lefties-in-a-row lineup *could* end up being a vulnerability, and that's what people focus on.

Let's think this one all the way through. Let's say that you've selected the nine hitters who will be batting for you that day. The best thing to do is to arrange them from best to worst so that the good ones get as many plate appearances as possible. Once you do that, you look on the lineup card and see that there are three lefties in a row at the top. This concerns you, so you start toying with the idea of bringing a weaker (but right-handed) hitter higher up into the lineup and giving him more plate appearances while pushing the stronger lefty further down. The solution to the "problem" has its own cost.

If you're considering hitting three lefties at the top of the lineup, the opposing *starting* pitcher is probably right-handed, and we know for certain that for the first few innings—when the runs count just the same—you will have your three best hitters, all with a platoon advantage, bunched up in a row and in the part of the lineup that comes to bat the most often. On the flip side, while we know for certain that the lefties *will* get to face the right-handed starter, it's not a guarantee that when the opposing manager is ready to go to his bullpen, your three-in-a-row lefties will be due up. Why base a strategy on something that *might* happen later in the game when you have an advantage that you know you can certainly take right now?

There are plenty of other baseball myths, and they all share the common thread of being based on fear and overly simplistic ideas that "sound right" rather than deep engagement with the data. This isn't a problem unique to baseball. Politicians of all stripes have relied on similar arguments for centuries to advance their own agendas. The nice thing about baseball is that we have a data set that makes checking out the truth of a lot of these claims easy. While myths and superstitions do serve a purpose in life, they are a bad starting point for making good decisions. I'm all for appreciating the human element of the game and maybe even a few wink-at-the-camera superstitions that everyone knows deep down are silly. It becomes dangerous when "the human element" becomes a cover story for engaging in baseless pseudoscience. It cheapens the understanding of the real human element in the game.

Often, when I talk about my lack of belief in "momentum," I hear the counterargument that "I've been in a big situation, and I've *felt* momentum affecting me." I have no doubt that people have experienced an emotional reaction to a big situation. I have no doubt that they attribute whatever happened next to that emotional reaction. If the data showed that momentum really did have an effect, I would be among the first to proclaim it. The problem is that those data aren't out there. Perhaps our own emotions are fooling us.

It's worth asking what "momentum" even means. If we say that one team "has the momentum," but that the other can "seize it back" by hitting a single to left, then "momentum" is just a silly word that means "the team which most recently did something positive." If we believe instead that "momentum" is some sort of mystical force that can propel a team to victory on the sheer power of an emotional high, then we have a different issue. We often think of "momentum" in terms of what it means for the team that hit the big home run, but rarely think of what that says about the team that *gave up* that home run. From that perspective, we are saying that because one bad thing happened to them, the losing team has somehow been mortally wounded. The momentum hypothesis presents a rather dark view of humanity, that we are essentially prisoners to whatever circumstances we find ourselves in and that we have no way of fighting back against adversity. That's the danger of accepting pseudoscientific nonsense. You end up selling yourself and your species short.

The reality of how humans handle crisis situations or playoff butterflies or walk-off home runs actually tells a much more uplifting story. People often report experiencing a brief moment of panic in a crisis, but then a sense of calm and even resolute determination. Even people who are not trained in crisis response are still commonly able to handle things. They often talk about being scared, but also realizing that something had to be done and then doing it. Humans are tough, resilient little critters, and *that's* the real human element in baseball. That's the human element that I choose to celebrate. That's why it's so important to do *real* research.

– 11 –

Dénouement

I WOKE UP ON THE MORNING OF OCTOBER 26, 1997, WITH A miserable cold. I barely had a voice. It was a Sunday, which would normally have meant that I could spend the entire day recovering, but this wasn't going to be a normal Sunday. The night before, Cleveland Indians pitcher Chad Ogea had done the impossible.

With the Indians down three games to two in the World Series, Ogea had drawn the assignment of facing off against Florida Marlins ace Kevin Brown, who the year before had finished second in the NL Cy Young Award voting. Ogea, who compiled a modest 8–9 record in 1997, with an ERA a tick below 5.00, was no one's idea of a postseason savior, but there he was on the mound, chucking changeups with the season on the line. Ogea and Brown had faced off in Game 2 of the Series, with Ogea and the Indians improbably prevailing 6–1 on the back of Ogea's 6 ⅔ innings.

Ogea's Game 2 was a nice story, but with the Indians now one game away from elimination and Brown back on the mound, I knew I was hoping for lightning to strike twice in the same place. And yet, Ogea delivered a thunderbolt. He held together for five innings, giving up only one run, and the Indians scored four runs against Brown, thanks in part to a two-run single in the second inning and a fifth-inning leadoff double which eventually led to a run, both off the bat of…Chad Ogea. The Indians went on to win Game 6 and to force a deciding Game 7 on Sunday night.

The Indians started rookie Jaret Wright in that Game 7, a game which, had it turned out differently, might have granted Wright immortality in Cleveland folk history. Wright had made his major league debut in June of that year, and was given the nod on three days' rest (Wright had started and won Game 4) over the Indians' fully rested Opening Day starter, Charles Nagy. Wright was fiery, cocky, and 21. He'd come to Cleveland at a time when it was desperate for a sports savior. The Indians had not won a World Series since 1948, and the last major sports championship that the city had reveled in was a 1964 Browns championship.

For Cleveland sports fans, the 1960s, '70s, and '80s had been a stretch in which mediocrity felt like success. From the beginning of divisional play in 1969, the Indians had never finished in the top three spots in the American League Eastern Division and had managed only three winning seasons between 1969 and 1994. Longtime Indians radio broadcaster Herb Score was often lauded as the man who had seen more bad professional baseball played than any other man alive. On top of that, the city's other sports franchises had their own streaks of lukewarm results. The Browns had stumbled through the '70s, but had a small renaissance in the late '80s when they made it to the AFC Championship game in three out of four years, only to lose each time to the Denver Broncos. The Cavs had their own run of greatness in the late '80s and early '90s, but had succumbed to the brilliance of Michael Jordan and the Chicago Bulls. The Indians themselves had made it to the 1995 World Series, only to be throttled back by Greg Maddux, Tom Glavine, and the Atlanta Braves.

But there stood Jaret Wright on the mound with a chance to win it all for Cleveland. He was an alpha male in a town with an inferiority complex on a team that almost had to turn to Albie Lopez earlier that year. During what seemed like an improbable playoff run, Wright had notched two victories against the heavily favored New York Yankees in the Divisional Series, as well as his Game 4 triumph four nights earlier.

Even though I'm an adult now and I should be better able to deal with silly things like this, it's still hard to rewatch the highlights from that Game 7. The Indians went ahead in the top of the third on Tony Fernandez's two-run single and Wright held that 2–0 lead into the seventh inning. As the Florida faithful sat down from what would be the last stretch break of the year, I had the thought in my very congested head that not only were the Indians about to win their first World Series in 49 years, they were going to do so by 11:00, so that I could go to bed and get some decent rest. Oh baseball, why must you do this to me?

Bobby Bonilla led off the Marlins' half of the seventh with a home run to cut the Indians' lead in half. Wright got another out via his seventh strikeout of the game, but was finished for the night when Mike Hargrove turned to veteran lefty reliever Paul

Assenmacher. Then something nice happened. Assenmacher quietly dispatched Kurt Abbott and Devon White back to their own dugouts, and a combination of relievers Mike Jackson and Brian Anderson set the Marlins down in order in the eighth and kept the Indians ahead by one run, leaving the ninth for Indians closer Jose Mesa. My entire family huddled ever closer to the television in the family room as if it would somehow bring us closer to Miami. Perhaps we could will the Indians on to victory. Even my mother was watching, and she doesn't much care for baseball.

By this point, I was somehow standing, despite the carpet of soggy tissues that surrounded me, powered only by the hope that "it" would happen. And it *almost* did.

Moises Alou singled off Mesa to start the ninth, and after a Bonilla strikeout, Charles Johnson hit a single to right, chasing Alou to third. With one out, Craig Counsell needed only a fly ball to the outfield to tie the game, and produced one to right field. The game was headed to extra innings.

The highlight clip of Edgar Renteria grounding a single up the middle in the 11th inning and Craig Counsell jumping down the third-base line into the waiting arms of his teammates at home plate gets played more than the average World Series highlight, because it's one of the few times that Game 7 of a World Series ended in a walk-off hit. It is the quintessential storybook ending to a baseball game and a baseball season. It's the way a good baseball movie is *supposed* to end, and yet no one ever tells the fairy tale from the point of view of the team that lost. In the movies, the director usually takes great pains to make sure that by the end of the story, the losing team has no fans, but that night we were out there. I was one of a million Clevelanders who ended that night with a broken heart.

After watching a few moments of teal-clad Marlins celebrating, my father turned off the TV and my mother comforted me and told me that I should probably go to bed. In the time honored funeral ritual for any baseball season she said the five words that needed to be said. "We'll get 'em next year." The next day, I woke up and went to school.

✳   ✳   ✳

IN 2016, AS THE INDIANS BEGAN ANOTHER PLAYOFF RUN which would end in the World Series, my friend Steve was in town visiting. As the Indians played Game 1 of the American League Division Series against the Boston Red Sox, we sat in a restaurant and watched the game, just like the good old days. We swapped dad stories. Because that's what two men watching a baseball game do. They talk about their kids. At one point, Steve pointed up to the screen and recited another poem. "If the Indians win the World Series this year, there's going to be a parade in Cleveland. I already told Anne that if they win, I'm going to get in the car, get on the highway, and go to Cleveland for that parade. Want me to pick you up on the way?"

I said yes.

On the night of November 2nd, 2016, I once again was there for the Indians in a World Series Game 7—this time in pristine health. The Indians, my childhood sweethearts, were matched up against my mistress, the Chicago Cubs. I sat on one of the two couches in my living room in Atlanta and listened to the radio feed from back home in Cleveland. I'd like to say that I was listening to the audio feed out of some high-minded principle that baseball is a game that is *made* for the radio, but the reality was that my wife and I were cord-cutters and didn't own a television.

The Indians were starting Corey Kluber that night on three days' rest, mostly because they had no other options. Prior to the postseason, the Indians had lost starting pitchers Danny Salazar and Carlos Carrasco to injury, and had run through the postseason using Kluber, who had won a Cy Young Award two years earlier, and the unheralded Josh Tomlin and Trevor Bauer as their starters. They had been carried this far largely on the left wing of reliever Andrew Miller and the right wing of closer Cody Allen. The Indians still hadn't won a World Series since 1948, and hadn't even been back since that night in 1997. While that normally would have awarded them "lovable underdog" status, they just happened to be playing a team that hadn't won a World Series since 1908 and hadn't even been there since 1945.

But there stood Corey on the mound, calm and ever-unflinching with a chance to win it all for Cleveland. He was an ace in a town with an inferiority complex on a team that almost had to dig up Albie Lopez earlier that week.

Even though I'm an adult now and I should be better able to deal with silly things like this, it's still hard to rewatch the highlights from that Game 7. The game didn't start off well, with Kluber surrendering a home run to Cubs leadoff hitter Dexter Fowler, though Carlos Santana tied the game in the third with an RBI single. The problem was that the Cubs scored the next four runs of the game and I sat across from my wife, sighing heavily. She knew what that meant. Even when the Indians scored two runs on a fifth-inning wild pitch that ricocheted off the mask of Cubs catcher David Ross, the outlook wasn't brilliant for the Cleveland nine that day.

In the top of the next inning, Ross redeemed himself with a home run off Andrew Miller, who up to that point in the playoffs had been the closest thing to an immovable object ever seen on a baseball diamond. In the bottom of the eighth, the Cubs turned to Aroldis Chapman, the guy who threw 100 mph on a slow day. It seemed like the Indians were doomed.

By this point, I was somehow standing, despite the fact that I had no reason to stand up, powered only by the nervous energy that came from hoping that "it" would happen. It happened, but only for a brief moment.

Brandon Guyer, whom the Indians had acquired at the trade deadline specifically because he hit lefties well, stroked a double off of the left-handed Chapman to score the green-haired Jose Ramirez. Then in a moment for which the word "euphoric" is far too pale a descriptor, Rajai Davis, a player known mostly for his stolen base totals rather than his power, hooked a ball down the left-field line and over the 19-foot wall at Progressive Field to tie the game at six. My wife saw me throw my head back in jubilation, and came over to join me, even though she doesn't really care much about baseball.

The Indians and Cubs traded outs in the ninth inning and the game was headed to extra innings. Oh baseball, why must you do this to me?

(But first, there was a rain delay.)

The highlight clip of Kris Bryant fielding Michael Martinez's slow roller up the line and throwing to Anthony Rizzo at first to finish off the bottom of the 10th inning gets played more than the average World Series highlight, because it marked the moment that the Chicago Cubs, lovable losers for more than a century, had finally won the World Series. It is the quintessential storybook ending to a baseball game and a baseball season. It's the way a good baseball movie is *supposed* to end. And yet no one ever tells the fairy tale from the point of view of the team that lost. Again.

After sitting for a few moments and listening to the sounds of Cubs players celebrating, I turned off the speakers and my wife comforted me and told me that I should probably go to bed. In the time-honored funeral ritual for any baseball season, she said the five words that needed to be said. "We'll get 'em next year." The next day, I woke up and went to work.

*   *   *

BASEBALL IS A HUMBLING GAME, ONE THAT HAS BROKEN MY heart more times than I care to count. Before my wife and I got married, I told her that I wasn't the kind of guy to go messing around with other women, but that she had to understand my relationship with baseball. She has learned to politely nod when I get "that look" in my eye. There's part of me that realizes that being a baseball fan makes no logical sense. As a therapist, I would often counsel people to avoid basing their sense of happiness and self-worth on something that they do not control. Yet, here I was becoming wrapped up in the efforts of 25 players who just happen to wear funny pajamas emblazoned with the name of the major city that I was born closest to.

Part of growing up as a baseball fan is the inevitable moment when you realize that those 25 guys who represent your hometown are just 25 guys. Some are amazing human beings. Some are complete jerks. You look back on your childhood heroes and realize that they were mostly just guys trying to make a buck by playing a game. Occasionally, you find out that one or two of them are now in jail. Then you realize that the team whom you spent so much time rooting against was just another collection of 25 guys, some of whom were amazing human beings and some of whom were complete jerks and some of whom are now in jail. Eventually, you learn to root for the good guys. You learn to be a fan of the game itself, even if you still feel a little tug to cheer for the hometown team because it's still part of who you were growing up. The truth is that no one ever really finishes growing up.

I've come to embrace another type of baseball fandom. Mathematicians define a fractal as a shape with a defined perimeter, but an indefinite amount of area. It's rather easy to draw one. If you draw a square, and then draw lines that cut it into four equal subsquares, the top right quadrant of that shape could be cut similarly into four equal parts, and so on. If you had a pen capable of making such fine lines, this could, in theory, go on forever. There are boxes within boxes within boxes, and whether you choose to focus on the original square or one of the tiny squares that were created by the 103rd round of divisions, there is still further complexity to explore within that space. Yet, there is a boundary beyond which it stops being "baseball." I am a fractal fan of baseball.

A single baseball game represents a fixed point in time. I can look back at a box score and not only recreate the game in my head, but also recreate myself as I was at the time. Yet, were a million monkeys sitting at a million typewriters for a million years, they might not reproduce a single box score that has ever actually happened. Anything *can* happen in a baseball game, but only one thing does, and that one thing becomes a marker for the rest of life. There's an entire lyrical subgenre of baseball writing on this very tension, and I am hard-pressed to better the masters of that art form. Instead, as a "data guy" I have my own preferred expression of the infinity/singularity dynamic.

Even after more than a century of what we have come to know as "Major League" baseball, the game is still consistently writing new line scores (i.e., the numbers of runs that each team scored in each inning). It's relatively rare for a unique *final* score to be recorded in a game. From 1901 to 2017, there have been 40 games which have ended in a score that had not happened before, nor has it been duplicated since. Not surprisingly, many of them are games in which one or both teams scored well into double digits, with perhaps the most famous being the August 22, 2007, game between the Texas Rangers (30) and Baltimore Orioles (3). Somehow, Rangers reliever Wes Littleton earned a save for his valiant effort in keeping the Orioles from overtaking the Rangers over the last three innings. The most common final score since

1901 has been a 3–2 win for the home team (3.5 percent of all games have ended this way), followed closely by a 4–3 for the home team (3.4 percent). Once we ask how they got to that 3–2 final, things get a bit more unique.

The most commonly played game from a line-score perspective (again from 1901 to 2017) is a 1–0 game in which the home team scores the only run in the bottom of the ninth. It's happened 296 times. It's followed closely by a 1–0 game in which the home team scores the only run in the *first* inning (269 times). On the flip side, in 2017, nearly 80 percent of all games ended with line scores that had never happened before in baseball history, and not because of strange games in which teams are combining for 30 runs. On the last day of the 2017 regular season, 15 games were played and nine of them featured historically unique line scores, including a fairly pedestrian 5–2 win for the visiting A's over the Rangers. Oakland opened the scoring with three runs in the third inning and pushed their lead to 4–0 with a run in the sixth. In the eighth inning, the A's scored one more, and despite a two-run Ranger rally in the bottom of the eighth, the A's went home winners. That had *never* happened before. Nearly every game has its own fingerprint.

Mathematically, it's not all that shocking. Consider a universe in which teams are able to score either zero or one run in an inning, with no multi-run innings. In this world, there are more than a quarter million (2^{18} = 262,144) possible line score outcomes, and there have been fewer than 200,000 major league games played from 1901 to 2017. Even if baseball games were mandated to end in a new line score every night, there

haven't been enough games played to get to all of the possibili-
ties, and that's before we allow that two runs could score in an
inning. Or three. As a fractal fan, I find that thrilling. There are
new things to discover and appreciate every day in the game of
baseball, much more territory than I or anyone else will ever be
able to cover. Baseball is at once familiar and novel, same as it
ever was and constantly shifting.

*   *   *

I'VE HIT A HOME RUN ONCE IN MY LIFE. MY DAD WAS PITCH-
ing me a whiffle ball and I was holding a plastic bat with an
over-sized barrel. I'm sure I hit plenty of foul balls back then, but
one day—and I recall this ever so clearly—I got hold of one of my
father's "knuckle-curves" and lined the ball over the chain-link
fence at the back of our yard. I was six years old and ready to take
over for Brook Jacoby. I haven't hit another one since.

When I started writing this book, I wanted to write a love poem
(with decimal points) to the game that has measured my life
from that first home run until now. I wanted to write about how
baseball has formed me and the experiences that have changed
how I look at the game. As a psychologist, I wanted to write how
concepts like thought and culture and ritual and language shape
the game. As a "data guy," I wanted to write a book where I could
separate out truth from sentimentality through a good, long look
at the numbers. It's a hard balance.

My father once told me—the contents of Chapter 1 notwith-
standing—that religion without a sense of humor is the most

dangerous thing in the world. It is, by far, the wisest sentence that anyone has ever said to me. It certainly holds true in the literal sense. Sadly, there are people who forget that every major religious tradition tells its followers to be humble and kind. My dad meant more than that. He meant it in a self-reflective way. When you think that you have all of the answers, you're in trouble.

I grew up in a Catholic family. We went to Mass on Sundays and I was even Altar Boy of the Year at my parish. Yet, my father always saved room for the occasional chuckle at the people walking around with ashes on their forehead on Ash Wednesday, even when (and perhaps because) he had ashes on his. After all, how is walking around with burnt palm branches smeared on the other side of your prefrontal cortex supposed to make you a better person? The message of the ashes is that we are merely dust and we will someday return to being dust. It's about humility... and it's also kind of silly if you take a moment to step back and look at it from another perspective. It's the kind of perspective that requires that ability to say, "Maybe I don't have all of the answers. Maybe I'm wrong."

There's a false sense of security that comes with "doing the numbers" and maybe even one that can manifest itself as something like religious fervor. Numbers are especially comforting specifically because they place a level of separation between a person and responsibility for giving bad advice. Despite the fact that I chose the data set, the variables, and the statistical methodology, it's easy to pretend that the numbers somehow represent an advanced form of knowledge that is completely free of bias, one somehow superior to mere humanoid assessments.

The truth is that I am fully capable of asking the wrong question and getting the correct answer to it. The fact that I got my answer from a spreadsheet doesn't make it any less dangerous.

If there's something that being a psychologist has taught me, it's that the humans are far worse at processing and understanding information than we fool ourselves in to thinking we are. I've learned that even when I think I *know* something, it's always best to get a second opinion, and the numbers are a place to find that sort of check on my own shortcomings. It leaves me in the uncomfortable position of knowing that both my eyes and my spreadsheet are quite fallible. While it has become trendy (and at this point, trite) to say that to understand the whole truth of baseball, one must combine observational and numerical data, at this point, I just hope that either one can point me in the right direction some of the time.

After my dad retired from the parking business, he took a job at a car dealership, greeting people who were coming in for service. As part of his job, he would ask the customers what problem they were having and write it down so that the mechanics knew where to start. He told me that a man once came in complaining that there was a funny noise coming from under the hood, but he wasn't sure what was causing it. My father's response was "Are you sure it's not the nut behind the wheel?" Confused, the man started looking at the steering column between the wheel and the dashboard until he realized that my father was making a joke. He was the nut behind the wheel.

For a long time, the controversy around the Sabermetric Movement has been about what counts as baseball knowledge.

When we hear old-school knowledge grinding its gears up against the results of a spreadsheet, each side runs to defend their data set and grabs on to the steering wheel to turn it as hard as they can in their direction. It's a natural human impulse. We all begin with the assumption that we're right. No one stops to think, "Maybe the problem is the nut behind the wheel."

*   *   *

WHEN I WORKED AS A THERAPIST, I HAD PLENTY OF PEOPLE who came to my office looking for advice or perhaps looking for someone who had all the answers. For some reason, people tend to confuse therapists with oracles. There are plenty of therapists who do little to stop them from continuing on in that belief. The job of a therapist, at least as I saw it, wasn't to give people advice, nor even to tell someone "how to think" about the problem. Instead, my job was to think *alongside* the person. Here's how I saw the problem from my own perspective. Sometimes those thoughts were hilariously wrong. Sometimes they were useful. Maybe once in a while, they were brilliant. Either way, I couldn't represent my thoughts as anything other than the observations of a fellow traveler.

I wanted to write this book in that same spirit. These are some of my observations on the ever-shifting game of baseball. I wanted to share pieces of my own story as a baseball junkie and a psychologist and a "data guy" and a Clevelander and a transplanted Clevelander and a public health worker and a dad and a husband and a thousand other things that make up who I am.

When you're trying to decide whether any of my thoughts made sense, it helps to at least know where they came from. My goal in writing this book isn't to tell you how to think about the game. It's to think alongside you about baseball, maybe in a different way than you're used to thinking about it. Maybe somewhere in my thoughts is a kernel of knowledge that you can use when you settle down to watch the game tonight.

Hopefully, I did my job.

See you at the ballpark. Footlongs are on me this time, Dad.

– *ACKNOWLEDGMENTS* –

A BOOK IS A COLLABORATIVE WORK, BECAUSE EVERY HUMAN being is—even in our existence—an act of collaboration. In sports, we often speak of the *Most* Valuable Player, and even outside the context of sports, people know what the abbreviation "MVP" means. There is a phrase in Latin, *sine qua non*, which translates as "who not without," that I prefer. Where baseball has one MVP Award, I prefer instead to think of SQN awards. Plural. While the words in this book spilled from my synapses through my fingers and onto my keyboard, there are some key people, *sine qua non*, the events that inspired my synapses would never have happened.

I owe the very existence of my synapses and fingers, my baseball fandom, and the fact that I survived to adulthood to my parents, Jake and Beth Carleton.

I owe my love of writing to a number of teachers who nurtured that part of me, including Ms. Jeanette Werner, Br. Joseph Chvala, C.S.C., Mr. Tom Carey, Mr. Grant Wanner, and Mr. Ross

Piché. I owe my ability with numbers to the work of my high school calculus teacher, Mr. Paul Bosley, and my college stats professor, Dr. Sarah Murnen. The debt of gratitude that I owe Mr. Daniel Cavoli is eclipsed only by the amount of time it would take to explain what exactly it was that Mr. Cavoli taught me. Oddly enough, this book probably owes the largest portion of its R-squared to the influence of my American History teacher, Mr. James Nieberding, whose advice to always seek out more data has quietly rung in my ears far beyond my teenage years.

I learned to be a proper researcher—along with a few lessons on human growth and development—under the kind guidance of my undergraduate research advisor, Dr. Linda Smolak. My graduate dissertation chair, Dr. Kathryn Grant, trusted me enough to put me in charge of the data team on a giant research project that had become her life's work. I got to learn on the fly how to be a data manager, and not just a data analyst.

Dr. Sheila Ribordy, may she rest gently, was the first in a long line of kind souls whom I met in Chicago when I was a terrified replacement-level adult. I can think of no better tribute than to place her name in the pages of a baseball book, even if she was a White Sox fan. Jeremy Taylor sat around with me in the Stress and Coping Project "dungeon" and we talked regression models, Cubs, and clinical psychology on more days than I can count. In Chicago, I even found my way to a church that doubled as a baseball fan collective. On Sundays, we would gather to discuss the important things in life, and also religion. At some point, Mike Dorosh, we are going to steal Fr. John's official hat and embroider a White Sox logo on it. I'm 95 percent confident that he'll think it's funny.

Evan Brunell asked me to join a small sports blog network that he had created as a sabermetrics writer after reading some of my work on Blogspot (hello, 2006!). At Statistically Speaking, I got to work with a lot of really cool people, some of whom went on to work for MLB teams, including Sean Smith, Mike Fast, Matt Swartz, Colin Wyers, and Brian Cartwright. When I took some time off after the birth of my oldest daughter and was thinking about getting back into writing about baseball, Eric Seidman asked me, "Would you be interested in writing at Baseball Prospectus?"

Kevin Goldstein and Christina Kahrl, and later Joe Hamrahi, were willing to take a chance on me at BP, which is the nerdy baseball writing equivalent of being asked to join the Beatles. John Perotto, Ben Lindbergh, Sam Miller, and Aaron Gleeman have, at one time or another, been willing to say yes to projects that started with "I have a crazy idea for an article…" Ben and Sam, who wrote a book together detailing how they ran an independent league baseball team in the Summer of 2015, indirectly spurred me to go through with this project. I figured that if those two could get a book published, it couldn't be *that* hard.

Dave Smith, who runs Retrosheet.org, an online repository of play-by-play and game data that stretches back into the 1930s, has made all of that data available for free to anyone who wants it. For this effort, he should be inducted into the Baseball Hall of Fame. I am not exaggerating.

I also owe Sean Forman at Baseball Reference a debt of gratitude for his work in putting together Baseball Reference, a data resource that I discovered in college and have been using ever since, including in this book. I used data from Fangraphs (thanks, David Appelman) and Baseball Prospectus (thanks, Dave Pease and Rob McQuown) as well.

Parts of this book originally appeared on the electronic pages of Baseball Prospectus and have been edited for publication here. Stephen Reichert and Sean Neugenbauer at BP helped me leap over some legal hurdles along the way. At BP, I have the luxury of picking the brains of some wonderful writers and collaborators, including Kate Morrison, Harry Pavlidis, Dan Brooks, and Jonathan Judge, all of whom sharpened the ideas that went into this book.

Jonah Keri introduced me to Adam Motin, managing editor at Triumph Books, and (spoilers!) that conversation went rather well. Mark Simon also gave me some friendly advice during the process. The fact that all of the sentences in this book have verbs in them is a tribute to Jesse Jordan of Triumph, who served as my editor. Clarissa Young also walked me through the contract process with aplomb.

I am also indebted to a number of "friends" inside Major League Baseball front offices who have kindly answered my questions when I have asked them. Special thanks go to Mike Chernoff and Keith Woolner of the Cleveland Indians, who gave me a chance to live out a childhood dream, if in a slightly altered form from the way that I had dreamed it up.

In the single nerdiest double *entendre* that I have ever made, I would like to thank William James.

Tanya Klimova ended up being one of the main characters in this book because she remains the most interesting person that I have ever met, despite the fact that she's not a baseball fan. When I told her that I was thinking about writing a book, she was the one who told me that I should do it and suggested that it be called *My Wife Is Awesome (Also, Baseball)*. Sorry, sweetheart. The publisher made me change it.

I am a fortunate man to have been carried so far by so many. May every kindness be repaid to you a thousand times over.